IMPOSTORS
in the
TEMPLE

Martin Anderson

SIMON & SCHUSTER

NEW YORK • LONDON • TORONTO • SYDNEY • TOKYO • SINGAPORE

SIMON & SCHUSTER
Simon & Schuster Building
Rockefeller Center
1230 Avenue of the Americas
New York, New York 10020

Copyright © 1992 by Martin Anderson
SIMON & SCHUSTER and colophon are
registered trademarks of Simon & Schuster Inc.
Designed by Edith Fowler
Manufactured in the United States of America

10   9   8   7   6   5   4   3

Library of Congress Cataloging in Publication Data

Anderson, Martin, date.
  Imposters in the temple / Martin Anderson.
    p.   cm.
  Includes bibliographical references (p.   ) and index.
  1. College teachers—United States—Intellectual
life. 2. College teachers—Professional ethics—United
States. I. Title.
LB1778.2.A53 1992
378.1′24′0973—dc20   92-12369
                                        CIP

ISBN 0-671-70915-1

To Professor George Taylor of Dartmouth College and Professor Eli Shapiro of M.I.T.—the two greatest teachers I have ever known—and to Glenn Campbell, the man who built the Hoover Institution.

Contents

CHAPTER ONE

TWO
INTELLECTUAL CLASSES

WE ONCE THOUGHT of universities and colleges as special places, places of teaching and learning, places for the pursuit of truth, but above all, as temples of integrity. Integrity is the soul of intellectual life; it infuses thinking and writing with soundness and veracity. In the intellectual world it is of particular importance, for, as Samuel Johnson noted over 230 years ago, "Integrity without knowledge is weak and useless, and knowledge without integrity is dangerous and dreadful."[1]

It has been quite a while since anyone spoke of the world of American higher education as a place of integrity. For good reason. Within that world, integrity is dead, having succumbed to the death of a thousand cuts. Each cut small and, by itself, not fatal. Each cut perceived as an aberration, an isolated case, an intellectual or moral transgression neither typical nor representative. Each cut seemingly unrelated to all the other cuts. But each cut, razor-sharp and deep, bled off some integrity, and the cumulative impact has been silent and deadly. Individually, each instance can be explained away as an aberrant human failing, characteristic of any human endeavor. But collectively, they cannot be explained away; instead they stand as an indictment of the institution of higher education itself. The death of integrity in the heart of higher education is the root cause of the educational troubles which afflict us today.

Our universities and colleges are the home of the high priests of the American intellectual world, the men and women we look up to and listen to and sometimes follow. Some of these intellectual priests are what we think they are—men and women of integrity, brilliant scholars with a passion for truth, conscientious teachers who love their craft. But today many of these academic intellectuals have betrayed their profession. They have scorn for their students and they disdain teaching. They represent their research and writing as important and relevant when much of it is not. Some have a passion for radical politics that transcends all else, and a few even have little regard for the truth.

They are the corrupt priests of America's colleges and universities and, while small in number, their influence is large and pervasive. They are the great pretenders of academe. They pretend to teach, they pretend to do original, important work. They do neither. They are impostors in the temple. And from these impostors most of the educational ills of America flow. Only when we understand these renegade intellectual priests, and take action against them, can America's full intellectual integrity and power be restored.

There are many alumni of America's colleges and universities, men and women who were once fiercely proud of their alma maters, who today are puzzled and pained, and sometimes embarrassed, when they hear of what goes on. Parents, instead of feeling keen anticipation when their children leave home for the university, today feel anxiety—anxiety about what they will be taught, anxiety about the moral values they will absorb, anxiety about the intellectual rigor of the classes. Today there are many students in the university who are surprised by the lack of intellectual challenge, and disappointed by the lack of integrity that demeans so much of higher education. There are even a growing number of professors and academic administrators who don't like what they see happening all around them.

And yet, at the same time, American intellectuals taken as a whole are probably the best in the world. They are the most numerous, the most influential, and, some may even argue, the brightest of any nation on earth. America's intellectuals have been the prime movers in the great debates of the twentieth century. Who led the battle against the ideology of communism and socialism? The intellectuals of Germany or Italy or Japan? The intellectuals of China or the Soviet Union? Or even France or England? No. It was mostly the Americans.

Who has dominated thinking in the fields of science and medicine, of economics and political science? Mostly American intellectuals. They were not alone, but they were and are the dominant intellectual force—the seminal thinkers, the winners of the Nobel prizes. And does anyone question the fact that intellectual debate and inquiry are freer and more robust and more influential in the United States than in any other country? Even our system of higher education, as corrupt as it is, is still considered to be the best in the world. Every year tens of thousands of foreign students fly to our shores to study and learn. In 1990 the president of Harvard University, Derek Bok, noted that according to a current poll eight of the twelve most outstanding universities in the world—Harvard, M.I.T., Princeton, Yale, Stanford, California (Berkeley), Michigan, and Cornell—are located in the United States.

True, America's high ranking may not be due so much to our distinction and excellence as it is to the dismal state of higher education in other countries. In our lifetime, most of the people of the world have lived in poverty and fear under the fist of dictators of one kind or another, in statist societies openly hostile to the open pursuit of truth. So while we may not be great, we are good enough to be the best. The sad part is that we should be great, and we are not.

Fortunately, America's academic intellectuals—the professors—are not America's only intellectuals. There are two major intellectual classes in America. The other class, the professional intellectuals, is, for the most part, composed of the writers and editors who work in the mass media and large publishing houses and a small number of fellows in the think tanks.

These two distinct intellectual classes—the academics and the professionals—derive naturally from the educational structure of the United States. The business of education in America is vast and sprawling—an untidy, complicated, multibillion-dollar enterprise of millions of men and women that can be best understood as two separate structures.

Think of education in America as two giant pyramids.

First, there is a pyramid of formal education, starting at the bottom with kindergarten and elementary school, then moving upward to encompass high school, college, graduate school, and post-graduate school. The higher we move up the pyramid of formal education the greater the breadth and difficulty of the learning, and the fewer the students and teachers. It is a formal, structured society of teacher and student, lectures and examinations, graduations and degrees. A huge bureaucracy runs it—millions of elementary and secondary school teachers, principals and members of school boards, college and university professors, administrators, and trustees.

The second educational pyramid is the jumble of intellectual activity we might call informal education. Teaching and learning occur in many ways. When we read a newspaper or a magazine or a book we are learning, and the writer is teaching us just as surely as the teacher lecturing in front of a classroom. In fact, most of us swim in a great pool of teaching and learning every day. We learn not only from printed sources, but from television and radio, plays and movies.

We often think of education as a process. It is not. The process is teaching and learning, and education is the result. Education is something that continues to occur long after we walk through those school doors for the last time. Some wags would argue that today it happens only *after* you exit those portals.

The informal educational pyramid is perhaps even more vast than the formal one. It is certainly more pervasive, ranging from local newspapers, small television and radio stations, and small publishing companies, all the way up to our premier newspapers, network television and radio, and international publishing houses. Like its formal counterpart, this informal educational structure is run by a vast bureaucracy—by reporters and publishers, editors and copywriters, directors and producers, and layer upon layer of administrators.

At the top of these two educational pyramids in America lie

the people who govern them—the respective intellectual classes who set the rules, define the policies, and act as powerful role models for the entire educational pyramids below them.

Inhabiting the highest reaches in the formal education pyramid, in the seats of prestige and authority, are the academic intellectuals—the professors. These are the men and women who decide ultimately what is taught and how it is taught. In the highest ranks of informal education are the professional intellectuals—the editors and columnists of newspapers and magazines, the writers and editors of commercial books, the writers and editors of journals of opinion, the fellows in think tanks, the pundits who do commentary and analysis on television and radio, and, to a lesser degree, the writers and producers of movies and plays. What professors are to the world of formal education, these men and women are to informal education. They set the standards and decide what is "taught" and how it is taught.

These two classes of intellectuals rarely overlap. They are like two separate societies (or tribes), each with its own rules, rituals, and ethical codes. But when speaking of the intellectual life of America, we often fail to make the distinction, blaming one class for what the other does, or crediting one for the other's successes.

America's intellectuals are America's educators. The reason why American education is in such trouble in the 1990s is that our educators are so troubled. The starting point for understanding the darkness that has fallen over education lies with those whose job is the teaching of our future educators, the next generation of intellectuals. At the heart of that darkness are our best universities and colleges. The ills of primary and secondary education are just distant reflections of the bad examples set in the ranks of higher education. If we are ever going to solve the deepening crisis of American education we are first going to have to understand and come to terms with our intellectuals.

The major factor that defines and separates the two intellectual classes in America is the effective society in which they work—the political structure of the organization they work for, the way in which their work is judged, and the people who judge them. In brief, America's academic intellectuals work in a quasi-socialist state, while our professional intellectuals, for the most part, work under bare-knuckle capitalism. Each of these distinct working environments has had for our intellectuals many of the same pluses and minuses of socialism and capitalism that we have all so recently seen play out around the world.

The academic intellectuals enjoy most of the material dreams of any socialist—a guaranteed job for life (tenure), excellent working conditions, recreational facilities, subsidized housing, and generous pensions. Professors do not have to worry about the whims of a tyrannical boss who might fire them. The only people to whom they answer, the only ones who effectively judge them are—other professors. Through the custom of "peer review," they have evolved a unique system in which they essentially judge themselves.

The primary calling of professors is to teach—the sacred responsibility to impart information and ideas to the young, to stimulate and excite them to intellectual effort, to develop their critical capacities, and to make them think. Teaching is what they get paid for, it is how they make their living. True, many academic intellectuals also contribute to our intellectual life through research and writing, but they rarely get paid directly for it. Sometimes professors will get paid more for producing academic writing, but salaries are almost always geared directly to their teaching responsibilities.

But curiously, what their students and colleagues think of their teaching, even what the trustees of the university think of their overall performance, is minor compared with the judgment their colleagues make on the quality of their research and writing. Unlike the professional intellectual, who is subject almost daily to the tough scrutiny of the buying public, the typical publishing professor must satisfy only a handful of "peers" or intellectual equals in his or her field of study. An academic book or a scholarly article is not expected to sell many copies, nor appeal to many people outside a select intellectual circle. Thus isolated, the typical academic intellectual operates freely, uninhibited by the judgment of outsiders, subject only to the verdict of colleagues who themselves are judged by the same narrow criteria. There is no objective measure of value, and all depends on individual honor and integrity.

The professional intellectual, on the other hand, is at the mercy of not only subjective judgments on the quality of the writing, but also its dollar value in the marketplace—how much money people will pay for it. The ultimate judge of the professional intellectual is the vast buying public, not the opinion of peers. If the professional intellectual does not produce serious, interesting, important work, it is just a matter of time before he or she will take up another occupation. No professional intellectual enjoys a guaranteed job; they can all be fired.

At the institutional level in the world of the professional intellectuals, entire newspapers and magazines, publishing houses, and broadcasting companies—unlike colleges and universities—can be bought and sold. Professional intellectuals operate in an intensely competitive world where their ideas are evaluated continuously; it is a rugged, vital process that prevents them from becoming insulated, inbred, or overly arrogant.

To the contrary, America's academic intellectuals are largely insulated from the discipline of free markets, each university or college a tiny oasis of quasi-socialism. They themselves decide what is good, whereas the professional intellectual must ultimately convince outsiders to buy his or her intellectual wares. As we shall see, the isolation of the academic intellectuals allows their natural hubris to flourish, whereas the marketplace will generally snuff out a flare-up of the hubris that also lies deep within every professional intellectual. And that is one of the major reasons why, paradoxically, the level of ethical behavior is substantially higher in the commercial world of the professional intellectuals than it is in academe. Most people will do the right thing if they have to, and professional intellectuals are no exception.

America's professional intellectuals are an expression of its capitalist society. They are the primary force defining the intellectual life of America, giving it a unique shape and form, color and texture. Professional intellectuals exercise their constitutional right of free speech with a vengeance. Deference to authority and tradition is an attitude foreign to them. They are inherently just as corrupt as academic intellectuals. In fact, their natural proclivity to ignore or break the rules is probably greater than that of their academic cousins. Few of the professional intellectuals have the temperament of scholars, few of them would take satisfaction in teaching young minds as a career, and they are every bit as intellectually arrogant as professors—with perhaps even greater leeway to indulge their passions and prejudices.

The left-wing political bias of America's professional intellectual class is legendary, confirmed by study after study. Their honesty and integrity are suspect to most of the public, and we often wonder if we are being deceived, not so much by what they tell us, but by what they leave out. They have nowhere near the prestige of the pipe-smoking, tweed-jacketed professor. They are seen as hard-living men and women, more interested in a sensational story and a big money contract than the pursuit of truth.

Yet there is a special kind of deep integrity that permeates the world of professional intellectuals. We rarely hear of one of them neglecting the essence of what they do, of ducking their duties as professional writers, or writing about trivial, unimportant matters. Plagiarism and fraud are so rare that when they do happen it is big news, universally condemned, and the perpetrator banished from the profession.

Yes, there is political bias and all other kinds of personal biases in their writings, but few professional intellectuals pretend to be objective and impartial. They usually have strong, deeply held beliefs and are not shy in prosecuting them. They rarely pretend to be what they are not. When they profess their beliefs they usually do it with integrity. Free speech can be as wild as a stormy sea, and the professional intellectuals daily push the limits of constitutional guarantees.

There is no question that if you selectively review the U.S. media you can find a steady stream of outrageously biased statements. If you string them together you could easily conclude there is a pervasive left-wing political bias. But if you look at the total output of the media, you will probably conclude otherwise. The diversity of views presented is striking. There is literally something for everyone. Politically they range from the libertarian right to the totalitarian left. True, there is not an even split; the tilt to the left predominates. For every two or three Anthony Lewises there is only one William Buckley.

The result is what one might call a sufficient balance. Not evenly balanced, not fairly balanced, but balanced enough so that it provides something that is crucial to a free society—a real competition of ideas. And, in the world of ideas, truth is not determined by counting writers, but rather by facts and logic which ultimately, somehow, manage to triumph most of the time.

There are few institutional scandals in the world of the professional intellectuals such as the recent exposés of price-fixing and fraudulent research overhead expenses charged to government-sponsored projects that have tarnished dozens of our finest universities. Personal transgressions may abound, but the institutional integrity of the professional intellectual world is surprisingly high. This integrity of the professional intellectual class in America can only be explained by the distinctive nature of the work they do, and the rules of conduct and economic forces that govern them.

Most of us think of the national media as one gigantic information and entertainment machine. It is. Except for one small, very important part: its intellectual component. Laced throughout the mass media are veins of intellectual work, a complex, multi-dimensional continuum of ideas and opinion. From the editorial pages of the daily newspapers to the weekly news magazines to the journals of opinion to serious commercial books to the pundits of television and radio, we get intellectual arguments in all shapes and sizes, fron concise ones that stress essentials to lengthy ones that consider every nuance.

The media machine of the United States is a powerful weapon, the most powerful one in the world, firing a steady stream of facts, information, and entertainment. While the intellectual threads of this vast media machine are relatively small, they are, when stripped out and bundled together, an intellectual powerhouse—pervasive

17

and influential. Its pundits are highly skilled, its focus is on timely, important issues, and its audience is huge.

There are not many professional intellectuals in the United States. In a country of 250 million people with approximately two-thirds of a million academic intellectuals, we would be lucky if we could identify 15,000 professional ones. No exact count is possible because the business of professional intellectuals is not one that lends itself to precise definition. But even a rough estimate shows the number is very small.

There are no more than several hundred national columnists writing opinion essays for our newspapers. There are several thousand newspaper editorial writers. The total number of men and women who write an op-ed article from time to time is several thousand or so. There are no more than a few thousand editors and columnists writing for magazines and journals of opinion. Editors working for major book publishing firms number in the hundreds. Those who write intellectual books for a living can be counted in the low thousands. Probably fewer than a hundred people are intellectual pundits on television and radio. The total number of fellows in the major private think tanks is somewhere between 250 and 300; if you add in government-supported think tanks, the number of fellows in major think tanks is still less than 1,000. Altogether, depending on how one defines them, the number of professional intellectuals in America runs from 10,000 or so to perhaps 15,000.

The power and reach of the intellectual veins that run through the mass media in the United States are extraordinary. The ultimate test of intellectuals is the lasting impact of their ideas. But an important, more immediate test is the size and importance of the intellectual's audience, and the readership of professional intellectuals is often measured in the millions whereas the typical academic writer is lucky to have an audience measuring in the hundreds. This vast disparity in communication power is one of the key distinctions between the professionals and the academics.

The top guns of today's professional intellectuals are the columnists and editorial writers for our leading newspapers. When A. M. Rosenthal or William Safire writes an 800-word essay for the *New York Times* or Robert Bartley writes an editorial for the *Wall Street Journal,* their thoughts are conveyed within hours to millions of readers. Like F-15 fighter pilots, they swoop and dive and strafe ideas on important issues several times a week, and their targets are the minds of many of the most influential people in the world—from politicians and business leaders to academic intellectuals to their colleagues in the media. Each of these newspapers alone has an estimated 3 million daily readers.

Altogether there are over 1,600 daily newspapers in America, ranging from the major, well-known ones—such as the *Washington Post,* the *Los Angeles Times,* and the *Christian Science Monitor*—to small, local papers. Their combined daily circulation is 63 million copies; their readership is substantially larger.

Another major branch of professional intellectual life is the world of periodicals—news magazines, business magazines, literary magazines, and journals of opinion. The heavy hitters of the periodicals are the news magazines—*Time, Newsweek,* and *U.S. News & World Report*—with circulations of 2 to 4 million a week and readerships in the 10-million-plus category. These magazines have their own special brand of pundits. While they don't have the steady impact of the writers on the major daily newspapers, the reach of their words is also sweeping. Whether it is Hugh Sidey and Strobe Talbott writing for *Time,* or Meg Greenfield and George Will for *Newsweek,* or David Gergen, John Leo, and Mortimer Zuckerman for *U.S. News & World Report,* they have an audience of millions. The same is true to a lesser degree for business and literary magazines. *Business Week* leads the pack with a circulation of 1 million copies a week, but a dozen or so others—including *Fortune, Forbes, The New Yorker, The Atlantic,* and *Harper's*—all have circulations in the hundreds of thousands.

The journals of opinion are in a special class, largely written by intellectuals for other intellectuals. Their circulations are relatively small, but what makes them influential are the people who read them regularly—especially other writers and political activists. Their political coloration ranges from left-liberal to right-conservative, from *The Nation* to the *National Review,* from the *New*

Republic to the *American Spectator*, from *Mother Jones* to *Human Events*. Their circulations tend to run in the tens of thousands. They are primarily sources of intellectual ammunition for other intellectuals, and their impact is significant, for they help to define the views of those who write and speak in more powerful, far-reaching media.

In spite of the enormous advances in electronic communication techniques, the printed page is still the most powerful way to transmit ideas. As it has been throughout history, the book is the tool of choice of our most influential intellectuals. It is the most effective vehicle yet devised for conveying large blocks of complex and interrelated material from one person to another. And if the columnists and editorial writers for the national newspapers are the F-15 fighter planes of the professional intellectual world, then the writers and editors of the big book publishing houses are the B-52 bombers. Book publishing is big business, and growing. Some 55,000 books are published annually in the United States. Just ten years ago, in 1982, total book industry sales were $8 billion. In 1990, annual sales hit $15 billion and are projected to be over $21 billion by 1995. By comparison, university press sales (academic publications) were only $246 million in 1990, a relatively insignificant 1.5 percent of total book industry sales.[2]

A dozen or so companies dominate the commercial book publishing world, and most of them are headquartered in New York and located within a few city blocks of each other. They are familiar if not household names: Random House; HarperCollins; Simon & Schuster; Viking; Harcourt Brace Jovanovich; William Morrow; G. P. Putnam's; Knopf; Little, Brown; Houghton Mifflin; the Free Press; and Basic Books. No one has ever researched the question of how many of the important intellectual books published in America were published for profit, but it's a pretty good bet that most were, and by a handful of the large publishing houses.

In the world of television and radio the number of intellectual programs is relatively small, but their audiences are tremendous. Over 10 million American households watch the three major network news programs every morning, and almost 30 million households watch them every evening.[3] Besides the slices of intellectual discourse that appear on the major news programs every now and then, the two most influential and prestigious discussion programs are *Nightline,* moderated by Ted Koppel, with an estimated viewing audience of 5.3 million households, and the *MacNeil/Lehrer News-Hour,* with an average of 4 million viewers nightly.[4] There are also weekly talk shows with large national audiences featuring prominent national policymakers, experts, and intellectuals of all stripes. *Meet the Press, Face the Nation,* and *This Week with David Brinkley* have several million households watching them on Sunday morning. On Sunday night, *60 Minutes* reigns supreme with up to 20 million households watching its weekly bag of commentary and analysis. There are smaller, more intellectual programs such as William F. Buckley's *Firing Line, Frontline,* and Bill Moyers' interview programs, but even these "small" ones provide intellectual ammunition every week to millions of faithful viewers. There is also a strong intellectual component in American radio, especially the talk shows where not only the audio pundits but also the listening audience participate in a free-for-all discussion. They range in size from national programs such as the *Larry King Show* and *Rush Limbaugh,* which have audiences running up into the millions, to small local broadcasts with audiences in the thousands.

Finally, there is a relatively new occupational group in America, called "fellows," that falls into the professional intellectual class. Their place of employment is the think tank, usually some variety of private research institution. They are professionals because thinking and writing, not teaching, is their occupation.

Perhaps the most striking thing about America's think tanks is their size. If we set aside two think tanks, the Rand Corporation and the Urban Institute, whose main client is the federal government, and the hundreds of tiny one- and two-person institutes, the private think tanks are, collectively, a very small business in the giant U.S. economy. The combined annual budget of the top dozen private think tanks in America—American Enterprise Institute, Brookings Institution, Carnegie Endowment for International Peace, Cato Institute, Center for Strategic and International Studies,

Heritage Foundation, Hoover Institution, Hudson Institute, Institute for Policy Studies, Manhattan Institute for Policy Research, Russell Sage Foundation, and Twentieth Century Fund—is less than $100 million. They employ fewer than three hundred fellows. Compared to the tens of billions of dollars expended by the national media and by universities and colleges, America's think tanks are a tiny David competing with intellectual Goliaths.

Yet the think-tank fellows have carved out a considerable role for themselves in the intellectual world of America. Perhaps the secret of the unexpected impact these several hundred fellows have had during the past two decades is the time advantage they enjoy over most of their intellectual colleagues in the media and in the university. Unlike professors, fellows can devote full, undivided attention to their research and writing, uninterrupted by classes to teach or meetings to attend. Fellows have almost total flexibility in their work life. If invited to testify before a congressional committee, or to write a column for a newspaper or magazine, or to shift gears completely to work for a political campaign, or even to set aside everything for years in order to research and write a book—they can do it without conflict. Not so for the typical professor, who is often committed many months ahead to a specific schedule of classes to teach and other obligations.

The think-tank fellows enjoy a similar advantage over media pundits. The time demands on anyone writing for a newspaper or magazine, or even a writer of commercial books, are merciless and relentless. The fellow has the uncommon luxury of setting his or her own schedule, of exploring at leisure an avenue of research, of rewriting again and again, of not letting go of the work until it is polished and complete. This combination of full-time devotion to intellectual work and the absence of deadlines is what gives the fellows an advantage over their colleagues in the university and in the media, and largely explains the intellectual influence of America's think tanks.

In summary, the world of the professional intellectuals is boisterous and thriving, providing a rich diversity of views on a wide range of issues. The largest, perhaps most important segment of this world is the national media. Contrary to the criticism that the media have created an intellectual desert of entertainment and sound-bite news and classified ads, there are small slivers of intellectual analysis and commentary that, when added together, form a mighty intellectual force, shaping and influencing the thinking of Americans and many others throughout the world.

The two classes of intellectuals, the academics and the professionals, coexist uneasily with one another. They don't understand each other very well; they like each other even less. A very few intellectuals are hybrids with one foot in each camp; but instead of being a bridge between the two camps, these bi-intellectuals are probably suspect by both. Travel between the two classes is quite rare. Occasionally a professor will turn in his or her tenure and become a professional intellectual, but it almost never happens the other way around. No matter how learned and brilliant, very few professional intellectuals are ever considered good enough to be invited to don the robes of academe.

Academic intellectuals, especially those on the faculties of our elite universities, enjoy very high status among the general population—much higher than professional intellectuals.[5] There are few other professions that can touch them in terms of occupational status. Most academic intellectuals have a degree of contempt (generally well concealed) for those professional intellectuals who write for money, referring to such efforts as "popular" writing, with the word "popular" implying work that can be comprehended by the general public and thus of a lower order of intellect. But their contempt is also accompanied by an envy (very well concealed) of the amount of money many professional intellectuals make.

The professional intellectuals would appear to acquiesce in this view of themselves. While appreciative of the money they make, they often seem to regard academic intellectuals as a superior breed, their work a more important and pure form of intellectual life, the kind of work they would like to do if money were not a consideration. But while the professional intellectuals might express admiration and respect in the abstract for the work of professors, they rarely read it. For mixed with the respect they feel they should have is a certain disdain for work that often appears exceedingly narrow and irrelevant to the larger issues they struggle with daily.

The professional intellectuals are seldom lionized in the academic journals, and they have relatively little status and respect in this intellectual world. All they have is most of the intellectual power and influence in our society.

It is a curious situation. The men and women who write for and speak to huge, important audiences have only a fraction of the status enjoyed by their academic brothers and sisters who write for and speak to small, select audiences. And yet almost all of what is wrong with American intellectual life today is in the academic intellectual part.

Just listen to some of the voices knowledgeable about the world of academics. In 1988 Yale University's nineteenth president, A. Bartlett Giamatti, wrote that "for almost two decades the American people have been aware of and dismayed by the gap in the nation's colleges and universities, the gap between grand, traditional, and almost unexamined professions of high principle, lofty mission, and splendid purpose—and institutional behavior that is often venal, self-serving, and shoddy."[6] Venal, self-serving, and shoddy? In 1990 Bruce Wilshire, a professor at Rutgers University, published a book entitled *The Moral Collapse of the University,* in which he wrote: "We must speak of the bankruptcy of the university as an educational institution. It is an humiliating admission."[7] Bankruptcy? In 1991 William Bennett, the former secretary of education, observed sadly that "in some ways universities are becoming increasingly irrelevant to the intellectual life of the nation."[8] Irrelevant?

When educational leaders openly use words such as "venal," "shoddy," "bankrupt," and "irrelevant" to describe the state of higher education in America, we can be sure that something is seriously wrong.

I am fifty-five years old. I have spent most of the last thirty-five years living among academic intellectuals, and I have spent a lot of time associating with professional intellectuals. During all those years I observed both tribes, even taking notes from time to time on things of especial interest. Without intending it, I became somewhat of an amateur anthropologist of American intellectuals. They fascinated me, and still do.

My early experiences with the academic tribe were excellent. The years I spent as an undergraduate at Dartmouth College from 1953 to 1957 lived up to the ideal of what higher education should be—stimulating courses taught by learned professors in a wide range of subjects, from physics to geography and philosophy, from English to foreign languages to calculus and art. The professors lectured us, argued with us, counseled us, made up their own examinations, and graded them personally. They were tough and demanding, and they were fair. They were all walking models of intellectual integrity. We were pushed far beyond what many of us thought possible when we first walked onto the college green. They taught; we learned. I thrived on it, was elected to Phi Beta Kappa in my junior year, and graduated summa cum laude when I was twenty years old.

Much has changed in the last thirty-five years. I am not confident, were I to return to Dartmouth today as a freshman, that I would receive half the powerful intellectual experience that could be had in the mid-1950s.

After Dartmouth I went to graduate school at M.I.T., studied economic theory under world-renowned professors (including two Nobel Prize winners), and received a Ph.D. in industrial management. I taught graduate courses in the engineering school at Dartmouth for a summer, studied on a fellowship for a year at the Joint Center of M.I.T. and Harvard, and then taught for six years at the Graduate School of Business of Columbia University. Since 1971 I have been a senior fellow of the Hoover Institution at Stanford University. During this time I have taught classes and seminars, supervised doctoral dissertations, attained tenure, served on faculty search committees, gone to innumerable faculty meetings, eaten at many faculty clubs, served on miscellaneous university-wide committees, helped design major research programs, and counseled students. I have written articles and books and op-ed pieces, spoken to large groups, and appeared on numerous radio and television talk shows. This intellectual world is my world, the world I live in. The intellectuals are my colleagues, the people I work with and talk to every day.

That is why this book is written with sadness and regret—and some anger. Because much of this intellectual world is wonderful, most of the intellectuals I know are men and women of high intelligence and great integrity. But today this world is badly flawed—and those flaws are almost exclusively in the academic world. Too many of our universities and colleges have acquired the trappings of an aging state—the same kind of smug arrogance that comes to people who are never seriously challenged, the kind of elitist mind-set that makes its leaders feel they are above the laws and values that govern others, the presumptuousness to believe that what they say is important is important, that what they say is true is true.

The avalanche of books and articles that have poured over us in recent years has demonstrated convincingly that not only is all not well on America's university campuses, but that some things are really rotten. Few defend the transgressions, and none deny they exist. We know about the smothering impact of "politically correct" thought. We know of the assault on the history and values of Western civilization. We know of the financial corruption. We know of policies that judge, not by intellect and achievement, but by skin color—all in the name of anti-racism. We know of the demise of teaching, how little it is valued by faculty and administrators. We know of the blatant abuses concerning student athletes. We know of the political bias—to the left—of most members of the academy.

Yes, we know all this. We deplore it. We fear for the kind of education our children will receive when they leave home and enter the hallowed halls of higher education. We may even fear a bit for the future of this great republic, as other nations sense our faltering intellectual lead and strive to overtake us.

But we hear very little about what we can do about it. We hear even less about why it is happening.

What is wrong with America's intellectuals?

I believe the answer—and the blame—lies not with our institutions of higher education per se, nor with the students, nor with the parents or the government. It does not even lie with most of the faculty and administrators. The answer lies, as it usually does with any institution that goes astray, with the relatively small group of men and women who are acknowledged leaders—the intellectual elite of America. It lies with the people who set the standards and values of intellectual life in America, with the intellectual role models, with the pacesetters. Perhaps if we look more closely at who they are and what they do and what they value, we shall have a clearer idea of why American education is in crisis today, and what specific things can be done to make it better.

I am reminded of a letter John Maynard Keynes wrote to a friend in November 1919 when Keynes was about halfway through writing *The Economic Consequences of the Peace,* a tough critique of the events that led up to the Versailles peace treaty. In that letter he wrote, "I personally despair of results from anything but violent and ruthless truth-telling—that will work *in the end,* even if slowly."[9] It is time to peel back the lid and peer into the top layers of the American academy.

CHAPTER TWO

ACADEME

UNIVERSITIES AND COLLEGES are now big business in America. Dwarfing in size the intellectual segments of the media world and the valiant band of think tanks, they roll along with a combined budget of many billions of dollars a year. The growth of American universities into big business has been recent and fairly sudden. In 1960 the total budget for our colleges and universities was $7 billion. During the next ten years it leaped to $25 billion, and kept accelerating through the 1970s. By 1980 it had reached $62 billion. In 1989 it was $130 billion, growing steadily at about $8 billion a year.[1]

Many universities are huge enterprises in themselves. Today the billion-dollar university is commonplace. All the top universities in the country have assets well in excess of a billion dollars. The assets of Harvard University, the largest of any U.S. university, were valued at some $5.9 billion in 1990. Stanford weighed in with assets worth $3.8 billion, followed by the University of Michigan at $3.7 billion, Yale at $3.5 billion, and Princeton and Columbia with $2.7 billion each. Even a relatively small college like Dartmouth was worth $914 million. And they all had annual budgets to match their wealth. Harvard, Stanford, Michigan, Columbia, and M.I.T. each spent over $1 billion in 1990. The wealth and spending power of our universities has never been greater.

The product the university sells is education, but curiously little of its annual revenues comes from the sale of what it produces.

Public universities receive only about 15 percent of their monies from student tuition and fees. Fully 60 percent of the funding comes from government—most of it from state governments, a substantial chunk from the federal government, and a little from local governments. The other 25 percent is derived from gifts, endowments, and miscellaneous sources, including various enterprises run by the university.[2] To a very large extent—some 60 percent worth—you are watching your tax dollars at work when you look at today's public universities.

The great private universities are only partially private; less than 40 percent of their revenue comes from tuition and fees, while another 40 percent may come from gifts, endowments, and miscellaneous enterprises. Private universities, even the elite ones such as Stanford, M.I.T., and Harvard, draw a significant amount of their incomes from the government checking account. Principally through funding for research, and grants and loans to students, government monies provide about 20 percent of the annual operating costs of private, independent universities. Almost all government support at private universities is federal; only 13 percent comes from state and local governments.[3] So even when you look at the private universities you still see quite a few of your tax dollars at work.

The faculty of universities and colleges now constitutes one of the largest occupational groups in America. Compared to the hundreds of think-tank fellows and the thousands of professional intellectuals in the media, the 665,000 men and women on the faculties of our universities and colleges make up one of the largest groups of academic intellectuals ever assembled.[4]

It is these two-thirds of a million academic intellectuals who today are the most suspect of America's intellectuals. They are an enigma and a paradox, very expensive ones. Most people know little of what they do and how well they do it, and much of what we do know often seems contradictory. But of one thing we can be certain. Their control of the centers of higher learning and research in our society gives them a potential power for either good or ill that is too important to ignore. For ultimately it is these people, our professors, who control the levers of formal education—and through it have a significant impact on the destiny of our country. And that is why the work of the academic intellectuals is too important to be left solely in their hands.

We know a lot about the work of professional intellectuals. We read their books and their articles and editorials in the newspapers, we listen to them on radio, we watch them on television. They write primarily for us, the reader—in clear, simple English—not for their intellectual colleagues. We may or may not agree with them, but we know what they do.

On the other hand, most of us have little idea what academic intellectuals actually do. We know they are supposed to teach and write, to impart knowledge to the young and to create some new knowledge on their own. Yet, except for the four or five years we spent in college classrooms, years that are for many of us only a dim, distant memory, we have no direct experience of what they teach and how well they do it. If we have sons and daughters in college we may get some hearsay tales, but little appreciation of their professors' actual teaching talents. When it comes to research and writing, which is now considered to be the most important thing these intellectuals do, most of us know nothing. Virtually all their work is published in scholarly journals, read almost exclusively by their colleagues and peers. Very few men and women outside the halls of academe ever read these specialized academic journals.

The result is that most of what we do know about the work of academic intellectuals—their teaching, their writing—we know from what they tell us. In essence, they rate each other and then announce their rankings to those outside the academy. When we say a professor is distinguished we almost always do so because other professors have told us it is so. This is a luxury of blind trust we can no longer afford.

The university's leap from a secluded retreat of quiet thought to one of America's bustling big businesses was not caused by some new intellectual awakening, by a thirst for knowledge on the part of its faculty. It was not driven by people banging on the doors of the university, wanting to join the faculty to pursue learning. What drove it was the explosive growth of the student population.

For a long time a college education was a rare privilege in the United States, something reserved for the brilliant and wealthy, and those otherwise drawn to intellectual pursuits. In 1870 there were only 52,000 college students in America, less than 2 percent of the 18-to-21 age group. Even in 1910, only 5 percent of the college-age population was enrolled in a college or university.[5] College graduates continued to be a small and elite group through the first half of the twentieth century.

As the appreciation of a college education grew, so did the demand, and the percentage of our young men and women attending college jumped sharply. By the beginning of World War II, 1.5 million of our children, over 15 percent of the college-age population, were in college. The end of World War II brought many changes, and one of them was a doubling of the number of college students. By 1950 the percentage of the 18-to-21-year-olds going to college had jumped to 29.9, then slowly increased until 1960, when 33 percent of our eligible youth, approximately 3.2 million of them, were in the halls of academe.[6]

Then came the explosive growth of the student body that transformed the world of the academic intellectuals. During the 1960s the number of college students leaped from the low 3 million range to 8.5 million; and between 1970 and 1975 it soared to 11.2 million, almost half of all the eligible youth in America. In just fifteen years, the size of the college population almost tripled, an increase of some 8 million students. From 1975 through the early 1980s the growth continued, but much more slowly, peaking at about 12.5 million in 1983, where it has held fairly steady. In fact, it is predicted to decline slightly in the years ahead to 12.2 million by 1996.[7]

There are many reasons for the explosive growth in the number of college students. One was a genuine increase in the desire for advanced learning and for the undergraduate and graduate degrees that were becoming so important for a successful career. Another was the substantial increase in the college-age population, the result of the "baby boom" that followed World War II. But part of it was also due to the turmoil and social unrest of the 1960s and 1970s, a time when young men felt mortally threatened by the possibility of being drafted and forced to fight in a war in Vietnam that many of them neither understood nor supported. Many fled to the universities to escape the draft, not necessarily to pursue higher knowledge. Finally, a substantial increase in federal programs provided the billions of dollars in grants and loans that enabled many more young men and women to join the ranks of those attending college. The combined impact of these forces resulted in a revolutionary change in the size and character of the college student population. For the first time in history, vast numbers of young men and women who would never have gone on to higher education were now there.

The 8 million increase in the number of college students from 1960 to 1975 hit the academic intellectuals like a tidal wave, and it caused much of the institutional trauma that plagues the university to this day. What was great for the young men and women of America was a terrible problem for the institutions. Who would teach these new throngs of students? Who would design the courses, and grade the exams, and counsel the students? Were there enough classrooms? Where would the students live? Well, the schools were up to the challenge. They absorbed the students, provided classrooms, and housed and fed them. But they may have paid a price. For in order to accommodate these students, they had to greatly expand their faculty and do it quickly.

Looking back at America's intellectual world since the end of World War II we can see there have been many notable changes— the vast increase in the influence of the professional intellectuals due to profound changes in communications technology, the growth of the think tanks, and the sharply increased demand for higher education. But none has been so notable or effected so much change in the nature of the intellectual world than the sheer increase in the number of academic intellectuals. Today, higher education is bursting its seams with two-thirds of a million restless, striving academic intellectuals, a mass of "thinkers" that probably far exceeds its natural size.

For most of our history, only a tiny fraction of the population answered the academic intellectual calling. Some two hundred and forty years ago, in 1750, the academe of America consisted of ten professors.[8] Gradually the ranks of the professors grew, slightly faster than the total population, but their numbers remained small. As late as 1870 there were only 5,553 professors in the United States, 4,887 men and 666 women.[9] As a proportion of the adult, eligible population in the nation, those between the ages of twenty-five and sixty-four, these professors were a quite tiny group—only four out of every 10,000. They were an elite group, by and large highly intelligent, many with a love of learning and a passion for teaching.

As the demand for higher education increased and the number of students expanded, so did the numbers of professors. By 1900 nearly eight out of every 10,000 adults were academic intellectuals. By 1920 the ratio had crept up to ten out of every 10,000. In retrospect these ratios seem to be reasonable, that five to ten men and women out of 10,000 would possess the special qualifications required of a university professor.

There are three main qualities that distinguish and define the academic intellectual. He or she must be blessed with high intelligence—at least in the upper 5 or 10 percent of the population, and preferably much higher. The hallmark of every intellectual, professional or academic, is that he or she is relatively smart. There is no such thing as a dumb intellectual; it would be a contradiction in terms. High intelligence does not necessarily imply wisdom or moral superiority, but it does mean the capability to understand and retain great amounts of information, to reason accurately and quickly, and to think creatively. It is the one thing common to all intellectuals.

But over and above raw intelligence, academic intellectuals need a couple of other attributes that need not be shared with their professional brethren. First, they must have the temperament of a scholar. Not all brilliant people like to do what academic intellectuals are supposed to do. In fact, most of those qualified by intelligence alone choose not to become professors. They become lawyers, doctors, entrepreneurs, artists, business executives, politi-

33

cians. Few people are suited by temperament to sit alone for hours in a musty library pursuing an obscure fact or a solution to a troublesome problem, and then reveling in its discovery. Few are suited by temperament to think for weeks or months, even years, only to come up with a new concept or idea that cannot be sold, but only shared, and yet still feel a profound satisfaction. And fewer still are suited to the anguish involved in capturing those vaporous thoughts and reducing them to the written word.

Second, the academic intellectual should be good at something that is unnecessary for the professional intellectual: classroom teaching. And he or she must like to teach. Teaching well is an uncommon skill, and many of those who are good at it don't like to do it. Most teaching involves direct, personal contact with much younger, less sophisticated minds. One must enjoy and value the pleasures of tickling those young minds, of watching the excitement of their growing awareness of intellectual power, of teaching them how to think.

Those individuals who possess all the necessary traits we have come to expect in an academic intellectual—high intelligence, studious temperament, love of teaching—are rare. The historical record suggests that perhaps less than one out of a thousand in our society qualifies on all counts. And that simple demographic statistic may be at the core of the difficulties we are experiencing in the academic world today.

As the demand for a college education has grown, we have been forced to find more professors. The increase in faculty has closely followed that of the student population: rapid growth during the fifteen years between 1960 and 1975, much smaller increases through the early 1980s, and a leveling off over the next ten years. Perhaps even more important than the absolute increase in numbers was the increase in their proportion of our society.

The number of professors per 10,000 adults in the United States—what we might call the academic intellectual ratio—has increased dramatically in this century. From 10 in 1920, the ratio moved up rapidly to 20 in 1940, to 28 in 1960. Then, as the student population explosion occurred over the next fifteen years, the ratio almost doubled from its 1960 level. By 1975 an estimated 52 out of every 10,000 adults in the United States had some faculty title. The ratio stayed slightly above 50 until the early 1980s, when it began to drop slowly, reflecting the leveling off of student population growth. Today, with some 665,000 college and university faculty out of the relevant adult population of slightly over 123 million, the ratio stands in the low 40s.[10]

By and large this dramatic growth in the number and proportion of academic intellectuals has been a male phenomenon. Male professors have outnumbered female professors by about three to one since the turn of the century.

The sudden increase in the size of our academic intellectual population during the fifteen years from 1960 to 1975 was an expected consequence of the growth of the student population, but it also may have had some unexpected consequences. When you more than double the number of professors—from 276,000 in 1960 to 628,000 in 1975—you run into the same sorts of problems any profession would encounter that attempted to increase its size rapidly. Where do you find 352,000 new professors in fifteen years? How qualified are they to teach and do creative, original research? How do you attract these men and women to the college teaching profession?

With a population base of over 200 million people at the time, numbers were not a problem, but qualifications were. It requires a rare blend of skills and temperament to qualify as an academic intellectual. If you suddenly and sharply increase the relative number of professors in any society—as we did during the 1960s and 1970s—you run into some intractable demographic problems. The nature of any population changes very slowly over time. Over the short span of a few decades such characteristics as the distribution of intelligence, a studious temperament, and a passion for teaching the young are not likely to change at all.

Many of the critical qualities that make a good academic intellectual cannot be taught. Skills can be augmented and improved by training, but no amount of opportunity or education can significantly alter the degree of intelligence or the kind of temperament that one must have to be a good professor.

What can you do when you need more professors quickly to fill the powerful new demands for higher education? You hire some people who may not be quite as intelligent as you would like, even though they may have a monklike devotion to intellectual work and love to teach. You may accept some people who, though brilliant researchers, really don't care that much for working with young students. You may even take some people who are highly intelligent and great teachers but who loathe research, study, and writing. Slowly, almost imperceptibly over the years, you compromise the standards of quality and take men and women who may be a little less intelligent, a little less capable of doing scholarly research, a little less devoted to teaching.

It is theoretically possible to sharply increase the size of the academic intellectual class in a society over a short period of time without either lowering its average intelligence or demeaning the quality of its temperament. In theory one could conceivably improve both. But this assumes the prior existence of many people who are qualified to be academic intellectuals but who are currently working in other fields—and further assumes they would leave these jobs and join the faculties of universities. Possible, but unlikely.

Today there is a real question as to whether we have watered down the quality of the academic intellectual stock by rapidly expanding the sheer number of professors in our society. There is no scientific evidence available to test this proposition, and there probably never will be. We don't regularly give intelligence tests to professors and track the scores over time. No one has yet devised a scientific test for measuring the scholarly temperament of intellectuals, let alone measuring the degree of their affection for teaching and their skill at it.

But we can make some personal, subjective judgments. The logic of the argument points to some degree of watering down. If you take any profession or craft that requires a special set of human skills and personality traits—whether it be professional baseball players, policemen, or rock musicians—and greatly expand the number of people in that occupation over a short period of time, you will almost certainly see a marked deterioration in the quality of work performed. The stars, those at the top of their profession, will probably perform as well or better than before; it is the average performance that is likely to suffer.

What I have observed personally, during some thirty years of working with academic intellectuals, has convinced me that there has been a slow but significant decline in the average quality of academic intellectuals. Personal observations are a rickety foundation on which to build any sweeping generalization, especially given the normal tendency to romanticize the "good old days." But when I compare the professors I knew when I was a professor at Columbia University in the early 1960s with the professors I know today, I see an increasing number who thoroughly enjoy the prestige of being professors but who dislike what professors are supposed to do. Most of them don't like to teach, few of them do important research and writing, and at least one or two aren't very intelligent.

Perhaps I was spoiled by some of the early encounters I had in my own intellectual career. I remember one night in the early 1960s when I was a young faculty member at Columbia. My wife Annelise and I had been invited to a small party at Professor Milton Friedman's apartment on the upper West Side of New York City. All the guests were professors and their spouses, and the discussion was lively. Around 11:00 P.M. I got into an argument with Friedman over some point of political or economic theory, the substance of which I cannot recall. What I do remember is the zest and exhilaration of that discussion. Arguing with Milton Friedman was the intellectual equivalent of attempting to climb Mount Everest. We went on until close to 2:00 A.M., most of the guests had left, and I finally admitted that I was tired and sleepy and had to go home. Friedman smiled, his eyes twinkling, and said, "All right, I win."

Milton Friedman, over and above his reputation as the world's best economist, is also an archetype of what an academic intellectual should be. Beyond his brilliant mind and his influential research and writing, he has a natural instinct for teaching. He teaches naturally, all the time, whether in front of a lecture hall or in personal conversation. He loves the play of ideas, loves challenging people, making them think, pursuing the truth wherever it leads. About him is an aura of pure intellectual integrity.

If we had an academic world peopled with men and women the caliber of Milton Friedman we would not have the problems that are now crashing down on us in the intellectual world. We would have what we should have: an academic intellectual community distinguished by brilliance, by important, relevant research, by teaching that crackled and sizzled, by integrity. We are far from that ideal, and getting farther away every day.

The question of whether the quality of academic intellectuals has been diminished may never be answered with certitude, and will probably remain in the realm of personal judgment in the foreseeable future. But if the thesis is true, that there has indeed been a watering down of our academic intellectual quality, it might go a long way toward explaining the often inexplicable, sometimes shocking things that occur on even our most elite university campuses. And if we can explain things, we may then be able to fix them.

Another notable, and perhaps unexpected, consequence of the powerful demand for professors during the last few decades has been a strong improvement in the working conditions of the faculty. No longer poor, threadbare idealists who seemed to care little for the material benefits of this world as they strove for truth and knowledge, today's academic intellectuals have perhaps the best combination of working conditions and pay of any large occupational group in America. In the multibillion-dollar industry that is higher education, the captains of that industry go first-class.

From the outside, today's universities look much like a large business corporation. They have hundreds of administrators and staff, boards of directors, thousands of professors, and tens of thousands of students. But they are not organized or run like a corporation. There is nothing comparable to stockholders to whom corporate boards and executives must ultimately answer. No one "owns" a university. Virtually all the major universities and colleges in America are mini-socialist states in which the trustees, administrators, and faculty answer only to themselves. True, there is a theoretical pecking order: the faculty answers to the administrators, the administrators to the trustees, but as a practical matter the academic intellectuals answer first to each other, and then to God.

The new academic intellectuals have used this privileged and powerful position to carve out some very good working conditions, especially at the more elite universities, conditions that would make any labor union leader of the twentieth century envious. Unlike any other employees in the United States, save for federal judges, tenured professors cannot be fired. The most unusual feature of being a professor is tenure, an almost ironclad form of job security.

Tenure is relatively new in America's universities, becoming a faculty right less than fifty years ago. Ostensibly put in place to guarantee academic freedom, to prevent a professor from being fired for such things as unpopular political views, tenure quickly transformed itself into a "job for life," immunity from being fired for anything but the most flagrant violations of conduct. Today, a professor's conscience is the main guardian of the standards of teaching and research, for if his or her only sin is not teaching very well or not producing important writing, not much can or will be done by the university administrators.

Tenure is what really separates the universities from business corporations. That, and the fact that there are no clear-cut owners to answer to, has created a free-floating, self-governing organization that pretty much can do as it wishes.

Other working conditions are what one might expect from a group that sets its own agenda. While most professors work hard, and for long hours, they have extraordinary flexibility as to when they do work. The times when they must be somewhere, such as teaching a specific class, are few, usually no more than half a dozen class lectures a week. The rest of their work—student counseling, research and writing, exam preparation and grading—they can adjust to their own schedule. Even in the midst of teaching a full range of courses they can almost always find an hour or two, or sometimes even a day or two, to tend to personal chores or pleasure.

To a significant extent academic intellectuals are their own bosses.

Their vacations are the longest in the land. Their summer vacation time can easily run three to four months. At Christmas and during spring break, they can usually pick up another week or two off. True, many professors do study and write during this time off, rather than play in the snow or sun. But the point is that they do so by choice, not because they must.

They are also well paid, some might say very well paid. Salaries vary greatly according to rank and seniority, the field of study, and the prestige of the school. At top universities the average full professor made over $80,000 a year in 1991, with a significant number of them earning in excess of $100,000. Even young assistant professors make well over $40,000 a year at these schools. The highest-paid professors are at Harvard, where their average salary was $89,000 in 1991. At the other end of the academic spectrum, the two-year colleges, full professors average about $45,000 a year and assistant professors $32,000. The pay range can vary by as much as 50 percent according to the field of study. For example, in private universities and colleges, professors of engineering, economics, and business make about one-third more than their colleagues in history, political science, and sociology, and one-half again as much as those in the fields of teacher education and theology.[11] A full professor at a medical school can make $150,000 or more.[12]

Beyond their base salary, many professors earn substantial amounts of money from private consulting, speaking fees, book royalties, and other miscellaneous work. Most universities and colleges allow their faculty the equivalent of one full day a week to do other things for which they can get paid. Professors do not punch a time clock, so it would be very difficult to check on exactly how they do spend their time. But that is not a problem, because rarely does anyone check.

Consequently, the opportunities to augment their income are plentiful. Some professors even run their own outside companies. In fact, "moonlighting" has become so widespread in recent years, to the detriment of things like teaching and grading and counseling students, that alarms are being sounded. In August 1989, Ernest

L. Boyer, president of the Carnegie Foundation for the Advancement of Teaching and one of the most respected authorities in the field of higher education, warned that "we need to strengthen oversight of entrepreneurial activities and ask hard questions about how many professors are engaged in outside activities."[13] But while we wait for the hard questions to be asked, and for the equally tough-minded solutions that should ensue, everything is wide open and running free.

The university salary is only part of the total compensation a professor gets. Fringe benefits for the faculty and staff of universities are close to being the most comprehensive and generous of any profession in America, except maybe for the members of the U.S. Congress. Their medical and dental insurance coverage is top of the line, and the university usually pays most, if not all, of the insurance premiums. Not even the federal government's retirement plan for its employees exceeds the generosity of the university retirement plan. It is completely portable from university to university. Once in the professor club, it does not matter where one teaches, the pension plan will follow.

The retirement pay is munificent. For example, at Stanford University a professor can salt away up to 5 percent of his or her salary every year into a retirement fund—the Teachers Insurance and Annuity Association College Retirement Equities Fund—and not be taxed on a penny of it while it accumulates. The best part is that for every dollar the professor contributes to the fund, the university double-matches it with two more dollars. Thus, for every dollar a professor saves, he or she gets three dollars invested in stocks and bonds—tax-free until retirement. Depending on how well the financial markets do, a professor retiring in the 1990s could well walk away with a nest egg of a million dollars.

Then there are the perquisites, the special bonuses one gets for being a professor. Many universities pay all or part of the college tuition for the children of their professors, even if they attend a college other than the one their parent works for. Most universities give subsidies for faculty housing. Automobile parking is cheap, often free. For example, at Stanford University where any parking is at a premium, a university sticker for the choicest parking locations is just $200 a year, or about a dollar a day for the normal nine-month teaching schedule.

The list goes on. Comprehensive life insurance policies with low premium rates. Same for automobile insurance. Excellent, subsidized meals at the faculty club. Substantial discounts when the professor rents an automobile from Hertz or Avis and flashes the university identification card. Special low rates at hotels. Full expenses paid for travel to conferences, often located in exciting domestic cities or exotic foreign lands. At the office there is free telephone, photocopiers, computers galore, fax machines. Professors have access to some of the best libraries in the world, secretarial help, and research and teaching assistants. About the only thing missing is door-to-door limousine service.

They also get free use of recreational facilities, from tennis courts, swimming pools, gymnasiums, basketball courts, squash courts, and weight rooms to, in some cases, an 18-hole golf course. Some universities near bodies of water have extensive sailing facilities. Stanford University owns a 72-foot yacht.

Many of the bigger universities and colleges have special recreational and conference facilities. Columbia University has Arden House, a dazzling estate the faculty often uses for conferences. Stanford University maintains a gorgeous resort on pristine Fallen Leaf Lake high in the Sierras. Dartmouth College has Moosilauke Lodge, used for camping and hiking in the White Mountains of New Hampshire. Then there are the special events, many of them closed to the general public—the lectures by famous and interesting people, the movies, the concerts and theater, the art exhibitions.

Taken all together, the package of pay and benefits and perquisites and general working conditions for academic intellectuals is better than that received by 99 percent of the workers in America.

The highest incomes in the academic world are usually reserved for the top administrators—our university and college presidents. The people who run the billion-dollar schools often live like the people who run billion-dollar corporations. For the most part, the responsibilities of their jobs justify what they earn, but it can nevertheless be enlightening to understand the full extent of their compensation. A survey by the *Chronicle of Higher Education* of presidential compensation in 1989 clearly shows that these educational leaders are not scrimping to get by.

Joe Wyatt, president of Vanderbilt University, was at the top with a whopping $300,000 salary—considerably more than the president of the United States earns. Michael Sovern, president of Columbia, was close behind with an annual salary of $297,000. Others included John Silber of Boston University ($275,000), David Gardner of the University of California ($243,500), Paul Gray of M.I.T. ($226,000), Hanna Gray of the University of Chicago ($222,500), H. Keith H. Brodie of Duke ($214,456), Donald Kennedy of Stanford ($194,375), Harold Shapiro of Princeton ($188,917), and Benno Schmidt of Yale ($187,500).[14]

Presidential salaries ranged from an average of $238,000 a year at major private universities down to $58,400 at small community colleges. But salaries are only part of the compensation of university presidents. A recent survey of 874 campuses found that an official residence was provided for 47 percent of these academic chief executives, 33 percent received a household staff, 67 percent got an automobile, 89 percent were fully reimbursed for all travel and entertainment, 78 percent were eligible for free tuition for their children, 16 percent received an annual bonus over and above their salary, and 63 percent held paid corporate directorships.[15] The result is a total compensation package that makes university presidents one of the highest-paid groups in America.

For example, take Stanford University. The president's salary is $194,375. Add to that the value of free housing. The president lives in a stately residence built by Herbert Hoover, a home that could be worth as much as $2 million in the California housing market. That translates into a housing subsidy of approximately $200,000 a year. Along with the free housing goes a retinue of servants—a cook, a personal assistant for the family, a housekeeper, two grounds keepers, and a house manager. When you add it all up, the total compensation package easily exceeds half a million dollars a year, and it is typical of what the heads of our big business-style universities earn in the 1990s.

When presidents step down from their perch at the top of the university they usually step into financially comfortable retirements. In one notable instance in 1991 the president of the University of Pittsburgh, Wesley W. Posvar, retired and was given (1) a lump-sum cash payment of $938,000, (2) annuities from two pension plans, and (3) a guaranteed annual payment of $201,000 for the rest of his life. That's even better than being a congressman.[16]

In summary, the hallowed halls of ivy have been radically transformed over the last few decades. From the rather small, quiet, dignified institutions of rarefied scholarly pursuits and the teaching of a select few, they have ballooned into sophisticated megabusiness machines, staffed by hundreds of thousands of men and women who call themselves professors, offering courses to millions of students, and paying themselves very well for what they do.

CHAPTER THREE

CHILDREN
TEACHING CHILDREN

In December 1990 the Carnegie Foundation for the Advancement of Teaching dropped the equivalent of a precision-guided bomb into the heart of academe. It was a small, 147-page report innocuously entitled "Scholarship Reconsidered." Written by the foundation's president, Ernest Boyer, the report was a scathing critique of college teaching. Boyer, former chancellor of the State University of New York and the U.S. commissioner of education under President Carter, concluded that "in the current climate, students all too often are the losers . . . in glossy brochures, they're assured that teaching is important, that a spirit of community pervades the campus, and that general education is the core of the undergraduate experience. But the reality is that on far too many campuses, teaching is not well rewarded and faculty who spend too much time counseling and advising students may diminish their prospects for tenure and promotion."[1]

Between the diplomatic lines was an acknowledgment of the secret shame of most universities and colleges in America: studied neglect of the teaching of students.

Boyer's bomb never exploded. Briefly noted in a few newspapers, the report was soon buried deep in the library stacks, there to be quietly forgotten. But the shame continues.

In the Alice-in-Wonderland world of today's academic intellectuals, the priorities are topsy-turvy. The teaching of students, the main reason for the existence of colleges and universities, gets—as the comedian Rodney Dangerfield would put it—"no respect." An increasing number of professors not only do not like to teach (and avoid it whenever possible) but, even worse, have little regard for the teaching efforts of their colleagues.

There is now a widespread contempt for teaching among the teachers on our university and college campuses. The immediate losers are the young men and women who are the students. The long-run losers are all of us, as the country loses all those things that might have been if the best and the brightest of our young people had achieved their potential.

It is difficult to explain how serious the contempt for teaching has become, so perhaps it is best to turn for a moment to a few of the experts and listen to the anguish in their voices. On April 5, 1990, Donald Kennedy, the president of Stanford University, gave an urgent address to the entire Stanford intellectual community, calling for a return to the main work of the university.

"It is time for us to reaffirm that education—that is, teaching in all its forms—is the primary task," said Kennedy. "We need to talk about teaching more, respect and reward those who do it well, and make it first among our labors. It should be our labor of love, and the personal responsibility of each one of us."[2]

Kennedy, to his credit, was one of the first to let out of the bag one of the best-kept secrets in America: the sorry state of university teaching. He is not alone. Everyone in the higher ranks of the universities knows the disrepute into which teaching has fallen, but few have spoken out as clearly as Kennedy did.

Now and then even a teacher has complained. James David Barber is a professor of political science at Duke University, a senior scholar who knows his academic colleagues well. Obviously disturbed and frustrated by what he knew, he let loose a sensational blast at his profession in January 1990. Barber charged that "the community of scholars" had so fragmented that it had "essentially destroyed any institutional responsibility for the quality of teaching, the rigor of student evaluation," and that "there are universities, including famous ones, where professional ethics are completely

46

neglected in faculty recruitment, so that this relatively civil line of work is warped by bullying and lying punks."[3]

No responsibility for the quality of teaching? Professional ethics completely neglected? Professors who are bullying and lying punks? It sounds preposterous, and I wish it were. But if one looks hard at the nature of university teaching, at who teaches, at how they grade and counsel students, it is difficult to disagree with the senior professor from Duke University.

Adding insult to injury, the university demands that parents pay dearly for the privilege. By the early 1990s the basic cost of attending one of America's better colleges—tuition, room and board—had soared to more than $20,000 a year.[4] That $20,000 is just for bare necessities; it does not include money for clothes, travel, books, and a little entertainment now and then.

What kind of teaching does $20,000 a year buy? Assume the typical student attends classes for three quarters during the school year. A quarter usually has ten weeks plus or minus a day or two for holidays. With a normal course load of three or four classes per quarter, and two to three hours of lectures per week for each class, there is a grand total of approximately 275 hours of classroom instruction a year. Stepping aside from the questions of how large the class is and whether or not it is taught by a professor or a student, a quick calculation shows you are effectively paying over $70 per hour for each class, whether you attend or not. That's more than the price of a ticket for a Super Bowl game or the best seat at the Metropolitan Opera House.

Teaching is what separates the academic intellectual from the professional intellectual. The first thing professors must do is profess, to teach special knowledge. That is primarily what they are paid to do: to lecture to students, to discuss and argue with them, to grade and judge them, to counsel and advise them. Everything else professors do—committee work, community service, scholarly research—is extra, above and beyond the basic requirements of their craft.

The teaching part of a professor's job, properly done, is tough, demanding work. This may sound like heresy, for it is contrary to the popular notion that university-level teaching is quite a leisurely, carefree way to make a living. After all, says the conventional wisdom, "they only teach six, maybe nine, hours a week," implying the rest is free time. Not true.

The hour spent in the classroom pacing back and forth in front of young students, challenging them, trying to stimulate them to think, is only the very tip of the effort that goes into teaching. I remember that during my first few years as a professor at Columbia University I easily spent eight or ten hours preparing for every hour of lecture, sometimes more. A seventy- or eighty-hour workweek was not unusual. In later years, when I taught the same course again, the preparation time was less, but it still took an hour or two for each hour of class to review my notes and update them.

University teaching is a three-legged stool, and class lectures are only one of the legs. The other legs are equally difficult and time-consuming. The classroom lecture is a one-way flow to the student and has limited value, perhaps not much more than watching a good videotape. The two-way flow between professor and student is where the real teaching is done. This interaction takes place when there is classroom discussion, a dialogue between the class and the teacher where students learn to test their own powers of thinking, presenting ideas and defending them.

The second major part of the student's learning experience takes place in the grading process. This is where the professor puts on his or her judge's robes and evaluates the performance of the student. It is an absolutely critical part of learning, because if you don't know what you are doing right, or what you are doing wrong, how can you make corrections and improve? Unfortunately, grading, properly done, is exquisitely difficult work, takes great skill, and much time: time spent in creating the examination, time spent in reading each student's labored answer, time spent in judging that answer and critiquing it in a way that does not discourage. When I taught, just making up an examination could take hours. Reading one student's exam, judging it, and writing a critique took at least half an hour. Simple calculation shows that grading one examination for one class of forty students can easily take twenty hours.

Multiply that by several classes dozens of times a year and you get an idea of the time commitment that proper grading requires.

The third leg of the triad is student counseling. Many students, even today, think of university professors as Thomas Jefferson thought of them, as "moral exemplars, persons of unusual virtue and wisdom."[5] Students want their advice on everything from the courses they should take to the life careers they should pursue. If the professor responds to the students' needs, as he should, it takes hours of time and effort. Each student's situation is unique, and advice must be given carefully because it will likely be followed. If there are any hours left in a professor's week after lecturing and grading they can be quickly absorbed by conscientious counseling.

But proper teaching creates a problem, a big problem. Teaching is low man on the totem pole of academic prestige. What counts today is research and publishing and certain kinds of administrative work. Professors get prestigious positions, promotions, and salary increases primarily on the work they do as researchers and administrators, not as teachers. So, being intelligent, rational beings, they have noticed that they don't get rewarded for doing something they don't like doing anyway. And many of them have sloughed off their teaching responsibilities with skill and dispatch.

The critical problem today is not so much that many professors don't teach very well, but that so few of them teach at all, that a significant part of the crucial teaching responsibilities of our universities has been handed over to people who are unqualified. It is the shame of the academic intellectuals, a shabby secret they are loath to discuss publicly. If senior professors were lecturing only six hours a week to a hundred or so students, but were preparing those lectures thoughtfully and thoroughly, grading the students individually with care, and counseling them wisely, then we would have no complaints. But more and more professors are not teaching or grading or counseling. As a former Stanford professor, John Kaplan, an excellent teacher himself, once observed, "Professors feel that students are the crabgrass on the lawn of academia."

Professors don't lecture or lead classroom discussion? Don't grade? Don't counsel? Then who does?

Students.

The clever solution that professors have come up with for the teaching albatross that grew around their necks in the 1960s and 1970s is the teaching assistant. These young men and women, usually graduate students, but sometimes undergraduates, do a large part of the teaching work of many of our universities. You won't find them listed in any college or university catalog by name, but they lecture, they lead classroom discussions, they make up examinations and grade them, and they counsel their fellow students.

We have recently had a growing problem in this country with children having children, a practice that threatens the stability of family life. We now have what may be an even worse problem, students "teaching" students, children teaching children. The extent of the scandal is difficult to know precisely because the records of student teaching are not publicized. Pick up any university catalog and you will find only the vaguest of references to these student teachers. Look at the detailed schedule of courses and you will not find their names among the listed instructors. They are nameless and unknown, unhonored and unsung in their own universities.

For example, if you examine the 1989–1990 catalog for the University of California at Berkeley, one of the finest universities in America, you will find the following descriptions of the learning experience that awaits the young men and women lucky enough to gain admittance. The very first page asserts that the faculty "is made up of some of the most distinguished teachers and scholars in the world," and that there are "more seminars and small classes, more creative challenges to the student."

Three pages later the Berkeley catalog boasts that "students who attend Berkeley have the benefit of learning from world-renowned theorists and researchers who are also often distinguished teachers." It continues to advertise the extraordinary teaching: "Every year, departments nominate many of their faculty as distinguished teachers. You will encounter excellent teachers in all departments, all disciplines, in large classes and in seminars. There is no one way to teach well; the styles you will encounter will be as varied as the courses you take, from eye-opening lectures to discussion sections in which you will clarify and define your own ideas. In teaching, as in every aspect of Berkeley, diversity is the key to a rich and challenging educational experience."

The impression given to a proud parent is clear and direct. Let your sons and daughters come to Berkeley, let them learn from some of the best professors in the world.

But when the professors sit down and talk among themselves they tell a quite different story about who teaches what. For example, on April 13 and 14, 1989, the University of California sponsored a conference for selected faculty and administrators entitled "Teaching Assistants and the University." In the keynote address, Carol Cartwright, a vice chancellor for academic affairs at Davis, spelled out the importance of student teachers in the prestigious University of California system:

> Teaching Assistants are a central part of the undergraduate educational experience at the University of California. TAs number in the hundreds on our campuses, thousands in the UC system. They are responsible for leading discussions, running instructional labs, evaluating papers and exams, and performing other critical functions. . . . Lower division students [freshmen and sophomores] will frequently find themselves interacting with TAs as instructors, academic advisors, and personal advisors.[6]

You won't find that description printed in the university catalog.

The reality of teaching is very different from that described in university advertising. If this were a business, or a profession such as law, would we stand for such false and deceptive advertising? Wouldn't we call it fraud?

One of the few systematic studies ever done on the use of teaching assistants was carried out at Berkeley in 1984. The report concluded that there were "at least 1800 +" graduate-student instructors at Berkeley, and that "in 1983–84 graduate students were responsible for 58% of the lower-division class meetings."[7]

Three out of every five class meetings for freshmen and sophomores being taught by other students should have been an acute embarrassment for Berkeley. But apparently not. Five years later the ratio had swelled to three out of four: an article in the *American Scholar* noted that "a two-day walkout of teaching assistants on the Berkeley campus of the University of California in the spring of 1989 caused the cancellation of nearly 75 percent of classes."[8]

This kind of intellectual deceit, baiting the catalog with tales of world-class professors and then switching to student teachers once the freshmen are safely enrolled, is not limited to the sunny campus of Berkeley. It is now accepted practice in many colleges and universities.

In 1987 the Center for Teaching Excellence at Ohio State University published a major report on the first national conference on the use of teaching assistants in the United States, ending once and for all the defense that some particular horror story of unqualified student teachers was "just an isolated example." The 359 participants in the conference represented 117 universities, located in forty-three states and the District of Columbia. Of the 117 universities represented, 95 of them ranked in the top 150 institutions according to total student enrollment.[9]

While conceding that "not all higher-education institutions employ graduate students as teachers of undergraduates," the report concluded that "TAs are a significant part of the teaching force across major universities. TAs are frequently responsible for a large percentage of class sections taught in lower-division courses and thereby directly influence the quality of education that undergraduates experience."[10] The teaching tasks assigned by faculty to these students were numerous, including: "discussion or recitation group leader; laboratory instructor; writer, grader, and/or feedback provider for tests and exams." Some teaching assistants performed in a "limited capacity under the class supervision of a senior professor or course leader," but others were "expected to teach entire courses on their own."[11]

Beyond identifying the key role of student teachers in our universities, the report also noted something that some might find disturbing: we know almost nothing about these teaching assistants. "[University] data systems seldom go beyond identifying the number of graduate students with TA appointments. We simply do not know, with any confidence, the specific tasks, competencies, and standards of performance that are expected of TAs as they are selected and assigned particular teaching duties."[12]

This type of professional irresponsibility, this benign neglect of the foremost duty of the professor, is not an aberration of a rogue university or two—it is shot through the entire system. According to Edward Jennings, president of Ohio State University, "Clearly, teaching assistants stand at the center of university education . . . we depend heavily on our TAs."[13]

The motivation for entrusting university teaching to unqualified youth is venal. Every class taught by a student is one less class that has to be taught by a professor, one more hunk of time freed for the professor to do what he or she really wants to do, be it research and writing or perhaps just contemplating. As Kenneth Eble, professor of English at the University of Utah and author of one of the papers in the Ohio State report, explains it: "A higher education system growing from about three million students at the beginning of the 1960s to 12 million in the 1980s obviously needed large numbers of TAs. The continuing withdrawal of professors from teaching at the lower division or from undergraduate work altogether added to the need."[14]

This, in turn, has led to what in Professor Eble's view is a system that would be "indefensible within any world slightly better than the one we occupy." While defending the TA system (as he ironically puts it) "as weakly as I am able," he ruefully confides that the system: (1) "fosters education on the cheap," (2) "exploits the TAs' teaching and the students under their tutelage," (3) "creates an underclass, temporary to be sure, but signifying a class system, pretending to be something else," (4) "fosters . . . a pedagogy of pooled inexperience . . . or no pedagogy at all," and (5) "supports faculty self-interest, neatly separating the drudgery of basic instruction from the glory of specialized scholarly pursuits." Eble concludes pessimistically that "the TA system is indefensible, like much in academia, and I think it will be not so much defended as kept in place . . . [one of the] subclasses to do our dirty work."[15]

The number of students teaching students at specific universities is stunning. At the University of Washington, for example, in 1980 teaching assistants were responsible for "almost 25 percent of the instruction in all undergraduate courses." According to Provost George Beckmann, "Many teaching assistants are expected to grade papers, conduct quiz sections, and teach undergraduate courses without adequate training or supervision."[16] By 1987 the number of teaching assistants had grown to 1,200 and represented "43.9 percent of the total faculty, a significant amount yet actually less than the averages of peer institutions,[17] which accounted for 53.5 percent in 1983."[18]

In university mathematics departments throughout the country, 45 percent of the classes are taught by teaching assistants or part-time faculty. At Ohio State University, which has 40,000 undergraduates, 39 percent of the instruction was provided by 2,200 student teachers. The University of Louisville in Kentucky had 150 student teachers. At Brigham Young University in Utah, 75 percent of the freshman English composition courses were taught by students. At Indiana University, the department of French and Italian employed 50 teaching assistants (called "associate instructors").[19]

They seem to be everywhere.

In November 1991, 2,200 student teachers at the University of Massachusetts went on strike for higher wages—thus forcing the cancellation of almost 60 percent of the undergraduate classes.[20] Even at some of our most elite universities—including Harvard, Yale, Princeton, and Columbia—there are hundreds and hundreds of graduate students teaching a substantial share of the undergraduate classes.

The student teacher phenomenon seems especially acute at the larger public universities. By 1988 the "student faculty" at Ohio State had swelled to 2,410, distributed as follows: 170 in the arts, 180 in the biological sciences, 91 in business, 115 in education, 240 in engineering, 466 in the humanities, 546 in mathematics and the physical sciences, 372 in the social and behavioral sciences, and 230 in miscellaneous areas.[21]

Qualifying to become a TA is fairly simple and straightforward for a student at Ohio State. First, you have to be admitted to graduate school, and second, you must score a passing grade on a test of *spoken* English. When a selected sample of the student teachers were asked to describe their primary role in the classroom, fully 66 percent responded that I "teach a course by myself."[22]

The practice of shifting university teaching onto the backs of graduate students is not a new phenomenon. The problem has been building slowly for some time. For example, in 1976 a study was done on the teaching load in the humanities and science departments at Stanford University. Even then the student teacher was becoming pervasive. One question asked in that 1976 study was: "What percent of a student's contact hours in a course were with professors or teaching assistants?" Teaching assistants accounted for over 40 percent of all contacts in the humanities and over 30 percent in the sciences. Teaching assistants at Stanford handled the following percentage of the teaching load in these courses: freshman English (100 percent), philosophy (31 percent), religious studies (53 percent), Spanish (73 percent), German (48 percent), English (59 percent), economics (25 percent), history (48 percent), political science (43 percent), psychology (50 percent), sociology (32 percent), chemistry (40 percent), mathematics (34 percent), and physics (38 percent).[23]

One of the first people to spotlight this growing problem was Charles Sykes in a 1988 book highly critical of higher education. Sykes, a reporter for the *Milwaukee Journal,* was incredulous at what he found when he peeked through the windows of our universities. "At Yale," wrote Sykes, "T.A.s make up more than 25 percent of the people teaching and in a recent year filled 1,521 teaching appointments."[24] In some of Harvard's largest and most important undergraduate classes Sykes found that "teaching assistants are crucial."[25] In 1992 there were approximately 800 students teaching at Harvard, 600 at Columbia, and between 500 and 600 at Princeton.

The use of foreign students is another factor that compounds the evil of using students to teach students. Most teaching assistants are graduate students, studying for the master's degree or the Ph.D. Many graduate students come from foreign lands to study in America. Therefore, many teaching assistants teaching in American universities don't speak, write, or understand English very well.

Fred Gottheil, a professor of economics at the University of Illinois, was brutally frank when he talked to Sykes. A popular teacher who often lectured classes with more than a thousand students, Gottheil lamented:

> I have 13 teaching assistants. All but one of them is a non-American. Some of them don't speak English. The whole structure of this department is not to put a qualified person in front of a class. It is to use the teaching assistant money to create Ph.D.s. . . . What he does in the teaching assistant sections, they [Gottheil's colleagues] have about as much interest in as in a soccer match in Bulgaria.
>
> So when I go complain and say, "You can't put that guy in my class," they say, "What the hell do you want me to do?" I say, "I want you to fire that son of a bitch because I want a person who can speak English." And they say, "Oh Freddy, give him a chance."[26]

Certain areas of study are more vulnerable than others. A survey conducted in 1986 for the Mathematical Association of America showed that one-third of the math teaching assistants were foreign-born. The 1984 study of Berkeley teaching assistants found that 13 percent of them had learned English as a second language.[27]

The problem of non-English-speaking instructors has become so serious that some states, including Florida, Minnesota, Missouri, and Ohio, "prompted by undergraduate complaints and by the ire of lawmakers," have passed laws restricting or prohibiting the use of teachers who cannot pass an English proficiency examination.[28] In 1990, following a flood of complaints from students and parents, Pennsylvania passed a law entitled "The English Fluency in Higher Education Act." It required "institutions of higher education to evaluate their faculties for fluency in the English language; provide for certification as to that fluency, and impose penalties" for not doing so.[29] Our universities and colleges have now reached the point where not only is much of the teaching being done by unqualified students, but some of that teaching cannot even be understood by the class.

It is still common practice for a professor to lecture to a large class, perhaps numbering in the hundreds, and leave the discussion with students to teaching assistants who later take smaller sections of the class. But in October 1991 Michigan State University announced a new teaching technique that may be the wave of the future: replacing the professor with a videotape.

Here's how it works. The six thousand or so students a year who study American history at Michigan State will meet three times a week in groups of fifty for a new, required course called "The United States and the World." First they will watch a history videotape for thirty minutes. Then the teaching assistants will take over and lead class discussion for the remaining twenty minutes of class. *Voilà,* neat, cheap, and no fuss—and no professor needed. Well, almost no fuss. Seven thousand students signed a petition protesting the new course as one step further down the "impersonal assembly line education at the university." Ben Emery, a junior, who led the petition drive to stop the videotape, summed up students' concerns, saying, "You can't look up to a television program." So far, the Michigan State students have been ignored.[30]

Another curious development that occurred during the rapid growth of academe in the 1960s and 1970s was the phenomenon known as grade inflation. Much of the sweat and anxiety went out of being a student as good and excellent grades were passed out like so many lollipops. It became almost impossible to fail. Almost no one flunked out of college. If you did your time and paid your money, you were pretty much guaranteed a degree. A good solid B replaced the old "gentlemen's C" as a standard grade in most courses, except in some of the more rigorous sciences like physics, mathematics, and chemistry, where the grader's judgment mattered less than the student's answer. Strings of A's became common, and few students complained of the pressure or hard work.

Many universities simply opted out of grades completely, replacing them with "pass" or "fail," and sometimes with the additional option of dropping the course from one's record if it looked as if you were going to pick up a rare failing grade. Even comprehensive examinations, which tested a student's general knowledge across a variety of fields and the ability to integrate that knowledge, have largely gone by the boards. At Dartmouth College, for example, they used to be a standard feature, but by the 1960s these comprehensive exams had become "unpopular among professors . . . who argued that their fields had become too specialized for such generalized tests. In 1967 the faculty voted to make the exams a departmental option, and by 1969 they were abolished altogether."[31]

In 1991 two professors, Richard Sabot and John Wakeman-Linn, both at Williams College in Massachusetts, published a study examining the extent of grade inflation between the early 1960s and the mid-1980s both at Williams and at a diverse group of eight other universities and colleges—Amherst, Duke, Hamilton, Haverford, Pomona, Michigan, North Carolina, and Wisconsin. The results were pretty much the same. At Williams the "mean grade in the introductory courses of eight large departments . . . has risen from . . . a bit above C+ in 1962–63 to roughly B in 1985–86; the proportion of students receiving less than B− has fallen from 47 percent to 26 percent." Seven of the other eight schools studied also "experienced substantial grade inflation . . . grades were relatively low and very similar across departments in 1962–63. In 1985–86, grades were higher and all seven exhibited the same phenomenon."

The most astonishing statistic is that in 1986 almost 73 percent of all the grades given at the eight fairly representative schools studied were either A's or B's. It's almost as if Garrison Keillor's Lake Wobegon line—"where all the children are above average"—has come to life in our colleges and universities.

The conclusion of Sabot and Wakeman-Linn is that grade inflation is a nationwide phenomenon.[32] We might also conclude that many of the grades received by students today are fraudulent, and that these phony marks of achievement reflect dishonor on the faculty, not the students.

The basic rationale for creating this intellectual Utopia was that students should study for the sake of learning itself, and not be engaged in the grubby process of competing for grades. As a former college student, I can understand the appeal of that rationale—I didn't like being graded and never met a student who did. As a former university professor, I can also understand the appeal of easy grading or nongrading—grading was one of the most difficult, time-consuming, mind-numbing aspects of being a professor, and I never met a professor who liked doing it.

But accurate, fair grading is an integral part of the educational process, an indispensable means of letting the student know how he or she is doing, and where to focus efforts to improve. A little competition for grades in the old days often served as a powerful spur to learning itself. Grading was part of the responsibility of teaching and was taken very seriously. No longer. Both students and professors can, and for the most part do, relax.

Of course, there is a bit of a problem. As grades lose their meaning and relevance, it becomes difficult to distinguish good students from bad students, an invidious thing to do perhaps, but the kind of judging that will happen to them once they receive their degree and walk into the outside world.

Today a college degree has become more a certificate of attendance than a badge of achievement, its worth devalued in the market. The demise of careful, accurate grading—of intellectual judging by one's intellectual superiors—has been a disservice to students at best, depriving them of a valuable part of what a higher education should be. At worst, it is a form of intellectual fraud, where students pretend to study and the faculty pretends to teach and grade. The students lose an education, and the faculty, in granting dubious degrees, loses its integrity.

The curious part of the demise of conscientious grading is how it came to happen. True, it was always a chore for the professors and a source of anxiety for the students, but those seem like slim reasons to pitch the whole process overboard. The real explanation may lie with the increasing use of students as teaching assistants, which meant that students, not professors, were doing the grading.

This presented the professors with a sticky dilemma: they could give out the grades awarded by the teaching assistants, or they could do all the grading themselves.

Neither alternative was very attractive. Many professors apparently had enough integrity to resist putting their names on grades given by a teaching assistant, yet they couldn't bear to sit down and grade all those examinations themselves. Moreover, the grades given by a teaching assistant don't count for much. Nobody really cares very much about what one student thinks of another student's work. So they seem to have muddled through and come up with a brilliant third alternative: give everyone good grades. At least two groups—the professors and the students—seem, for the most part, quite pleased with the solution.

The studied neglect of teaching students in the university during the past few decades may have led to other, unforeseen consequences. Grades have not been the only thing to suffer from inflation; so too has the time taken to earn the bachelor's degree. Virtually unnoticed, one of the trademarks of American higher education—the four-year college degree—has all but disappeared. Most students now take more than five years to earn their degree.

In 1990 the National Institute of Independent Colleges and Universities published the results of a two-year study of college students during the 1980s. Based on a large national sample, the study focused on those students who went to college on the traditional path—defined as full-time enrollment, directly after high school, at a four-year college or university. The results were surprising.

Only 20 percent of the students earned the degree in the "normal" four years. Twenty-six percent took either five or six years. Another 12 percent were in their seventh year, still at it, when the study closed down. (Forty-two percent had dropped out.)

The study concluded: "Degree completion after four years is no longer the norm, if it ever was. . . . The average bachelor's degree recipient now may take five years or more to complete the degree."[33] As the director of the study, Oscar Porter, later remarked:

"The five-year degree is becoming the standard . . . the four-year degree has become part of history."[34]

This is crazy. There is no reason why so many young men and women spend five, six, or more years of their life earning a college degree. The basic costs of a college education are money and time, and the opportunities we forgo when we use up that time. When the time to earn a degree jumps to five or six years, not only are thousands of dollars more spent in pursuit of that degree, but precious years of the students' lives may be wasted. A six-year degree is not worth a dime more than a four-year degree; the intellectual content is the same. The only major difference is that some young men and women have spent two years of their lives as dependent students when they could have been spending those years as independent, productive adults.

A few schools seem to have resisted the trend toward the stretched-out college degree. At Yale University, for example, more than 90 percent of the students finish in four years or less. The reason is simple; besides the high cost of going to Yale, the school has a strict policy that impels students to earn their degree and leave. According to Mark Landeryou, the acting associate registrar at Yale, "Except in rare situations, students are not allowed on campus more than four years."[35]

The stretch-out of normal college education to five, six, or more years is costly for our society—in terms of dollars spent, time wasted, and opportunities lost. The stretch-out came up on us slowly, unsuspected, as we were busy with what appeared to be more pressing matters. But it has now become too serious to ignore. Time to snap it back to where it should be—four years, with an exception now and then for health or financial reasons. Once again the four-year degree should be standard policy at our colleges and universities, a policy most of us thought had never changed.

Today, the teaching system in America's universities is three-tiered. Some teaching is done by professors, some of it by part-time, ad hoc faculty, and some of it by students. The amount of teaching done by students is now so large and pervasive as to threaten the validity of a university education.

Maybe we have been blaming the wrong people for the disastrous decline in the quality of university teaching in America. Perhaps it is the student teachers who bear much of the responsibility.

Why don't students complain? Why are they so docile about being taught and graded by other students? Basically, they don't have much choice. Who are they going to complain to—the professors and administrators who set the system up and who ultimately determine whether or not the student gets a degree?

One explanation was offered by Ernest Boyer. These kids arrive "all wide eyes and hopeful," he said. "Then they begin to see that they are not being well served and a certain resignation sets in. They figure, 'If these are the ground rules, and if I'll get a blue-chip degree and will have a good time in the process, let's go for it.' Instead these students should march into the dean's office and demand what the catalog promised them."[36] This is what they should do, but how many undergraduates are that strong?

The university world will argue that many student teachers are qualified, that they do possess the knowledge, the teaching skills, and the maturity to teach undergraduates. In some cases that may be true, but then we should insist that the university do the right thing: promote them to the faculty, pay them a decent wage, and give them the title for the work they do. Or stop pretending.

The seamy practice of allowing, and sometimes coercing, students to teach students is one of the most significant forms of academic corruption, and one of the easiest to correct. Prohibit all student teaching. Simply adopt a policy that says all classes will be taught by professors, all discussion sections will be led by professors, all examinations will be made up by professors, all examinations will be graded by professors, and all counseling of students will be done by professors. There is nothing radical about this. A few major schools—Amherst College and Dartmouth College, for example— have always done it this way. In fact, most people in America think that professors already do this.

Such a simple change would have an immediate, far-reaching impact. Students and parents would no longer feel cheated, duped by the rhetoric in the college catalogs. Students might even take more interest in their courses if they were taught by real professors, not one of their beer-drinking buddies. Because students, graduate students especially, would be prohibited from teaching, they could devote more time to their own studies, complete their degrees earlier, and add to the pool of professors available for teaching. Professors, required to spend more time on what they were originally hired to do, would have less time to spend on spurious research and writing, thus tending to increase the quality of intellectual output.

It will be argued that no single college or university could afford to make this change because of the great competitive disadvantage it would experience. Professors required to teach would simply move to schools that allowed them to continue as before. But universities and colleges could get together and decide to implement such a policy collectively, so that none would be at a competitive disadvantage. If some of our finest institutions of higher education can get together to set financial aid awards, they are capable of getting together on the simple matter of requiring professors to teach.

Any attempt to banish the widespread use of student teachers can be expected to meet adamant hostility from professors. Much of this opposition stems from the fact that so many of today's professors do not have the temperament of teachers. Teaching is an old and honorable profession, but many professors consider teaching no longer a fitting vocation once they get to be thirty-five or forty years old. These are the academic intellectuals who are excited by the play of ideas among equals or near-equals. Publishing an article in a prestigious academic journal, participating in an advanced seminar, debating colleagues in a panel discussion: these are what stimulate their intellectual juices.

Teaching teenagers, no matter how bright and precocious, the same subject matter, year after year, some professors find demeaning and boring. As they get older and their intellectual powers grow, they want interaction with older, wiser people—in graduate schools, think tanks—who can challenge them.

The art, and the satisfaction, of being a good teacher is to convey some complex knowledge, previously unknown to the student, in the most simple, clear, elegant way possible. The state of the art attained and the degree of satisfaction experienced are directly affected by the capabilities of the student. Rare is the undergraduate who has the knowledge and understanding to appreciate the full range of intellect of a sixty-year-old genius. A university teacher with the right temperament does not find this distressing, and takes great pleasure and satisfaction from teaching young students.

The issue of student teachers is so taboo at most universities that it is beyond discussion or debate. For example, in 1986 the University of California set up a special "Task Force on Lower Division Education" to investigate "the quality of teaching and learning." Its conclusion on teaching assistants was clear and unequivocal: "So the main question is not whether the University makes use of ancillary teaching personnel [i.e., students]; that question would appear to be beyond debate, given the legitimate research functions of the faculty, given the general budgetary limitations on the University, and given the unreality of the idea that enough additional resources might be available so that all teaching could be done by regular faculty."[37]

That statement could be the operating philosophy of almost every college and university in America. To paraphrase it slightly, it says: "Given the money available, and the greater importance we place on doing research, we just don't have enough time to teach students. The students will have to do that." What is truly unacceptable is the attitude that the issue is "beyond debate." It is not.

Students are not qualified to teach. They do not possess enough knowledge. They do not have enough judgment and maturity. They rarely know how to teach. Some of them, incredibly, can't even speak English well. They have powerful conflicts of interest, for in many cases they must teach and grade some of their friends, or even the young men or women they date. To pretend that students are qualified to lecture other students a scant few years behind them, to grade and judge them, and to counsel them is to mock the essence of higher education.

Children teaching children is unconscionable.

The spectacle of students playing at being professors is keenly embarrassing to many faculty, but others are quick to defend the practice. In defense of the use of students as teachers, faculty fall back on several rationalizations. They emphasize that teaching assistants are supervised by professors who have the ultimate responsibility for the conduct of the courses. They claim that being a teaching assistant is good experience for a future college teaching career, and that the use of teaching assistants makes it possible to have smaller classes. These claims are true, but they fail to go to the essence of what is wrong with using student teachers. The size of the class, and how valuable the experience is for the young instructor, and whether or not a senior professor has oversight responsibility say nothing about the quality of the teaching experience—the lecturing, the dialogue, the examinations, the judging, the counseling.

While most professors prefer to pretend the issue does not exist, some have gone to great lengths to defend the use of teaching assistants. For example, a comprehensive report prepared by the Committee for Graduate Studies at Stanford in 1991 simply resorted to the old "black is white" technique, stating that the "employment of graduate students as teachers greatly *strengthens* undergraduate education. Teaching by graduate students *enriches the interaction between faculty and undergraduates* [italics added]."[38]

The most effective part of the learning experience in the university is the dialogue that takes place in the classroom between the teacher and the taught, in the taking of examinations and the feedback the student gets from thorough grading, and in direct, one-on-one personal counseling. Sitting in a large, cavernous lecture hall, as one of hundreds of other students, peering at a tiny figure behind a podium hundreds of feet away is generally not the most enlightening or stimulating experience. Some large lectures are good, and some rare students can get more out of reading a book in a library than from hours of intense discussion with a learned professor. But these are the exceptions. Most students benefit from dialogue, a give-and-take discussion, exams, the feedback of grading and counseling.

It is also true that professors give most of the large lectures and the teaching assistants are usually reserved for the smaller discussion and recitation sections. It is here the student teachers do the work of teaching. They lecture the class, lead the discussion, grade the examinations, and counsel their fellow students. This is the essence of the problem. The heart of the teaching/learning link between professor and student is broken. It is a teaching assistant, not a professor, who decides what issues are to be raised in class. It is a teaching assistant who grades essays and exams, the results of which can determine the career paths of beginning students. It is a teaching assistant, often only a few years older than his or her charges, who counsels them on important, critical matters of intellectual substance.

The result is a university learning experience that is barely one step above the learning that takes place in a bull session in a dormitory. Maybe that is the way it has to be. But then why don't the universities at least be honest about what they are peddling? Why don't their catalogs sing the joys of students being taught by students, graded by students, and counseled by students? Perhaps because some parents would think again about paying so much money for that kind of education for their children.

Student teachers are used today because the universities have discovered they can get away with it, and because student "professors" are cheaper than real professors. The University of Wisconsin–Madison, with its 1,600 teaching assistants, has a typical pay scale for student teachers. In the late 1980s a teaching assistant holding a half-time appointment was paid $10,831 a year. Add to this the opportunity to participate in a low-cost health plan and you have a total compensation package of perhaps $12,000 a year.[39] Some universities pay more, some less. But compared to the total compensation package of a professor, which, when one adds in the cost of retirement plans, housing subsidies, comprehensive health insurance, and all the other benefits, can easily run to $65,000 or $70,000 a year or, in the elite universities, to over $100,000—the teaching assistant is a terrific bargain.

Yes, the use of teaching assistants does free professors who dislike teaching to pursue more rewarding interests. But the use of students as pseudo-professors debases the university education, and it defrauds all those young people who enter the university believing they will be taught by learned professors.

One puzzling question remains. Where on earth do they find all those students willing to teach other students, usually for very meager wages? Going to graduate school is a full-time job; so is properly teaching university courses. How do university officials persuade so many of their graduate students to forgo their studies— sometimes for years—to pick up the chalk and eraser?

Simple. They coerce them. The exploitation of graduate students in American universities is the mental equivalent of the old sweatshops, long endured in silent agony by their victims. The typical candidate for an advanced degree is in a terribly difficult position to complain to anyone about anything, but we are beginning to hear some murmurings of protest. And sometimes a professor or two, especially an older one, will tell the truth.

In 1991 Jacques Barzun, a doyen of the American professoriate and one of the most distinguished intellectuals of this century, bluntly attacked the use of students as teachers. Referring to "the university practice of paying graduate students a pittance to teach undergraduates," he recommended that "the use of slave labor should be abolished":

> These young scholars have reached the hardest stretch of their studies; they either neglect them or scamp the so-called teaching they are ill-fitted to perform. . . . It may be predicted that if the ancient abuse were done away with, the undergraduates who register for a course with the great scholar, only to endure the inadequacies of his substitute, would send up a large cheer.[40]

The Ph.D. process is the incubator of the academic intellectual world. This is where young professors are hatched, nurtured, and trained. It should be an inspiring, memorable time. Ideally, it works like this: The newly minted college graduate enters graduate school, takes advanced courses in his or her special field of interest, studies under some of the most learned people in the country for two years or so, and then takes and passes comprehensive written and oral examinations demonstrating mastery of a wide and deep range of knowledge. The final step is to write a dissertation, a Ph.D. thesis, an original piece of work that demonstrates a capability to conduct thorough, rigorous research, and that is itself a significant contribution to knowledge. After a full year of research and writing, the dissertation is submitted to a small jury of professors, defended orally, and then, soon, the young scholar is the proud possessor of a handsomely engraved document that confirms that he or she is the recipient of "the degree of Doctor of Philosophy in recognition of his [her] scientific attainments and ability to carry on original research as demonstrated by a thesis."[41]

By robe-wearing time the person should be about twenty-six years old, with a comprehensive, solid education and a bright future ahead. No longer a lowly student, a dependent person of little power, the Ph.D. recipient is transformed, butterfly-like, into a paragon, addressed as "Doctor" or "Professor," a certified scholar earning good money, with a career virtually guaranteed for life, a career that also enjoys some of the highest prestige in the land.

That's how it should be. That's how most people think it is.

But it's not. The hard reality is dismally different.

Today the Ph.D. process in America is, in effect, a long apprenticeship, a throwback to the medieval guild system in which a master craftsman could hold his apprentices in virtual bondage. With exceptions here and there, today's Ph.D. students are similarly beholden, as apprentices to professors. Their numbers are large. In 1988 there were 33,456 Ph.D. degrees awarded in the United States.[42] Listen to one of the most respected professors in America, the Harvard paleontologist Stephen Jay Gould, describe that system in his 1989 book, *Wonderful Life:*

Universities operate one of the few survivors of the old apprenticeship system in their programs for awarding doctoral degrees. . . . In some fields you must abandon all thought of independence, and work upon an assigned topic for a dissertation . . . in any case you are an apprentice, and you are under your mentor's thumb . . . the system does produce its horrors—exploitive professors who divert the flow of youthful brilliance and enthusiasm into their own dry wells, and provide nothing in return.

Many students don't understand the system. They apply to a school because it has a general reputation or resides in a city they like. Wrong, dead wrong. You apply to work with a particular person. As in the old apprenticeship system of the guilds, mentor and student are bound by mutual obligations. . . . The work of graduate students is part of a mentor's reputation forever . . . this system is largely responsible for the sorry state of undergraduate teaching at many major research universities. . . . For researchers ever conscious of their reputations, there is no edge whatever in teaching undergraduate courses. . . . Your graduate students are your extensions; your undergraduates are ciphers in your fame.[43]

Well said by the Harvard professor, and the only time I have seen it acknowledged publicly. But even Professor Gould does not want to change this cozy setup. "When it works, as it does rather more often than a cynic might expect, given the lack of checks and balances, I cannot imagine a better training."[44] And when it comes to the "sorry state of undergraduate teaching," he just shrugs and says, "I wish that this could change, but I don't even know what to suggest."[45] Nevertheless, there may be a few things we can do.

The driving force behind every system of apprenticeship is simple. It is not the benevolent idea of training young men and women to help them succeed in the world. There were no altruists in the guilds. The main purpose of having apprentices is to have them do as much of your menial, boring, repetitive work as possible, for as long as possible. The old medieval guilds did this openly and guilelessly. The apprentice "learned his trade as he practiced it under the instruction and supervision of a master. . . . Typically, a boy was bound to a master at the age of 14 and served for 7 years. . . . As an apprentice he began by doing the most menial jobs. . . . Gradually, he was trusted with more responsible tasks."[46] The apprentice earned the title "master craftsman" after he had completed his training and had "demonstrated his ability by examination or by preparing a masterpiece."[47]

If you substitute the words "professor" for "master," "graduate student" for "apprentice," and "dissertation" for "masterpiece," it's surprising how close the two systems are. The medieval apprentice served his master for seven years; the typical American Ph.D. student spends seven years in residence at the university studying with his or her professor.

How has it come about that so many university classes are taught by students, leaving the professors free to pursue other things, such as the writing of journal articles? Ever wonder how the faculty manage to convince so many students to don the hat of professor and take over classes? The answer lies in the student apprentices, the students pitifully beholden to the professors. Graduate-student apprentices perform two critical tasks that many professors consider menial, boring, or repetitive: (1) teaching undergraduates and (2) undertaking much of the drudgery of research.

In the apprentice system a student's future career can ride on the judgment of a single professor. That judgment or opinion is often subjective, subject to no test or recourse. If professors are wise and fair there is no problem, but if they are not so wise and not so fair, there is an awesome potential for abuse.

Let's say the professor supervising your doctoral studies "suggests" you teach an undergraduate course. Do you say, "Sorry, I'd rather concentrate on my studies, get my degree, and then compete with you"? If a little psychological terror does not work, there is always economic coercion. Need financial aid while you are working toward the Ph.D.? No problem. Just sign these papers and we will make you a teaching assistant. Teach and get paid. No teaching, no money. In 1988, 44 percent of all university financial support for Ph.D. students was tied to their teaching.[48]

Many universities have stopped fooling around with implied

threats and economic coercion. In some areas of study they simply *require* that every Ph.D. candidate teach for a certain amount of time in order to qualify for the degree. For example, in 1990 the economics department of Stanford University stipulated that every Ph.D. student "must serve as a teaching assistant for at least one quarter." In the political science department at Stanford, "A candidate for the Ph.D. in Political Science may be asked to serve as a teaching assistant (TA) in the department for three quarters. Two quarters must be served."[49]

The unholy combination of implied threat, economic coercion, and specific requirements has been effective. Lots of graduate students working toward the Ph.D. degree take time out to teach, not because they want to but because they have to. Preparing and teaching a class, making up examinations and grading them, and counseling students is a full-time job and leaves little, if any, time to study and work on a Ph.D. Compelling Ph.D. students to teach before they are ready is, at its core, mean, base exploitation of graduate students by professors.

Making them teach is not the only way professors exploit their young apprentices. They also make them do research. Again, the professor in charge of your Ph.D. program "suggests" you might like a job doing some of his research work. What do you say? "I would rather concentrate on my own research so I can finish my dissertation and enhance my reputation, not yours"? Not likely, unless your intellectual mentor possesses a rare streak of integrity. Plus there is always the money involved. In 1988 fully 38 percent of all university financial aid to Ph.D. students was paid to research assistants.[50] Just as with teaching: no research work for the professors, no money.

Altogether these "assistantships"—teaching or research—account for over 80 percent of financial aid given in graduate school. In fact, only about 13 percent of financial aid to graduate students comes in the form of string-free fellowships. The rest, in essence, is tied to some kind of work that professors don't like very much.[51]

The idea of apprenticeship is an ancient rite of passage from childhood to adulthood. It is a medieval concept of exploitation, subtle and powerful, that has been adapted by today's academic intellectuals to make selfish and unethical use of hapless graduate students. While Ph.D. students are used as teaching assistants, while they do boring and repetitious research work for their professor-mentors, they are not progressing toward either mastering their chosen field of study or producing a piece of original research of their own.

Pauline Maier, a professor of history at M.I.T., observes that there is an "enormous power teachers have over students." And that "power can be used for good, to release energies and develop talents, or for evil, causing (even inadvertently) an unwarranted and crippling sense of failure and incapacity."[52]

All of us have heard Lord Acton's famous maxim, "Power tends to corrupt, and absolute power corrupts absolutely," so often that we probably no longer pay any attention to it. But there is a lot of wisdom in what Lord Acton wrote to Bishop Mandell Creighton in 1887. Academic intellectuals are no more immune to the seduction of power than anyone else.

Today there is a ritual abuse of Ph.D. students. What they need most is *time* to pursue their advanced course work, *time* to master their field of study, *time* to learn how to conduct original research, to write, and to finish a dissertation. Instead, the professors rob them of that time, demanding that students free them from much of their teaching and research responsibilities. The professors exploit their graduate students with great skill, concocting a long teaching and research gauntlet that must be run by anyone who wants a Ph.D.

Studying for an advanced degree should be an exhilarating time, but for many it is a debilitating one. Because of the effective requirement of doing someone else's teaching and someone else's research, it now takes an excruciatingly long time to earn the Ph.D. degree, an unconscionably large chunk out of one's life. In 1988 the median number of years it took to get a Ph.D. after graduating from college was 10.5. Even if you just count the median number of years the students were actually enrolled in graduate school it is a very long time: 6.9 years.

In the social sciences (anthropology, economics, political science, sociology, et al.) the median number of years spent in graduate school is 7.4. For the humanities (history, classics, philosophy, religion, et al.) the median time stretches out even further—8.5 years in graduate school, and 12.2 years total time to the degree.[53]

If we break down these numbers by sex and race, the results are even more disturbing. While the median number of years it takes to get a Ph.D. is 10.5, men manage to do it in 9.7 years. But women take 12.3 years, 27 percent longer than men. And African-Americans take 14.9 years—more than 50 percent longer.[54]

Of note here is the growing controversy in the academic intellectual world over the noticeable lack of black professors, in spite of some twenty years of affirmative action programs by the universities. As we enter the last decade of the twentieth century, only 2.6 percent of university faculty are African-American. Almost all members of the faculty are white—90.5 percent—while 2.9 percent are Hispanic, 3.3 percent Asian, and 0.7 percent are American Indian.[55] When challenged on the glaring discrepancy, the professors usually defend their white enclave by pointing out there are relatively few African-Americans earning doctoral degrees, at least not enough to provide the numbers they profess to want. It might help to reduce the "shortage" a great deal if it did not take fifteen years for an African-American college graduate to earn a Ph.D. degree.

There is no good reason why a Ph.D. should take more than three, or at most four, years of work beyond the bachelor's degree. Experts have agreed on this for years, ever since the Ph.D. was created just before the Civil War. Yale University awarded the first three American Ph.D. degrees in 1861. The requirements at the beginning were: (1) two years of course work past the bachelor's degree, (2) a comprehensive final examination, and (3) a written dissertation.[56] The quality of the thought in the dissertation, not its length, was what counted. One of the first three men to receive the Ph.D. in America was James Morris Whitton, and his Yale dissertation was "a six-page handwritten thesis in Latin on the proverb *Brevis vita, ars longa*" (Life is brief, the arts endure).[57]

For most of the next one hundred years there was agreement on just how long it should take to earn a Ph.D. In 1990, in an article brilliantly critical of the American Ph.D. system, Theodore Ziolkowski, a professor at Princeton University and dean of the graduate school, traced the stability of the Ph.D. system since its inception:

> The American conception of the Ph.D. has remained remarkably constant throughout most of the century. In 1964, the Association of Graduate Schools and the Council of Graduate Schools issued a joint statement summarizing their view of the normal course of study leading to the doctorate: a year or two of lectures and seminars followed by a general examination and a dissertation. The entire course of study should normally involve no more than three or, at most, four years beyond the baccalaureate. The four-year norm has been affirmed by most writers who have analyzed the situation. [58]

The gap between what should be and what is exacts a fearsome price. When young men and women are forced to spend not three or four years, but ten, twelve, or even fifteen years to earn the Ph.D., the entire process becomes corrupting. Those extra years are critical ones that are ripped out of the productive life of the young scholars. At a time when they should already have the degree and be teaching at a university, earning substantial amounts of money and enjoying the prestige and satisfaction of being independent, they are, instead, struggling students. As the years roll by and they grind on in their studies and research and writing, they must by necessity hold part-time and temporary jobs. They marry, they have children, they grow old—and yet they are still students.

The average graduate student is thirty-four years old before he or she breaks free of the cocoon of dependency that is the Ph.D. process. [59] Thirty-four years old before they get to be practicing adults. Others their age have a ten-year jump on them. Psychologically, some remain students for life, never quite getting used to the idea of making decisions on their own. You might say they remain in a state of arrested social development. And, of course, these are the relatively lucky ones. Some take many more years to earn the degree. The average African-American is almost thirty-nine years old when he or she receives the Ph.D. They give up fifteen years or more to get that coveted piece of paper. Fifteen years of career advancement, fifteen years of increasing income. Fifteen years of being an independent adult.

There is an unseen cost to this exploitation of graduate students. What we see are 33,000 middle-aged men and women groggily grasping the Ph.D. degree every year. What we don't see are the tens of thousands of brilliant minds who would not tolerate the abuse, the students who would not submit to the humiliation and exploitation. Tragically, this probably includes many of the best minds in America. For it is these strong souls who would have been much more likely to advance the thresholds of knowledge, more likely than the ones who followed the rules and meekly surrendered so many years of their lives.

In 1992 Neil Rudenstine, president of Harvard, and William Bowen, president of the Andrew W. Mellon Foundation, published a major new study of doctorate education in America, *In Pursuit of the PhD*. Perhaps the most startling finding of this work is that *fewer than half* of all students who enter Ph.D. programs ever get the degree—more than half drop out along the way. They don't drop out casually, but more likely "after pursuing degrees for anywhere from six to twelve years."[60]

This terrible waste and abuse of some of America's finest talents has been going on silently, virtually unnoticed, for decades. Perhaps why so little has been written about it can be explained by what a clinical psychologist, Dr. Frederick Stern, told Bowen and Rudenstine in the course of their study. Having done his own doctoral dissertation on the effect psychological factors have on the length of time it takes students to complete a dissertation, Stern suggested that "the *traumas* associated with pursuit of the Ph.D. may even have discouraged many scholars from returning to such a personally painful subject [italics added]."[61]

If this all sounds farfetched, try something. The next time you get the opportunity to talk to someone who has run the Ph.D. gauntlet, or even better, someone who started but dropped out, ask him about his experience. Did he find it fair, challenging? Did he think he was treated well, with respect? There is no better way to understand what is involved than to listen to the pain and anguish of one who has experienced it.

But it shouldn't be this way, and it doesn't have to be this way. In fact, the things that would fix it are simple.

First, we have to stop this business of students teaching students. Not only is it disastrous for the younger students who are taught, it is also disastrous for those who teach. The time a graduate student spends in teaching is of very limited benefit. It may puff the egos of some students who enjoy the temporary power and position, and it will give them some hard-won experience they can use if they ever go on to become professors. But the cost they pay is too high.

Second, we have to stop this business of professors using students to conduct their research. We don't have to get rid of all research jobs, some of which are proper and needed, but we do need to stop the practice of students doing research for the professors who supervise their doctoral programs. The conflict of interest is self-evident. There is too much pressure to put the professor's interests before the interests of the student.

Third, we should do everything we can to shorten the time needed to get the degree and to free up the student's time to focus on his own work as much as possible. Universities should increase the paltry amount of financial support they now give in fellowships and grants.

Universities should also expand their loan programs. One widespread myth is that Ph.D.s are saddled with large debts when they graduate. Not true. In 1988, over half (53 percent) of the Ph.D. graduates had no debt whatsoever related to the ten-plus years of their education. Another 17 percent owed less than $5,000; only 13 percent owed more the $20,000. And no wonder, since most of them were forced to teach and do research instead of being allowed to borrow money to pay for the cost of their graduate education.

Fourth, the apprenticeship system, with a single professor as mentor, should be dismantled. Students should be evaluated by review boards composed of many professors and by more standard-ized examinations, all designed to remove the student from the clutches of any one professor. When power is dispersed, it tends to be more benign.

Fifth, the dissertation should be treated realistically for what it is, a demonstration of the student's ability to conduct rigorous research. It is time to drop the pretense that Ph.D. theses must constitute an important, original contribution to knowledge. Very few Ph.D. theses can meet this test. Very few ever have. Almost none of the tens of thousands of theses completed each year are published, and even fewer are ever cited as important contributions to knowledge. There is nothing wrong with this, because this is what one would expect from beginning scholars.

Something is wrong with pretending that everyone should, and that almost everyone does, make an important contribution with his or her first major piece of research. That is the first step down the slippery slope of intellectual deceit, a fallacy that eats away at intellectual integrity. It is a curious concept, but the idea of making an original, significant contribution to knowledge as something one must do to become a professor is branded in the mind of every Ph.D. candidate. Few of them ever forget it. Most of them never achieve it.

The ability to do original, important research has nothing what-soever to do with superior teaching. Yes, a new discovery or two can add immeasurably to the classroom experience—but the truly new is truly rare. What is critically important to superior teaching is a mastery of the field. It helps a lot if the teacher knows what he or she is talking about. It does not help a lot if the teacher has demonstrated the ability to conduct research. As Andrew Hacker, a professor of political science at Queens College in New York City, commented in 1990, "I have never seen why a Ph.D. should be a requisite for college-level teaching. Indeed, very few professors con-tinue with serious research after they get their doctorates."[62]

Indeed, it is a question that has been posed many times over the years, but perhaps never more cogently than by William James, in his classic 1903 essay "The Ph.D. Octopus." In 1903 America produced just 337 Ph.D.s, one percent of the number we produce today.[63] But James, based on his experience as a Harvard professor, deftly seized on the live nerve that still jangles when touched in the graduate schools of America. "Is not our growing tendency to appoint no instructors who are not also doctors an instance of pure sham?" he asked. "Will any one pretend for a moment that the doctor's degree is a guarantee that its possessor will be successful as a teacher?"[64] James's telling question was ignored then, just as it is ignored today.

What we need to do is award the Ph.D. degree in two models— one with the written dissertation and one without. Sort of like the President's Medal of Freedom, the most prestigious award that can be given to an American. The Medal of Freedom comes in two varieties—the regular one and one "with distinction." Almost no one knows the difference, because they are both extraordinary honors.

The basic Ph.D. degree should be awarded for mastery of a field of study, after passing written and oral examinations to demonstrate that mastery. It should not take longer than three years of intense study. Possession of this degree should qualify one to be a college teacher.

The second type of Ph.D. degree would be reserved for those students who had demonstrated the ability to research and write. If, and only if, the student elected to write a thesis and the thesis was accepted as a clear demonstration of the student's ability to conduct serious research would the Ph.D. degree be granted "with research distinction." Moreover, if someone who had received the regular Ph.D. later produced a piece of good, original research, the notation "with research distinction" could be added to the earlier degree.

These simple changes would dramatically shorten the time necessary to earn the Ph.D. and open up the profession of university teaching to tens of thousands of men and women who may not be researchers but who have the temperament and brilliance to be superb teachers of our children.

CHAPTER FOUR

THE GLASS BEAD GAME

IF TEACHING—the *raison d'être* for being a professor—has fallen into such disrepute among academic intellectuals, then what does command their affection? The answer is scholarship. Today the most important prize in the world of academic intellectuals is a scholarly reputation, recognition that one has made an important contribution to knowledge. The degrees and nuances of such recognition are many, but appreciation is largely confined to one's peers; rarely do scholarly reputations reach such heights that the general public is aware of them. For most professors the surest route to scholarly fame (and some fortune) is to publish in the distinguished academic journals of their field. Not books or treatises, for these are rare indeed, but short, densely packed articles of a dozen pages or so.

The successful professor's résumé will be littered with citations of short, scholarly articles, their value rising with the prestige of the journal. These studious articles are the coin of the realm in the academic world. They are the professor's ticket to promotion, higher salary, generous research grants, lower teaching loads, and even more opulent office space.

The articles are rarely speculative essays. Mostly they represent the summing up of hours, months, even years of research. Often packed with arcane mathematical equations, they bristle with words most of us never use. These strange words are jargon, the special code words that represent meaning only to the cognoscenti who reside in that particular part of the academic world. Amid this turgid prose, the mysterious formulae, charts, and graphs, one sometimes finds a nugget of intellectual gold.

Few Americans are familiar with these articles. When was the last time you read an article in a prestigious academic journal? When was the last time you heard of someone else reading one of these articles? Say, for example, a businessman or a reporter citing some sliver of wisdom from the latest issue of the *American Economic Review* or the *Journal of Political Economy* to drive home a point? Perhaps that is an unreasonable question. These are supposed to be scholarly pieces at the cutting edge of new knowledge written by the men and women at the top of their fields, and not everyone should be expected to appreciate the complexities and subtleties of such work.

But now I must confess something. Many years ago, when I read these articles regularly as part of my academic training and during my early years as a professor, I was bothered by the fact that I often failed to find the point of these articles, even after wading through the web of jargon, mathematical equations, and turgid English. Perhaps when I get older and wiser I will appreciate them more, I thought. Well, I am now fifty-five years old and the significance of most academic writing continues to elude me.

In recent years I have conducted an informal survey. Whenever the opportunity presents itself I ask scholars about their academic journal reading habits. For example, I recently asked a colleague, a man with a solid reputation as a scholar, what he considered to be the most important academic journal in his field of study. An economist, he immediately replied, "the *American Economic Review.*"

"Let me ask you a question," I said. "Take, say, all the issues of the last five years. What's your favorite article?"

I was 99 percent sure what his response would be. I had asked the same question of many dozens of scholars, from many different fields, during the past two or three years. This particular journal, the *American Economic Review*, is published four times a year, with a dozen articles or so in each issue. So he had about 240 articles from which to choose his favorite.

Sure enough, he answered like all the rest. There was silence for a few seconds; then he cleared his throat at bit and, looking somewhat guilty and embarrassed, said, "Well, I haven't been reading it much lately." When pressed he could not name a single article he had read during the past five years that he found memorable. In fact, he probably had not read any articles but was loath to admit it.

He is not alone. There are exceptions, of course, a handful of men and women in every field who do read these articles and try to comprehend any glimmers of meaning or significance they may contain. But, as a general rule, nobody reads the articles in academic journals anymore. They may skim the table of contents of a journal to acquire enough knowledge—authors and titles—to carry on a decent cocktail party conversation, but they rarely sit down and study them and, even more rarely, use what they have studied.

There is a mystery here. For while these academic publications pile up, largely unread, on the shelves of our university libraries, their importance to a professor's career continues unabated. Scarcely anyone questions the value of these proofs of erudition on a résumé. They are treated with respect, and every article authored in a prestigious journal in a scholar's field of study is like a notch in the six-gun of an Old West gunfighter, a proof of talent and a visible building block of the academic intellectual's reputation pyramid.

One reason why these research articles are automatically accepted as significant and important is that they have often survived the criticism of "peer review" before being published. Peer review means that a submitted article must be approved by at least one and often several people who are considered to be not only experts in the field, but peers in reputation and learning. Often the peers doing the reviewing are referred to as referees, and the articles are called, reverentially, "refereed articles."

Some of the manuscript reviews are done "blind," with the author's name stripped off, while others are not and the reviewer knows exactly whom he or she is evaluating. Given what is at stake in peer reviewing—often the career hopes of a budding young scholar—it would not be unreasonable to worry a little about corruption sneaking in.

But these questions are not explored. The fact that some fields of study are small enough so that the intellectuals involved in them are all known to each other, or that friends review friends, or that reviewers repay those who reviewed their own writings favorably in the past—all these potential problems are ignored. Peer reviewing is treated with the same respect as confession in the Catholic Church. It is held unthinkable that anyone would ever violate the canons of the craft. Well, maybe. But someday the whole practice of peer review should be opened up and studied, and the techniques of scientific analysis so prized by academic intellectuals applied rigorously to the process.

This still does not explain why the academic journals are so seldom read. Two reasons are usually given. First, it is alleged that the splendid growth of intellectual research has led to such an enormous output of important, relevant material that no one really has time to read it all anymore. And second, that many of the articles, especially those heavily laced with mathematical equations, are too difficult for most people to understand.

It is true that an astounding number of academic journals are published every year. We don't really know how many there are because no one as yet has had the inclination or the fortitude to count them. One estimate has at least 40,000 scientific journals published worldwide, generating over 1 million articles every year. That's 2,740 every single day. The *New Republic*, one of America's leading magazines for professional intellectuals, estimated in the late 1980s that the field of sociology alone produced 2,400 scholarly articles a year in the United States.[1]

It is also true that no academic intellectual could possibly read everything published in his field. But that is true for almost everyone. The incredible explosion of publications everywhere has produced so much information that none of us can possibly keep up with everything. But that does not prevent us from reading a lot of what is published, especially those things we find interesting, important, and useful. Moreover, academic intellectuals are generally faster and better readers than the average person and are fully capable, both in terms of time available and intelligence, of reading forty or fifty journal articles every year. But they don't.

The most widely accepted reason for the benign neglect of scholarly articles in prestigious academic journals is that they are too mathematical. The complicated mathematical equations used to spin out the intellectual's speculations are thought to be beyond the comprehension of most people. And it is true that during the last thirty or forty years there has been a massive shift toward the heavy use of mathematical formulae, and away from English prose. To many people, encountering an article heavily studded with mysterious equations is equivalent to trying to read Chinese. The meaning of the article is a mystery locked behind unfamiliar symbols. In the research world of the academic intellectuals that mystery only adds to the allure. Not being able to comprehend something that is important and profound, that has been given an intellectual seal of approval by peers, only deepens the mystery and enhances its value.

Still, there is a danger in all mysteries. We cannot ever fully trust what we do not know or cannot explain. What if what is hidden beneath those thick words and intricate equations is wrong or inaccurate, or worse, trivial?

Impossible. Preposterous. Everyone "knows" that most academic research consists of important, significant contributions to knowledge. Many of us may not understand or appreciate the contribution, but no one questions the contribution. That conviction has been long held. It was an article of faith when I first entered the world of the academic intellectuals in the late 1950s. Sure, every now and then there was an article that was a clinker, an aberration, an exception to excellence. But not everyone is so complacent anymore. In fact, questions are being raised by some of the most noted intellectuals in the world.

On March 6, 1991, Donald Kennedy, president of Stanford University, sounded an alarm on the quality of scholarly research. In an address to his faculty, he called for "significant changes in the process of appointment and promotion, so as to decrease the pressure on the quantity (not quality) of research production," and stated bluntly that he hoped "we can agree that the quantitative use of research output as a criterion for appointment or promotion is a bankrupt idea. The overproduction of routine scholarship is one of the most egregious aspects of contemporary academic life: It tends to conceal really important work by its sheer volume; it wastes time and valuable resources."[2]

Bankrupt? Overproduction? One of the most egregious aspects of contemporary academic life? What is this man talking about? The research efforts he scornfully dismisses as "routine" have been the heart and soul of academic life for as long as any of us can remember. Does he know something that most Americans don't? Perhaps. The seriousness of Kennedy's concern led him to go so far as to propose a limitation on "the number of publications that can be considered in appointment or promotion."[3] Sort of an academic equivalent of the acreage allotments in the federal farm subsidy program.

Concern about the quality of academic research is not unique to the president of Stanford University. His is just one of a small but growing number of voices who are challenging the most sacred myth of the academic world: that academic publications represent important, original contributions to knowledge.

One of the most eminent voices to say the unthinkable is that of Professor Maurice Allais, a world-renowned scholar from the economics department of the École Nationale Supérieure des Mines in Paris and the 1988 winner of the Nobel Prize in economics. Writing in the Fall 1989 issue of the *American Economist*, Allais condemned the quality of the research his colleagues were turning out:

> While many literary theories cannot be considered scientific, the same can be said of a great number of theories, purely logical, with no real link to the facts. . . .A new scholastic totalitarianism has arisen based on abstract and a priorist conceptions, detached from reality; this kind of "*mathematical charlatanry*" had already been denounced by Keynes in his "Treatise on Probability."[4]

No real link to the facts? Charlatanry? The noted French economist seems to be charging many of his colleagues with intellectual fraud, of engaging in mathematical games with as much connection to the real world of poverty and prosperity as the game of Monopoly, and pretending they are serious economic theories. Similar charges were made a few years earlier by another eminent scholar, Professor Wassily Leontief of Harvard University. Also a Nobel laureate in economics, Leontief wrote, in a blistering letter to *Science* magazine in 1982, that "page after page of professional economic journals are filled with mathematical formulas leading the reader from sets of more or less plausible but entirely arbitrary assumptions to precisely stated but irrelevant theoretical conclusions."[5]

Arbitrary assumptions? Irrelevant conclusions? These are damning criticisms of accepted scholarly work, and one might have expected a firestorm of controversy to erupt. But nothing happened. There was little note taken of Leontief's charges, little note taken of Allais's condemnation. They were ignored. If this were the world of politics we might call it stonewalling. The academic profession absorbed the Leontief and Allais arrows and plodded stoically on. But Allais and Leontief are right and, if they err at all, they err on the side of being too timid in their criticisms.

The dirty secret of the academic intellectuals is that much of what they write and hold up to themselves and to the rest of the world as the highest expression of what they do is inconsequential and trifling.

The work of scholars that is relevant to the critical issues facing Americans is almost nonexistent. As Derek Bok, president of Harvard University, wrote in 1990, "Armed with the security of tenure and the time to study the world with care, professors would appear to have a unique opportunity to act as society's scouts to signal impending problems long before they are visible to others. Yet rarely have members of the academy succeeded in discovering emerging issues and bringing them vividly to the attention of the public."[6]

Taken as a whole, academic research and writing is the greatest intellectual fraud of the twentieth century. There is a simple way to test this proposition.

First, obtain a recent issue of any prestigious academic journal. I have in front of me the September 1990 issue of the *American Economic Review*. Second, pick any article at random and read it for whatever you can get out of it—important insights into theory or policy, something that might actually have a significant impact on one of the big issues facing the nation. Four articles, written by professors from Stanford, Princeton, Rutgers, and Harvard, that caught my eye in this issue were: "The Origins of American Industrial Success, 1879–1940"; "Unexpected Inflation, Real Wages, and Employment Determination in Union Contracts"; "Margin Requirements, Volatility, and the Transitory Component of Stock Prices"; and "Tying, Foreclosure, and Exclusion."

The most obvious thing about articles like this, something that strikes you as soon as you have read a few words, is that they are the product of much time and effort. They are not done lightly. Written laboriously, footnoted extensively, they go on and on in dogged detail, summing up hundreds of hours of intensive work. Unfortunately, when one considers the many important economic problems confronting us, what most of these academic articles prove is that it can take just as much time and effort to write something of relatively little value as it does to write something of significance.

The people who probably know more about academic journal articles than anyone are the journal editors, the people who get to read hundreds of manuscripts a year in order to choose the few dozen that get published. Robert W. Clower is the Hugh C. Lane Distinguished Professor of Economic Theory at the University of South Carolina and served for a time as editor of the *American Economic Review*. "The experience," reported Professor Clower in 1989, "turned out to be shattering. What was remarkable was the absolute dullness, the lack of any kind of new idea, that predominated in the selection of papers I got. Close to a thousand manuscripts a year—and I swear that the profession would be better off if most of them hadn't been written, and certainly if most of them hadn't been published."[7]

But, you will say, this is unreasonable. How on earth could

so much be written by so many people, and so few notice how worthless it all is?

The main reason, I believe, is the normal tendency of all of us to be embarrassed about admitting ignorance. Virtually all of this pseudo-research is written in two languages that are obscure to many people, the language of mathematics and the jargon of particular fields of study. Rather than admit they don't understand the mathematics or vocabulary, most people prefer not to ask, let alone presume to criticize something they do not understand.

The first inkling I had of the pretense that infects the upper reaches of the academic world occurred while I was a graduate student at M.I.T. in the early 1960s. One day at a seminar, attended by both faculty and graduate students, a senior economics professor, Sidney S. Alexander, stood up and lavishly praised the work of Paul Samuelson, one of his renowned colleagues. His remarks were to the effect that Samuelson's book, published by Harvard University Press in 1947 and called *Foundations of Economic Analysis,* was a profoundly important contribution to economic knowledge. What was jarring was that Alexander prefaced his praise with the embarrassed admission that, of course, he "didn't understand any of the math." Everyone laughed and Samuelson graciously accepted the compliment. Alexander's comment was said in jest, but it contained an awkward truth.

Samuelson's 447-page book was virtually one long mathematical equation. If you didn't understand the mathematics, you had absolutely no idea what he was saying. There is nothing inherently wrong with the use of mathematics. There are times when an equation, properly understood, can cut to the heart of a matter faster and more effectively than words. There are even times when you can say something in mathematics you cannot say in words. In fact, in a course on economic theory I later took from Professor Samuelson it was his use of mathematical equations, combined with a brilliant teaching style, that confirmed my suspicion that a capitalist economy was far more efficacious and just than a socialist one.

But the use of mathematics as legitimate language is not the issue. The issues are whether or not people understand the language, and what ideas are being conveyed by that language. How could a professor with integrity praise something of which he admittedly knew nothing? It bothered me at the time, and it still does.

Soon thereafter I had another personal experience that further convinced me of just how powerful the infatuation with mathematics was among academic intellectuals, especially among those who did not understand mathematics. One of my major areas of study in the graduate school of M.I.T. was economic theory. This put me in direct competition with dozens of graduate students who had majored in economics during their undergraduate years. I was fresh out of the engineering and business schools of Dartmouth and had taken only one introductory course in economics, a few years earlier. My anxiety vanished when I discovered that most of the graduate courses in economics at M.I.T. were short on economic principles and facts and long on mathematics, something I had studied extensively.

In the fall of 1959 I signed up for a year-long course in international economics, taught by one of the country's noted experts, Charles P. Kindleberger. He had written a classic textbook in the field and was a scholar of integrity and wit. But as the course progressed, it became obvious that he was not on the cutting edge of the use of mathematics in economics, nor was he an original theorist. Years later, when he was almost eighty, he confirmed this when he lamented that "thirty years at MIT have produced books rather than articles. What is irritating, however, is a reputation based on a moderately successful textbook, written to help educate a large family, rather than an original work. Textbooks are syntheses of work of others."[8] Sad. Even at the twilight of an illustrious career, he couldn't take satisfaction in what he had done, but yearned instead for the academic prestige of "articles" and "original work."

But back in the fall of 1959 I did not realize the deep undercurrents that bedeviled so many academic intellectuals, and when the time came to write a term paper for Professor Kindleberger I chose a nontheoretical, nonmathetical, straightforward exposition of the terms of trade with West Germany in the years 1950–1959, complete with nice clear tables and charts. It was a good paper, something that Kindleberger could understand easily, and I was confident of a good grade. In graduate school any grade below A, especially for those of us on fellowships, was not considered good. In fact, it was pretty bad.

My grade on that first paper was a B, accompanied by some comments to the effect that it was "a little light on analysis" and the notation "empirical" next to the grade. Puzzled, I asked Kindleberger for an explanation. Yes, he conceded, it was a good empirical paper (i.e., no theory or mathematics), and there were some issues that I could have usefully explored, but the primary reason for the low grade was that the paper "didn't have it." What was *it*, I wondered.

Then it became clear to me. First-class, A-level work was theory written in mathematics. Facts and economic principles written in English, no matter how good, could never aspire to be more than B work. While Kindleberger did not say this directly, his meaning was clear, even though he seemed somewhat uncomfortable with it. I thanked him for his insight and counsel, and began to think about the second semester of his year-long course.

When the time came to write the term paper for the final grade, I determined to give the professor what he wanted. The title of the paper I submitted in May 1960 was "The Effect of a Customs Union on Direct Investment." The theory was breathtakingly simple. When a customs union exists between two or more nations or states, tariffs and quotas are reduced and sometimes eliminated. For example, the fifty states of the United States constitute in effect one large customs union. My "theory" was that direct investment in a foreign country was determined by economic incentives, the general economic environment, and the national economic policy of the country in which one might invest. Drawing on all my previous mathematical training, I translated these simple principles into symbols to which I applied calculus, taking derivatives, integrating, manipulating until I had generated eighteen complex mathematical formulae, one of which I proudly noted ran a half-page all by itself. The conclusions of my "theory," following twenty pages of mathematical analysis, were also pretty simple: the formation of a customs union (1) will usually increase direct foreign investment, and (2) is likely to improve world welfare.[9]

I handed that paper in with a certain foreboding. The theory was so simple, so trivial, that, if clearly understood, it could be laughed at. But, on the other hand, I was confident that Kindleberger would not understand the mathematical equations I had used in the exposition of my "original theory." A few days later I got my grade: an A, with the written comment "I like it" from Professor Kindleberger.

That was the last mathematical, "original theory" article I ever wrote.

The disenchantment with mathematical expressions of so-called original economic thought has grown and spread over the years, and more and more distinguished scholars are expressing concern—much to the consternation of many of their colleagues.

In 1988 the American Economic Association set up a commission to examine the nature of graduate economics education in the United States. Its conclusions, if reached in any other profession, would have been a scandal. One member of the commission, Professor Alan S. Blinder of Princeton University, conceded that: "Our surveys found widespread dissatisfaction with graduate education in economics—and a fairly consistent pattern of complaints. Both students and faculty find economics obsessed with technique over substance, or too theoretical, or too mathematical, or insufficiently connected with the real world, or too removed from policy and institutional context. . . . Only 14 percent of the students report that their core courses put substantial emphasis on 'applying economic theory to real-world problems.' This strikes me as a devastating critique."[10]

"Devastating" is not an overstatement. When leading academic intellectuals in the field of economics admit that what they are practicing and teaching is "obsessed with technique over substance" and "insufficiently connected with the real world," it is equivalent to a confession of intellectual bankruptcy. If there is no substance to what they teach and research, no significant connection to the economic problems that challenge the world, then it can be truthfully said that these academic intellectuals themselves are of little consequence.

The American Economic Association study was prompted by an earlier study conducted in the late 1980s by two economists—Arjo Klamer, an associate professor at George Washington University, and David Colander, a professor at Middlebury College. Their book, *The Making of an Economist*, is a path-breaking, disturbing report on the condition of graduate economics study in America. The book is based on a comprehensive survey of 212 graduate students enrolled in the Ph.D. programs at six of the most elite universities in the country—Columbia, Harvard, M.I.T., Stanford, Chicago, and Yale—and augmented by a number of in-depth interviews.

They found clear evidence that the content of the courses taught by the eminent professors at these schools was as trivial and irrelevant as most of their writings. The authors concluded, somewhat sadly, that "we see a group of intelligent, sympathetic, caring, and sincere students who find themselves in an academic situation where they are presented with a highly challenging field of study—but one of dubious relevance to reality," that "there was a strong sense that economics was a game," and that "the façade, not the depth of knowledge, was important."[11]

The tragedy is what happens to these students. Answering the anonymous questionnaire, most of them (53 percent) confessed a desire to become involved someday in policy formation, and said that desire was "very important in their decision to attend graduate school."[12] Their keen interest in the real world was soon crushed. Among those surveyed, 43 percent now "believed that a knowledge of economics literature was unimportant," and 68 percent "believed that a thorough knowledge of the economy was unimportant."[13]

Many of the students were cynical and bitter. Speaking candidly, off the record, they made comments like these:

Don *(M.I.T)*: "The people are very smart, and the work may show a lot of brilliance, but it seems that they're not dealing with the issues."

Vicky *(Harvard)*: "It is kind of funny. This semester we are learning model after model, but we learned so many things that don't work in reality."

Claire *(M.I.T)*: "If you go down the index of the *Journal of Political Economy* what percentage of articles would most of us think are not stupid? It's pretty small."

Janet *(Harvard)*: "We learn what all the recent theories are, look for little holes in them, and write our Ph.D. theses on that. . . . You don't really care if you come up with solutions to a real problem. It seems so strange."

Rick *(Chicago)*: "I now think that the profession in general is too mathematical. When I look at the journals, I get sick."[14]

Even stranger is what was done after Klamer and Colander's work came out, after the results of the American Economic Association's own study were published. Robert Solow, professor of economics at M.I.T., admitted ruefully after reviewing Klamer and Colander's work, "To say something is wrong with graduate education is to say something is wrong with the economics profession."[15] Yet nothing significant was done. No changes, not much beating of breasts, just business as usual, a calm indifference to shaming charges. It is symptomatic of the widespread cynicism and lack of integrity that mark so much of the academic world today.

The extent of intellectual bankruptcy is wide and deep. As Klamer and Colander observed in 1990, "Disillusionment and cynicism are not conditions limited to graduate students. Many members of the profession appear to lack faith in what they do. They will confess, usually at unguarded moments, that their highly sophisticated research produces ultimately meaningless results—but they will demand their students follow their lead anyway. 'Of course this assumption is absurd,' a well-known economist noted during a recent seminar, 'but, hey, isn't all we do absurd and utterly unrealistic?' "[16]

The trivial substance of much academic research and its blissful irrelevance to the vital problems of the world was perhaps best illustrated by the response of the academic economists to the problems that pummeled the United States in the late 1970s and early 1980s. I felt this keenly, for I served as Ronald Reagan's policy adviser on a wide range of issues including economic policy during the presidential campaigns of 1976 and 1980, and a year and a half in the White House.

Remember what it was like then? Inflation racing out of control, close to 20 percent during some months in 1980. Interest rates soaring up into the same 20 percent range. Waiting in gasoline lines for hours. Taxes and government regulations multiplying with no end in sight. People becoming more and more fearful that the economic mess would turn into a permanent disaster, with the United States going the way of some of the irresponsibly managed economies of Latin America. The specter grew of even our national security being undermined by a declining economy. Then, in the 1980s, the international communist empire began to crumble. Profound, unprecedented change crackled through China and the Soviet Union and dozens of other totalitarian economies.

There were lots of big problems for economists to wrestle with, to analyze, and to address with solutions and recommendations. For example, there was a clear need for a comprehensive program to halt the nation's accelerating economic decline. When the presidential race began in 1980, one of the first questions thrown at every serious candidate by the press was, "What is your economic program?" As far as help from academic journals was concerned, every candidate was on his own. There simply was nothing there that was of much use or relevance to the economic difficulties engulfing us. I know. I looked.

The critical economic problems of the nation were obvious to everyone by the end of 1978. But if you examined the scholarly articles published in the most prestigious economic journal, the *American Economic Review*, during the 1980s, you would gain only the barest clues to the economic roller-coaster we were experiencing, from the depths of a recession to the greatest economic expansion in our country's history. In particular, you would find not a single attempt to spell out a comprehensive economic policy for the United States. There were hundreds of articles on subjects of limited, peripheral importance, and some that were just mindlessly irrelevant.

Fifty-two major articles were published in the *American Economic Review* in 1978. They included nothing on the pocketbook issues beginning to hit every American family, nothing on the control of federal spending and tax policy and the crushing burden of government regulation of business. Here's a sampling of what the economists were writing about: "Some Results on Incentive Contracts," "Optimal Fiscal Reform of Metropolitan Schools," "An Analysis of the Changing Location of Iron and Steel Production in the Twentieth Century," "A Model of Agenda Influence on Committee Decisions," "Optimal Investment Strategies for Boomtowns," and "American Indian Relative Ranching Efficiency."

Shades of Nero fiddling while Rome burned. The academic economists fiddled while the U.S. economy crumbled in the 1970s. And they kept right on fiddling through the 1980s. For the next eleven years, through some 450-odd articles, they managed to maintain their folly—proudly, arrogantly.

Not a single piece on comprehensive economic policy. Not one article on how to manage the unparalleled transformation of totalitarian states into free economies. Not a blessed word about the U.S. economic expansion from 1982 to 1990.

Yes, they did continue to publish articles such as "Appropriative Water Rights and the Efficient Allocation of Resources," "Labor Supply Functions in a Poor Agrarian Economy," "The Design of an Optimal Insurance Policy,"[17] "Welfare, Remarriage, and Marital Search,"[18] "Taxing Tar and Nicotine," "A Structural Model of Murder Behavior,"[19] "The Homogenization of Heterogeneous Inputs," "The Economics of Risks to Life,"[20] "The Economics of Superstars,"[21] "The Economic Consequences of Cognitive Dissonance," "The Demand for Leisure and Nonpecuniary Job Characteristics,"[22] "Property Rights and Efficiency in Mating, Racing, and Related Games,"[23] "Coping with Complexity," "Gambles and the Shadow Price of Death," "Marx and Malthusianism,"[24] "The Demand for and Supply of Births,"[25] "Golden Parachutes, Shark Repellents and Hostile Tender Offers,"[26] "Prizes and Incentives in Elimination Tournaments,"[27] "Ski-Lift Pricing, with Applications to Labor and Other Markets,"[28] "The Economics of Rising Stars,"[29] "A Study of Fashion and Markdown Pricing,"[30] and "In Quest of the Slutsky Diamond."[31]

By December 1989 the *American Economic Review* had descended to publishing an article on basketball scoring, entitled "Does the Basketball Market Believe in the 'Hot Hand'?" Seems that some people who watch basketball games believe "players who make a shot are more likely to hit the next shot than players who miss a shot." Is this true? Four pages of dense analysis are devoted to answering this weighty question. For those who care, the answer is yes, but unfortunately, the author concludes, the effect is so slight that you cannot make money betting on it. Well, there's always horse racing.

After reviewing the twelve-year output of America's most scholarly economics journal I understood more clearly a phenomenon I had witnessed during four years of government service, first on President Nixon's White House staff and then as President Reagan's economic and domestic policy adviser. Not once in all those years, in countless meetings on national economic policy, did anyone ever refer to any article from an academic journal. Not once did anyone use a mathematical formula more complicated than adding, subtracting, multiplying, or dividing.

There was much debate about economic principles, about statistics, about human motivations and incentives, about the overriding issues of economic growth and job creation. But as far as the *crème de la crème* production of the academic intellectuals was concerned, it was as if it did not exist. Those who had the responsibility for advising and making decisions held no animosity toward the work of academic intellectuals. They just did not think of it.

The same pattern of irrelevance held firm even as revolutionary economic changes swept through most of the world during the 1980s. The collapse of communist economies was barely mentioned in the prestigious academic journals. Nor will you find in them any analysis of the determinants of economic growth and job creation in the 1980s, when the United States set historical records.

In the September 1990 issue of the *American Economic Review* you will find "The Economics of Product Patents" by a professor from the University of Reading in England, but you will not find anything on current national economic policy. You will find "The Origins of American Industrial Success, 1879–1940" by a professor from Stanford University, but you will not find anything on the origins of our economic successes in 1982–1990. You will find "A Theory of Managed Trade," but you will not find anything on how the Soviet Union can break free of its managed economy.

Unfortunately, the irrelevance that infects so much of the academic intellectual world, and whose key symptom is the mathematical equation, is not limited to the field of economics. It is everywhere.

Robert Alter is a well-known scholar, a professor of Hebrew and comparative literature at the University of California at Berkeley. In 1989 he published a book dealing with academic intellectuals in the field of literature. The book begins with these words: "Peculiar things have clearly been happening in the academic study of literature."[32] Professor Alter continues, "The most central failure, I think, is that so many among a whole generation of professional students of literature have turned away from reading."[33]

Many of us have always believed the study of literature meant reading. Alter's conclusions about students of literature is comparable to students of religion turning away from the Bible or the Koran, or mathematicians giving up equations. This is hard to believe, a situation even worse than that of the economists.

But Alter is serious. "For many of the new trends in literary studies," he charges, "the object of the preposition 'about' is often no longer literature. . . . One can read article after article, hear lecture after lecture, in which no literary work is ever quoted and no real reading experience is registered."[34]

Then what are the articles about?

Alter gives as an example a discussion on Stephen Crane, the famous American novelist of the early twentieth century who wrote *The Red Badge of Courage* and died when he was only twenty-eight years old. Here is what one of today's literary intellectuals had to say about Crane's writing:

> The becoming-visible of writing must be considered in terms of a programmatic equation of identification that, I want to suggest, underwrites realistic discourse. This equation involves the perfect "fit" between the ontology of writing and the specific material—the historically specific subject-matter—of the social body–machine complex, the perfect "fit" between the (apparently non-historicizable) ontology of writing and a historically specific biomechanics.[35]

Stephen Crane, being dead, is fortunate to be spared this bizarre analysis of his work.

Lynne V. Cheney, chairman of the National Endowment for the Humanities, sadly described the situation in July 1991: "If we are completely honest about it, we must admit that the overemphasis on research has—in the humanities as in other fields—meant a lot of useless activity, a lot of publishing that serves no purpose beyond expanding the authors' c.v.'s [curricula vitae] . . . many publications will mainly gather dust on library shelves."[36]

The scientific literature also has been infected by the virus of inconsequentiality. As scientific articles tumble off the printing presses, concern with their quality grows. In the scientific world "horror stories of studies rendered useless by mad methodologies, improper use of statistics, shoddy data, sloppiness, or fraud are legion."[37] Some of the practitioners themselves are becoming alarmed. Speaking of "bad statistics" used in some scientific articles, Gabriel Weinreich of the University of Michigan says, "It's not a minor violation—it's really rather horrifying."[38] And Walter Steward, a National Institute of Health researcher, goes even further: "I've never met a scientist who didn't believe that 80 percent of the scientific literature was nonsense."[39]

A reporter for *Science*, David Hamilton, concluded at the end of his examination of the value of academic research that "an unfortunately large percentage of what passes as the bedrock of academic achievement more closely resembles intellectual quicksand."[40]

One measure of the importance of a published piece of academic work is the number of times other writers cite the work. As we shall see, counting the number of times a work is cited is a rather weak standard by which to measure importance, but the practice is widely accepted among academics today. Measured by even this admittedly questionable yardstick, most academic publications flunk.

According to a 1990 survey of all the articles published in journals covered by the database of the Institute for Scientific Information, the citation bible for academic intellectuals, a disturbing number were never mentioned after publication. The percentage of the journal literature that remains uncited for five full years after publication varies from field to field: 22.4 percent of the articles in science journals, a whopping 48.0 percent of the articles in social science journals, and a hard-to-believe 93.1 percent of articles in the arts and humanities journals just faded from sight.[41]

Even the research efforts of professors at the more practically minded graduate business schools are coming under critical questioning. As Richard West, dean of New York University's graduate school of business, bluntly put it in October 1990, the writing in these academic journals is "often crap. They say nothing in these articles, and they say it in a pretentious way. If I wasn't the dean of this school, I'd be writing a book on the bankruptcy of American management education."[42] Regrettably, the dean of one of America's leading business schools is dead right, as anyone can easily determine for himself by picking up a current learned journal such as the *Journal of Strategic Management*, which Dean West was referring to specifically. It is something the academic intellectuals in the field have known for a long time.

While not all of today's academic research and writing is irrelevant or pretentious, a disturbing amount is. Scott S. Cowen, dean of the School of Management at Case Western Reserve University, estimates that "as much as 80 percent of management research may be irrelevant," and wonders "if the majority of it is of any significant value to executives in terms of influencing their daily actions, behaviors, or business practices."[43]

The powerful vested interests that produce this pseudo-research will leap to defend it by citing example after example of important articles. They will be right, of course, but that is not the point. As Edward Fox, dean of Dartmouth's Amos Tuck School of Business Administration, says, "The point is that a lot of what passes for research has no value."[44]

And yet, it seems that as the research product becomes weaker, the efforts to produce more of it are redoubled, placing great demands on the intellectuals. There are dozens of academic journals in the management and business field, and the articles therein soak up a lot of time and effort. That time is stolen more and more from teaching. As Donald Jacobs, the head of Northwestern University's Kellogg School of Management, the number one ranked business school in the country in 1990, told an interviewer: When he joined the faculty as an "assistant professor of finance in 1957, he was required to teach *nine* courses a year. By the time he had become dean in 1975, the teaching load had shrunk to only *six* courses, to allow faculty more time for research. Today, the average is *four* courses a year. If a professor is editor of a journal . . . it's only *three* courses [italics added]." In summing up what has happened in our graduate business schools, Dean Jacobs concludes: "The demands have shifted from the classroom to research output."[45]

Page Smith is an eminent American historian, the author of twenty books, the founding provost of the University of California at Santa Cruz, a man who earned his Ph.D. at Harvard and then taught at the university level for twenty-one years. In his book *Killing the Spirit*, Smith summed up what he had learned about the scholarly research of his colleagues during a lifetime spent in the top ranks of the American academy:

> The vast majority of the so-called research turned out in the modern university is essentially worthless. It does not result in any measurable benefit to anything or anybody. It does not push back those omnipresent "frontiers of knowledge" so confidently evoked. . . . It is busywork on a vast, almost incomprehensible

scale. It is dispiriting; it depresses the whole scholarly enterprise; and, most important of all, it deprives the student of what he or she deserves—the thoughtful and considerate attention of a teacher deeply and unequivocally committed to teaching.[46]

Almost as disturbing as the lack of substance and relevance in much of today's academic research and writing is the attitude of those turning it out. Gone is the enduring search for truth, gone is the concern for relevance, for the essence rather than dross. Instead, there seems to be a sense of arrogant defiance, an attitude that says "This is important because I say it is important, and how dare you or anyone else question it?"

Sar Levitan is a noted economist, born in 1914, the author of numerous books on social policy and a member of the faculty of George Washington University. The prestigious journal of his field is the *Journal of Human Resources*. For years he had watched with consternation as the journal declined into what he labeled "obscurantism," a word that is defined either as "positive opposition to enlightenment or the spread of knowledge," or "a policy of deliberately making something obscure." Either way, it is not a particularly nice thing to say about an intellectual journal.

But by 1989 Levitan's patience had run out, and he made that charge in a stinging letter to the editor, a young fellow, then forty-one years old, Robert Moffitt. "Enough is enough," Levitan wrote. "I wouldn't be surprised if other subscribers share my frustration with JHR's propensity to abuse, if not torture, the English language. . . . If you ever decide to publish the JHR in English again, please let me know and I will be happy to renew my subscription."[47]

Moffitt, now a professor of economics at Brown University, was not amused. In a fit of *lèse-majesté*, the young man of far less distinction essentially told his intellectual better to go fly a kite. "Dear Professor Levitan," Moffitt wrote back. "To quote the familiar opinion of J. Willard Gibbs, 'Mathematics is a language.' . . . I hope that you will renew your subscription to the JHR after you have expanded your vocabulary."[48] To which Levitan graciously replied, "There is no need to get testy. The issue is neither my disadvantaged education status nor whether mathematics is a language."[49]

That is precisely the point. The issue is whether or not there is any merit to the ideas being expressed, and whether the very possibility of judging that merit is being deliberately and cunningly obscured by the use of mathematics and jargon.

The main problem is not that much of the writing of academic intellectuals is too mathematical, but that it is insignificant, unimportant, trivial. If the ideas were significant and important ones couched in the language of mathematics, that would be fine, for presumably it could be reworked into English. But if the writing is devoid of any merit, expressing it in plain English would expose the intellectual sham.

The intellectual corruption of the academic world is so deep and widespread that some of those concerned about it have resorted to using wit to expose the vice and folly of it all. One intrepid professor, J. Scott Armstrong at the University of Pennsylvania, reviewed the literature analyzing scholarly publications and came up with a tongue-in-cheek "author's formula" for publication success in the academic world. Academics writers should: not pick an interesting topic, not challenge existing beliefs, not obtain surprising results, not use simple methods, not provide full disclosure, and not write clearly.[50]

An amusing satire on the state of research in the medical world was written in 1988 by Dr. Durmond Rennie. As senior editor of the *Journal of the American Medical Association*, he speaks with the confidence of one with special knowledge, the person who gets to read all the research papers submitted for publication. According to his experience, "There seems to be no study too fragmented, no hypothesis too trivial, no literature citation too biased or too egotistical, no design too warped, no methodology too bungled, no presentation of results too self-serving, no argument too circular, no conclusions too trifling or too unjustified, and no grammar and syntax too offensive for a paper to end up in print."[51]

Pyrite, a naturally occurring iron disulfide mineral, is called fool's gold "because its colour may deceive the novice into thinking he has found a gold nugget." It is useful mainly in making sulfur, although it does emit hot sparks when struck by steel, leading some archeologists to believe it was a primitive means of making fire.[52] Much of the academic writing that glitters and gleams in the academic journals is intellectual pyrite, perhaps good only for making fire.

Some may say "So what?" Who cares if the scribblings of academic intellectuals are often trivial and irrelevant? There are at least two reasons for concern. One is the tragic waste of so much brainpower. Professors—even the least talented and least enthusiastic ones—generally work hard. When career advancement is at stake, the pressure to publish can be all but irresistible.

Second, and perhaps even more important, is the corrosive impact of producing trivial, irrelevant research and then pretending that it is important. Writing for publication is now the essence of what the academic intellectual does. It is the self-selected standard by which academics judge each other and themselves. When they pretend that each other's work is important when it is not, that it is relevant when it is not, that it is a significant contribution to knowledge when it is not, they violate the integrity of who and what they are. If a man or woman repeatedly publishes or praises work that is essentially worthless and pretends it is not, there is unavoidable damage to his or her self-esteem. Knowing that one is to some degree an intellectual fraud can create powerful feelings of anxiety and guilt.

Let me make one point as clear as I can. I am not talking about all professors in our universities and colleges. Many of them are what we think they are. They are brilliant, learned men and women, they love teaching and do it well, they research and write about important, relevant things, and they do it with insight and skill. But this kind of academic intellectual appears to be dwindling in number and influence, increasingly crowded out by a distressingly large number of newcomers who share neither their temperament nor their mental powers. They are the ones who now dominate, and who deserve our scrutiny. They are the ones who have created the bizarre intellectual world of today's universities in which the highest value is trivial, irrelevant publication and the lowest value is teaching.

There are some interesting parallels between America's academic world in the 1990s and the world of Hermann Hesse's 1943 novel, *The Glass Bead Game*. The novel is an ironic parody of the intellectual world as Hesse saw it then, and is remarkably prophetic of our own time.

The glass bead game in Hesse's book was exactly that—a game. But it was played with such intensity that it gradually took over the professional lives of the intellectuals who played it. As they played the game with increasing skill and fervor, they retreated further and further from the concerns of the real world. In effect, the intellectuals in Hesse's *Glass Bead Game* created their own fantasy world that transcended reality, and as they earned respect and honor for their game skills, as being the highest possible level of intellectual achievement, they soared off into ultimate irrelevance.

In Hesse's words, the glass bead game was designed to be deliberately elite, open only to the brilliant few who worked hard and surrendered themselves to its charm:

> The only way to learn the rules of this Game of games is to take the usual prescribed course, which requires many years . . .
>
> The Game . . . was capable of expressing mathematical processes by special symbols and abbreviations. The players, mutually elaborating these processes, threw these abstract formulas at one another, displaying the sequences and possibilities of their science. This mathematical and astronomical game of formulas required great attentiveness, keenness, and concentration. Among mathematicians, even in those days, the reputation of being a good Glass Bead Game player meant a great deal.
>
> At various times the Game was taken up and imitated by nearly all the scientific and scholarly disciplines. . . . Each discipline which seized upon the Game created its own language of formulas, abbreviations, and possible combinations. Everywhere, the elite intellectual youth developed a passion for these Games, with their dialogues and progressions of formulas. . . .

> The Glass Bead Game, formerly the specialized entertainment of mathematicians in one era . . . now more and more cast its spell upon all true intellectuals. Many an old university . . . turned to it . . . the Game rapidly evolved into what it is today: the quintessence of intellectuality and art, the sublime cult. [53]

Academic life in America today bears a chilling similarity to the fantasy Hesse created in 1943. Our academic intellectuals play an elaborate game whose markers of success are not small glass beads, but the number of articles published in academic journals and the number of times those articles are cited in other articles written by their colleagues.

In theory this makes good sense. Judging any piece of written work can be a highly subjective business, and judging objectively many different pieces of work by many different authors can be all too taxing. The idea seems to be that a count of the articles written and a count of the number of citations received is a good proxy for measuring scholarly output. After all, journal articles that are reviewed and approved for publication by one's peers should be superior work. And if one's work is cited by another academic intellectual, the clear inference is that it must have been important enough to influence his or her thinking, and thus is a contribution to knowledge.

Unfortunately, the theory of article counts and citation counts rests on the silent assumption that the articles counted are important, relevant, and contain significant, original contributions to knowledge, and that citations counted thus measure the dissemination of that knowledge. The assumption is false. Only a tiny portion of academic articles come close to meeting the multiple criteria of importance, relevance, and originality.

Sadly, a sensible idea has become corrupted. The shortcut to measuring quality and lasting impact has turned into a short-circuit of valid judgment. Though the article counts and citation counts are wildly popular among the aficionados of today's intellectual fashions, they have little validity. But if you think of them as brightly colored glass beads in a game that values glass beads, then they have great value when exchanged for promotions and salary increases and intellectual reputations in the academic world.

It is a relatively simple matter to keep count of the journal articles anyone writes. Most academics keep detailed, up-to-date lists that they attach to their résumés and can provide you with almost instantly. But citations, those references to one's published works in the writings of others, are a more elusive quarry. So much is published that it would be a monumental chore for anyone to track down all citations of his or her work. Beyond that, any attempt to assign meaning to that count, to attach importance or significance to work cited, would be even more difficult.

On the other hand, important, significant work does tend to be referred to by later writers and, in some instances, can be a true reflection of the power and scope of the work being cited. For example, in economics the works of Adam Smith and Karl Marx are still being cited many years after their deaths. The same is true of more recent economists such as Alfred Marshall, John Maynard Keynes, Ludwig von Mises, and Milton Friedman. But the logic of citation is one-way. While important, significant works are often cited, it does not follow that frequent citation necessarily means the works cited are important and significant. That simple point seems to have been lost in today's academic intellectual world.

It is tacitly assumed that a citation is the intellectual equivalent of a small glass bead that can be hoarded and tallied up, and eventually cashed in. Not unexpectedly, close attention is paid to something that valuable. In fact, there is a small industry serving the academic world that does nothing but sift through the millions of pages that roll off the academic presses each year and record, analyze, and print the results.

The preeminent citation counter is the *Social Sciences Citation Index* (SSCI), with the intimidating subtitle "An International Multidisciplinary Index to the Literature of the Social, Behavioral and Related Sciences." First published in 1973, the index is a multimillion-dollar business. The published version is sixty-five volumes, each volume containing hundreds of pages densely packed with fine print. The whole set takes up about eight feet of shelf space. And it is not cheap. An annual subscription to the printed index costs $3,950. It is also available on computer, making searches much easier. The software costs $4,500 a year.

While the SSCI index can be used for a variety of research tasks, its primary use is to set forth a comprehensive accounting of when and where a writer's work has been cited by others. Say you have written several articles during the past ten years and are curious to know how often others have cited your work during the past year. No problem if you have a subscription to the SSCI. Just look up your name, and the listing of citations follows. It's a useful tool for administrators wanting to check the research production of their faculty, and it is particularly good for satisfying one's own curiosity. Of course, the index is a very expensive way to slake your vanity, and few individuals can afford it. But many universities add it to their libraries and, beyond its limited usefulness in scholarly research, it is available to faculty as a perquisite. The index has close to one thousand annual subscribers.

The index is good at what it does. It indicates the literature which mentioned your work and the author and date. In 1989 the index listed a total of 1,646,742 citations, sifted and culled from 4,700 academic journals.[54] But that's about it. It doesn't count how many times different people cited you; that you have to do yourself. It doesn't indicate how many times you were mentioned in any specific article; just one count per article.

There are some serious deficiencies. If someone's work is cited in an article, it counts as a citation; if it is mentioned in a book, it doesn't count. Books are not listed in the index, nor are any references to other books or articles that appear in books. Thus, if you write books, arguably the most important, most basic source of facts and ideas, or your work is referred to in other books, you are automatically excluded from the index. (Once the SSCI index did count citations in books, but the practice was discontinued in 1982.) However, if someone writes an article for an academic journal and mentions a book, then the book and its author would be cited.

Perhaps the most grievous lack is that the index doesn't say whether you were mentioned favorably or unfavorably. You could have been roundly denounced for uttering the dumbest proposition of the decade, but it would still count for one citation. You could have been cited a dozen times in one article by an outstanding scholar, and it would count for one citation. You could have been cited a dozen times by a dozen fourth-rate scholars, and it would count for twelve citations.

The citation index shows no more discrimination than someone with a mechanical counter conducting a traffic survey. The person counts cars, period, not what make of car or how many people are in the car. The index counts mentions of a work with not the slightest attention paid to the content of that mention. Sometimes, even the count can be misleading.

To test the index, I looked up my own name in the 1989 edition. On page 356 was the entry "ANDERSON M" followed by sixty-two citations. Well, not exactly. It seems that I am not the only M. Anderson cited. Any Anderson whose name begins with M gets lumped under the same heading—whether it is Michael or Martha or Martin. Since I of course knew what I had written, I picked out the eight entries that were citations of my work. But any other user of the index could not have done that without looking up each and every citation, the very kind of tedious, laborious work the index is supposed to eliminate. The eight citations all referred to books I had written, which had been cited in journals by other writers.

One of the unwritten rules of social science research that has come increasingly in vogue is that if you cannot measure what is important, then you do the next best thing and analyze what you can measure. Citation counts are of doubtful validity, but they are easy to quantify and researchers have analyzed them avidly. For example, in 1989 the *Journal of Economic Perspectives* published a list of the "top 25 young [under 40 in 1985] economists in the nation." How were they chosen? By the importance and significance of their ideas? By their teaching skill? By the quality of their government service? By their usefulness to big business? No. They were "ranked by the number of total and mean citations."[55]

Sixty percent of the "top 25 young economists" came from the top ten universities. Some of them were very good, demonstrating that some distinguished intellectuals do get cited a lot. For example, number nine on the list was Michael Boskin of Stanford with 483 citations. Boskin was then chairman of the Council of Economic Advisers for President Bush.[56] But most of the people on the list you will never hear of, demonstrating that counting citations is a shaky way of measuring intellectual distinction.

A further indication of the importance of counting citations in today's academic writing is the changing practice of how citations are made. The normal practice has been to footnote. You refer to someone else's work, you put a little number in the text, and anyone interested in the source turns to your list of footnotes, either at the bottom of the page or at the end of the work. Most people like this system. They don't want to read every footnote, and it is not necessary. But normal footnoting practice does not highlight the reference to another's work, and the reader may well skip reading the footnotes. To fix this, many of today's academic writers have adopted a new practice.

They put the citations right smack in the middle of the text. Not the full content of a footnote, but the name of the author cited and the year the work was written. Just to make sure we do not miss what is of crucial importance in their writing—the citations—they interrupt with bracketed lists of sources. For example, an article in the December 1989 issue of the *American Economic Review*, co-authored by Steve Dowrick and Duc-Tho Nguyen, has right after the very first sentence, "(See, for example, Roger Kormendi and Philip Meguire, 1985; Moses Abramowitz, 1986; William Baumol, 1986; Fred Gruen, 1986; Steve Dowrick and Duc-Tho Nguyen, 1987)."[57]

Leaving aside the shameless self-quoting in the last entry, and the obvious pleasure it gives to those mentioned, that citation form gives us no useful information. Unless we are intimately familiar with all the literature of the field, we don't even know what works they are referring to unless we turn to the list at the end of the article. But this list does provide all the information necessary to make a full entry in the published citation indexes. You could easily get the impression that the main purpose of many academic articles is to produce citations, not to explore and propound important ideas.

Some writers now even dispense with the brackets and run the citations into the text. Here is the first sentence of an article by Professor James N. Brown from that same issue of the *American Economic Review:* "Nearly 200 years after Adam Smith's original statement, the 'human capital' model of earnings was extended in the work of Milton Friedman and Simon Kuznets (1945), Jacob Mincer (1958, 1962, 1974), Theodore W. Schultz (1960, 1961), and Gary S. Becker (1962, 1964)."[58]

Citing long lists of names and dates in the text itself is aesthetically ugly and makes for deadly dull writing, but it does help ensure that those who count citations for a living will be kept busy. Although it does border on the bizarre to cite eight references in the very first sentence, at least Professor Brown didn't quote himself until the second page.

In pursuit of citation counts, perhaps the most shameful practice is quoting oneself. In that December 1989 issue of the *American Economic Review* there were fifteen major articles. In eleven of the fifteen the authors cited themselves, in four cases three or more times. Professor Olivier Jen Blanchard of M.I.T. managed to refer to his own writing seven different times. But a citation is a citation.

One of the most serious problems in the academic world today is that the measure of quality is quantity. Academics are rarely ranked by the power and range of their work, by its importance and significance. To an increasing degree they are measured by the quantity of their work only, by how many articles and books they publish. For example, in 1988 the *International Social Science Review* published a study which assessed the research done by the graduate departments of "80 U.S. universities—20 each in physics, chemistry, sociology, and political science." The quality of the intellectual research done was measured by three criteria: (1) "total articles per faculty member," (2) "total articles in leading journals per faculty member," and (3) "total books per faculty member."[59]

The academic intellectuals have learned one lesson well. If they are going to be judged by the number of citations bearing their name, they will do whatever is necessary to maximize the number of citations. When the first *Social Science Citation Index* was published in 1973, the average number of references per article was nine. As more and more academic writers caught on to this game, that citations were being tabulated and published, and that they were valuable counters toward academic prestige and even salary increases, they responded as one would expect rational, intelligent people to respond. They began to maximize the generation of citations. During the past fifteen years the average number of citations per article has increased steadily from nine to sixteen, an increase of almost 80 percent.[60]

As the work of the academic intellectuals became more and more obfuscated by mathematics and jargon, and more to be counted than read and analyzed, those who were writing adjusted. Normally, one of the most jealously guarded prerogatives of any writer is authorship—sole authorship. Thinking and writing is a solitary vocation, and virtually all original, important ideas—especially in the social sciences—spring from one brain. Committees rarely author new concepts or write essays, and when they try they usually fail. For most intellectuals the sense of territory, of proprietorship, in something they have created is instinctive. What they write they want stamped with their name. They are loath to share credit, particularly undeserved credit. Yes, there are those rare instances of effective collaboration, where two or more people contribute roughly equally to a piece of work, where multiple authorship is justified and welcomed. But not often.

And yet, in spite of the natural territorial imperative that writers feel toward their work, there has been a sharp and pervasive increase in multiple authorship over the past decade or two. More and more work, especially in the academic journals, is signed by two people. Sometimes three, four, or more affix their signatures. The practice is far more widespread than could be reasonably explained by genuine collaboration. It is a baneful practice, for it adds one more dense layer of fog over much academic work. You have no way of knowing who wrote a particular passage, who thought of the key ideas, whose insight organized the work. As a consequence all the authors listed receive equal intellectual credit.

The virtues of multiple authorship were quick to be recognized by the academic world as increasing emphasis was put on the number of articles written and cited, and less emphasis on the content of what was written. It does not take a rocket scientist to figure out that if, say, three people each write an article and publish it under their own names they will each get one publication credit. If those same three people worked together, shared ideas, and agreed to sign all three articles, then each of them would get three publication credits. One minor drawback to multiple authorship is that the major citation index, the SSCI, will list only the name of the first author.

The chances of three people contributing equally to any intellectual piece of work are virtually zero. One may have thought of the key idea, one may have done most of the writing, one may have done the editing. It is a neat, efficient way of mass-producing published work that gives fraudulent credit to its authors.

The result, whether consciously intended or not, is to give people credit for work they did not do. This practice is notably abusive when someone with stature and reputation agrees to coauthor the work of a less well known colleague—for example, an older, established professor agreeing to place his name on a piece of work done primarily by a young professor or research assistant. In this Faustian bargain the young, unknown scholar trades sole credit for his or her work for the association with the more distinguished scholar, which will increase the chances that the work will be published. The senior professor trades his reputation for a partial share in work he did not do. Both parties to the bargain gain in terms of academic prestige; only integrity loses.

The way some intellectuals turn out written work is similar to the way some of the old master painters and sculptors used to turn out their work. They used assistants to rough out the works, and the paintings and sculptures, while not forgeries, were also not sole, original works. They were better known as belonging to the "school of so-and-so."

With so much coauthored academic work being produced, credits are multiplying like rabbits. Until the practice is stopped we will never really know who the parents of the ideas are. Perhaps instead of giving equal credit to all multiple authors, we should give no credit whatsoever for coauthored work, saving that for works that have a clear and distinct parentage.

Over the last thirty or forty years an almost impenetrable cocoon has been spun around most academic writing, until today it is almost as tough and dense as fiberglass. The fiendish combination of writing in the language of mathematics and jargon, of breaking up whatever shreds of recognizable thought remain with long streaks of citations in the text, and then hiding any personal accountability behind multiple authorship, has created a secret world in which we are all guilty of complicity. We might not have the foggiest notion of its worth, but we generously assume its worth is considerable. That is a mistake.

This glass bead game has even spread to the world of the graduate business schools. As an article in *Business Week* reported, "As many as 100 journals—some of them barely read by the academics themselves—now exist in the B-school world, as much to allow junior faculty to gain credits for promotion and tenure as for anything else. The papers are largely written to please an inner circle of academic experts who must approve an article before it can be published. Morris Holbrook of Columbia University has called the lengthy review process 'a socially approved form of intellectual sadomasochism.' "[61]

Hermann Hesse must be smiling in his grave.

With no effective check from the outside, academic intellectuals—who generally refer to themselves as representing a "field" of study—have in effect been left to regulate and judge themselves. Those who produce the work judge the work. And if they say it is important—and no one else reads it—who's to say it is not important?

Within many so-called fields of study there is widespread logrolling. Many of the fields are small enough so that most of the members know each other. I remember one incident that occurred when a committee I served on was reviewing a fellow for promotion at the Hoover Institution. Someone asserted he was "one of the top ten men in his field in the United States." Not being familiar with the "field," I innocently asked how many were in the field. "Oh, about six" was the reply. This was said partly in jest, but only partly.

A particular field of study is often such a closed, incestuous little society that its members are reluctant to criticize one another. In fact, they usually go to the opposite extreme. They lavishly cite one another, building up credits with their colleagues, expecting with good reason to be cited in return. It is a tricky trading game they play because if they overcite a competitor they can upset the delicate pecking order of academic prestige in their field.

During the past thirty years I have sat in countless committee meetings charged with evaluating intellectuals—hiring or promoting them either as professors or fellows. Rarely does the evaluation of research work get beyond an article and book count, although conscientious members of the committee will often skim an article or two and read the titles of the rest. Of course, sometimes the candidate is so distinguished and well known that counting publications or citations is irrelevant. At times one book or one article will stand out so much that it alone is enough. And often the candidate will be personally known to members of the committee, sometimes for a period of decades, and that personal testimony will be an overwhelming factor.

But the regrettable thing is that, somehow, we have gotten to the point where, all other things being equal, we are giving disproportionate weight to the quantity of intellectual production, not its quality. It is unprofessional, it is wrong, and it is the most significant cause of the decay that is eating through the academic intellectual world.

To the outside evaluators of academic intellectuals—to the administrators of their university who pay their salaries, to intellectuals in other fields, to the general public—the value of what they do is accepted on faith. We trust them when they say that what they do is important, and sometimes we check them by counting their output. By doing only that we have contributed powerfully to the decline of important, significant academic research. Once it became acceptable to shroud one's ideas in jargon and mathematics, the potential for abuse proliferated. When it was no longer possible to determine whether or not an idea made sense because we could not see through the mathematics or jargon, we were forced to trust to the judgment of the handful in each field who did know.

There are two other characteristics of academic writing that reinforce the notion that, as Gertrude Stein once said of Oakland, California, "There is no there there." In commercial publishing, a new work by an established author is anxiously awaited by enough people so that two things happen. First, the work is published promptly, and second, the author is paid for his or her effort. Not so in academic publishing.

In the first place, academic journals do not pay fees to their writers. Writing is more or less done for the honor and glory of it all. You could argue that most of what the academic journals get is worth exactly what they pay for it. And perhaps Samuel Johnson was right when he wrote in 1776 that "no man but a blockhead ever wrote except for money."[62] Actually the situation has gotten worse. Today not only do academic writers not get paid, but many in effect pay to get published. Not a lot, but they do pay.

Some scientific journals charge their would-be contributors by the word or page. Even the venerable *American Economic Review* has something euphemistically called a "submission fee" that must be paid by anyone sending in a manuscript for possible publication. The fee is $50 for members of the American Economic Association and $100 for nonmembers. To the degree that writers pay, academic publishing is vanity publishing. There is nothing intrinsically wrong with vanity publishing, but it does tell us something about the demand for and the worth of the writing.

Moreover, some of the most important academic journals are not sold on a public subscription or per-issue basis. Normally one gets them as a matter of course after paying dues to an academic association. This has further masked the real demand for the work and, in effect, creates a captive subscriber list, making it possible for the publisher to boast of reasonably large circulation without getting into the sticky questions of readership or whether people would actually pay for a subscription in the real world.

Finally, the publication schedule of academic journals is notoriously slow. Years can pass before you will ever see the printed page. As Professor Kenneth Arrow, winner of the Nobel Prize in Economics in 1972, remarked in 1990, "In the 19th century, you'd find that people used to get their material into print within a month. Now to get a paper published in a journal takes a year or two."[63] Arrow is one of the few people who ever publicly complained about the lengthy publication process that sometimes makes even the U.S. government look efficient. The lack of concern is probably not misplaced, because for most of what is published in the academic journals it just doesn't make much difference when it appears— except of course, for the author, who needs the "glass beads" for promotion and salary increases.

The importance placed on the publishing productivity of professors varies greatly in American universities and colleges. It has always been either assumed or suspected that the publication of academic work was far more important in our large research universities than in the liberal arts and two-year community colleges. Now we know. In 1989 the Carnegie Foundation for the Advancement of Teaching conducted a comprehensive national survey of randomly selected faculty in 306 colleges and universities. Its findings confirmed the conventional wisdom concerning academic publications, and added some powerful new insights about how professors view the relative importance of research and teaching.

The pressure that professors feel to publish is strong and pervasive, especially in the large, more prestigious universities. When asked if it was "difficult for a person to achieve tenure if he or she does not publish," 95 percent of the faculty in our major research universities said yes. The professors obviously have responded to that pressure. Ninety-six percent of the research university faculty said they had published at least one article in an academic journal; and a somewhat astounding 63 percent boasted of publishing eleven or more articles. Sixty-two percent of them had either published or edited a book or a monograph, but only 4 percent managed to do it eleven or more times.

But how do the professors feel about all this academic publication? Do they think it is judged fairly? Would they rather do something else? Forty-two percent of the professors agreed that at their schools "publications used for tenure and promotion are *just counted,* not qualitatively measured [italics added]." Just counting, and not judging, academic publications in determining tenure and promotion is fraudulent, it is dishonest. And yet 42 percent of our finest professors seem to be saying, "Yes, that's the way it is." In the poll, 9 percent of the professors were neutral—so only 49 percent thought their school was intellectually honest about the evaluation of academic research.

Perhaps even more intriguing was what the professors answered when they were asked whether their interests lay primarily in research or teaching. Only 18 percent flatly answered "research," and 48 percent said they "leaned toward research." Thirty-four percent responded "teaching" or "leaning to teaching." Twenty-one percent even agreed that teaching effectiveness, not research productivity, should be the primary criterion for promotion of faculty.

The conclusion one draws from this is that there is strong pressure to publish in the large, research universities. Virtually all of their faculty respond to those pressures by writing articles for the academic journals, and a few write books. But a high percentage take a cynical view of the publication charade, and a small, but still surprisingly high, percentage value teaching.

When we look at the responses of professors in the four-year universities and colleges that focus on undergraduate education and do not grant doctoral degrees, we find an even more jaundiced view of academic research and a substantially greater fondness for teaching. At the "non-Ph.D." schools we find that 66 percent of the professors in universities and 40 percent of those in liberal arts colleges still feel that it would be difficult to achieve tenure if they did not publish. And though these professors are not at research universities, they publish a lot. Eighty-one percent of them have published at least one article, and 43 percent one or more books; at the liberal arts colleges 68 percent of the professors have published one or more articles, and 33 percent one or more books. Regrettably, they are just as cynical as their colleagues in the research universities about academic publishing: 33 percent of the liberal arts college professors and 54 percent of the university professors believe the articles are just counted and not seriously read and judged.

On the other hand, the interest in teaching among the faculty of non-research universities and liberal arts colleges is very high. Seventy-seven percent of the university faculty, and 83 percent of the liberal arts college faculty, say they prefer teaching to research—in spite of the extensive pressure on them to publish.

In the two-year community colleges and technical colleges the research/teaching balance is reversed. Only 6 percent of the faculty think it would be difficult to get tenure if they have not published. Less than half the faculty has ever published even one article in an academic journal, and less than one-third a book or monograph. Even so, 19 percent of them feel that what they did publish was only counted, not qualitatively measured. And they clearly see themselves as teachers first and foremost; 93 percent state that their primary interest lies in teaching students.[64]

Undoubtedly the most brazen claim made for research and publishing is that it helps to make one a better teacher, that it really helps students. One of the most unshakable axioms of the academy is that if you are a productive scholar, you are a better teacher. "A teacher teaches better if he's at the forefront of his field," asserts Peter Koehler of the University of Pittsburgh.[65] "If one is not a world-class researcher," says Professor Richard Scheller of Stanford, "it is impossible to teach the type of course students at Stanford expect. . . . Teaching and research go hand in hand."[66]

Much of this is nonsense and a blatant attempt at justification for the immense amount of time and energy that academic intellectuals expend on "research." Yes, there will be a case now and then of a brilliant researcher bringing the excitement of his findings into the classroom. But that is the exception. A great teacher is a master of his or her field, of existing knowledge, a person who can communicate that knowledge skillfully, who can stimulate students, who can make them think. There is no essential connection between these talents and those of a researcher, however distinguished.

Even if we were to assume that most academic research is important, that most academic intellectuals do a lot of research, and that they all teach, there is no logical inference that a skilled researcher will be a better teacher for it. In fact, there is a great deal of evidence that indicates research has little if any impact on one's teaching ability. In 1987 Kenneth A. Feldman, a sociologist at the State University of New York at Stony Brook, reviewed and analyzed forty-two separate studies, conducted over twenty years, on the relationship between the research productivity of professors and their effectiveness as teachers. The consensus of these forty-two studies was stark and simple: there was no clearly discernible relationship between research productivity and teaching skill. As R. A. Hicks, the author of one of those studies (459 faculty members at San Jose State University), concluded, "While research productivity may not be of great benefit [to teaching], it certainly does not seem to interfere with effective teaching."[67]

The evidence is clear. Because someone happens to be an excellent teacher does not mean he or she will be a great scholar. Conversely, because someone happens to be a powerful researcher does not mean that he or she will be a better teacher. The opposite is just as likely to be true.

Moreover, since we know that most academic research done today is not important or relevant to begin with, that most professors don't do any research, and that an increasing number of them have delegated their teaching responsibilities to students, the claim that research contributes importantly to the quality of teaching is really outrageous. It is one of the great myths of the academic intellectuals.

The research ethos that now dominates the academic world has been tragic for many professors. They delude themselves when they claim their research is important, a significant contribution to knowledge—when most of it is irrelevant and unimportant. The tragedy is that most of them probably know what they write is not important. And when they act as if it were, when they allow others to assume it is, when they accept promotions and salary increases because of it, they are engaging in a subtle form of intellectual corruption. They begin by lying to others, and end up lying to themselves.

Perhaps the larger part of the tragedy is what does not happen. The things not studied, the knowledge not acquired, the classes not taught, the counsel not given, because of the terrible time and energy demands that any research makes, regardless of its importance.

The useless research that now gluts the academic world is largely a result of two powerful, impersonal forces that pressured the professors into their current unseemly state.

The first was the simple fact that as fields of intellectual study aged, it became more and more difficult to discover new, important ideas. Sort of like a gold mine that has been gleaned of all the big nuggets. The physical sciences will yield important discoveries forever; we will continue to explore and redefine the world of matter. But in other fields, especially in the social sciences with their focus on the study of man, big, new, important ideas are increasingly unlikely with each passing day.

It is difficult to improve on Aristotle, Shakespeare, or Adam Smith. We do make discoveries and advances in many areas of intellectual thought, but rarely of the fundamental nature of the ones we inherit. Take, for example, the field of economics. Perhaps 80 or 90 percent of the economics you need to know to make decent economic policy in the twentieth century was figured out and written down in the eighteenth and nineteenth centuries.

The second force was the explosive growth in the number of academic intellectuals. During the last forty or fifty years the number of men and women searching for intellectual nuggets increased enormously, while the finds were becoming ever more scarce.

It was accepted without question that doing research, making original, important contributions to knowledge, was the essence of what academic intellectuals did. It was a daunting standard, but people tried their best to achieve it. If their research was not very important, they would redefine it so that it was. If there were not enough publishing opportunities to go around, they would create them. They have been immensely successful.

In effect, the academic intellectuals have created their own world, with their own rules and journals and publishing houses—a world in which their creations, their research and journal writings, almost regardless of importance or relevance, can be turned in for the prizes of the real world—money, promotions, prestige. And all it cost them was their integrity.

Such systematic corruption is going to be difficult to stop. The academic intellectuals have developed such a tight-knit scheme of intellectual logrolling that their evaluations of the merits of scholarly work have become, for the most part, worthless—especially those based on article or citation counts. There needs to be a strong reemphasis on quality—on the importance and relevance of research and writing—instead of quantity. We need to establish independent reviews of academic publications, free of the conflicts of interest that permeate the current review procedures.

The professors will argue that they, and only they, are qualified to judge their peers. Don't believe them. Their vested interest is too strong. The judgments of intelligent, disinterested outsiders will be far more likely to assess the intrinsic worth of someone's research and writing than the judgments of colleagues who are looking down the road to the time when they, the judges, will become the judgees.

But before any lasting, effective change is wrought in our colleges and universities, we will have to address the fundamental organizational structure that has contributed so significantly to the current situation. As long as professors have guaranteed jobs, effectively immune from dismissal even for poor performance, and as long as they are expected to produce research we will have the abuses that abound today.

The first institutional change to consider is to stop granting tenure. Tenure is a relatively new innovation in American higher education, but we have lived with it long enough, almost fifty years. It is time to pass judgment. Like a lot of bad ideas, it began with good intentions—the preservation of academic freedom and the protection of professors from outside political pressures. Today that threat is obsolete and the effect of tenure is the opposite for which it was created. Tenure is corrupting; it gives academic intellectuals almost unlimited license to do as they please with no fear of consequences. Its major effect is to encourage sloth. In a nutshell, professors who are good don't need tenure, and those who need tenure usually aren't very good.

In fairness, we should "grandfather" those who already have tenure; let them keep it. They have expended too much of their lives to obtain this prize to take it away from them now. But no more. All new members of college and university faculties should be given what we might call "continuing appointments," jobs they keep as long as they do their work skillfully and conscientiously.

We should also consider some fundamental changes in the way faculties organize themselves. The main business of higher education should be teaching and learning. There is a great pretense today that its main business is the production of new learning, new knowledge. That pretense is pernicious myth. Very little new knowledge of any worth or substance walks out of the university gates these days. In fact, the main business of the university is what it has always been—the mastery of a growing body of human knowledge, the continual shifting of that knowledge into ranked divisions of relevance and importance, and the enlightened transmittal of learning to the students.

We should reorganize the university into new job categories that accurately reflect what the faculty should be doing. Today they are all professors. Yet some do nothing but research and writing, some rarely teach, others primarily teach but do little if any research and writing. We could end this confusion if we created two new categories of college and university faculty.

First and foremost should be the teachers. Teaching is what faculty are supposed to do, and "teachers" is what they should be called. To be a college or university teacher is an honorable calling, and it should be recognized as such by title as well as monetary rewards. Being a teacher should be the most prestigious post on campus, and the most highly paid.

Second, there is an important role on college and university faculties for those whose primary interest and capabilities lie in research and writing. But let us not pretend that they are teachers, nor subject students to the torture of trying to learn from someone who despises and resents teaching. For those relatively few men and women whom we would like to have on the campus as they pursue their lonely paths of research and writing, let us reserve the title of "fellow." It is a title already used by all the think tanks in America, and it would clearly denote someone who was primarily a writer and researcher, someone who would not be expected to teach (though the person might if he or she liked it and was good at it), someone who would be judged solely on the quality of the research produced.

Of course, such a radical scheme will be emphatically rejected by virtually every one of those hundreds of thousands of men and women who wear the title of "professor" today. Here again, as in tenure, some grandfathering would be in order. Allow all professors who wish to continue to do a little teaching, a little research and writing, to retain their titles.

A new kind of university, whose faculty was mainly full-time teachers with only a few fellows here and there, would be a bracing intellectual environment, one in which both teaching and research were defined and appropriately respected. All the students would love it, most of the faculty would love it (after a while), and even the administrators might learn to appreciate it.

CHAPTER FIVE

HUBRIS

WHAT IS MOST PUZZLING about the loss of integrity in the academic intellectual world—the loss of respect for teaching, the loss of standards of excellence in research and writing—is how and why it could happen. Why do men and women ostensibly committed to a life of reason, the people to whom we entrust our children's education, act this way? Of all people in our society, these people— highly intelligent and free to pursue the life of the mind—should be among our best. Instead, their professional lives are often a lie. Collectively they have brought our great colleges and universities to their knees. But why?

A large part of the answer lies in a human weakness that the ancient Greeks knew well, and feared—a flaw that they, unlike us, studied deeply and tried to ward against. The Greeks called it *hubris* and considered it one of the most dangerous of human flaws. Today, in modern America, the word has fallen into disuse and the subject is barely mentioned in polite discourse, especially among intellectuals. But hubris is here—in full measure.

Today, "hubris" refers generally to a haughty pride, an arrogant disdain for the thoughts and feelings of others. It had a richer meaning in classical Greek ethical thought thousands of years ago. Hubris was considered an "overweening presumption suggesting impious disregard of the limits governing men's actions in an orderly universe . . . the sin to which the great and gifted are most susceptible and in Greek tragedy it is usually the basic flaw of the tragic hero."[1]

The driving sin of our academic intellectuals is hubris—unchecked intellectual arrogance. Like gravity it is invisible. We can't see or touch it, but we can feel its effect. It is a deceptive force. Some people feel that politics lies behind much of the turmoil and intellectual decay in today's academic world, the rise of the notion of "political correctness," and the decline of academic freedom. But that's not it. The toleration of corruption and unprofessional conduct cannot be laid at the doorstep of a handful of political ideologues. In many instances of misconduct there is nothing to gain politically, and some of the worst offenders don't have a political bone in their bodies.

In the academic intellectual world there is a deeper force than political passion, a force that is unique to this world: intellectual elitism. "Elitism" normally refers to social elitism, a notion held by people who believe they are socially superior, the kind of people who prefer the company only of those listed in the Social Register and who rarely associate with those whom they consider lesser men and women. Intellectual elitism is a smaller, more virulent phenomenon, shared by a group of people who feel superior to others solely by virtue of their higher intelligence and learning.

The very essence of a modern university is intellectual elitism—the elitism of the mind. Academic intellectuals are generally not only more intelligent than average people, but are more learned than almost everybody, because they devote much of their professional lives to acquiring knowledge. Being intellectually superior is as much a part of being a professor, especially at one of our top universities, as being strong and powerful is part of being a professional football player. A proper self-appreciation is neither wrong nor damaging.

Unfortunately, many academic intellectuals wrongly conclude that because they may be more intelligent and more learned, they are better. They believe that because they can think faster and reason more deftly that this somehow means they are wiser and morally superior, that they are natural leaders who should be followed by their intellectual inferiors.

There is a wide streak of snobbery in almost everyone who considers himself or herself an academic intellectual. Their feeling of natural superiority is important for us to understand, for it infuses all that they do. Some of their actions, which may seem unprofessional, unethical, and sometimes even bizarre, will take on a certain rationality when viewed through the lens of dogmatic intellectual elitism.

It is not all their fault. Academic intellectuals are the only large group in our society that is certified smart, whose intelligence has the equivalent of the Good Housekeeping Seal of Approval. They are usually stamped twice, once with the Ph.D. when they complete their doctoral studies, and then again with the title "professor" when appointed to a university or college faculty. Others may be as smart or smarter, but only the academic intellectuals get to add the three little letters "Ph.D." after their names, and "Professor" or "Dr." in front. Most of them know they were pretty intelligent to begin with, but the act of being formally certified smarter than most, and then being addressed daily as "professor" or "doctor," getting to tag on "Ph.D." every time they sign their names, can prove to be an intoxication from which some of them never recover.

That natural feeling of intellectual superiority is an emotion that can be difficult to control. It gives one a sense of power and rightness that can easily lead to both arrogance and resentment— the arrogance of contempt for the judgments of other people, the resentment when one's intellectual powers and wisdom are not recognized and deferred to, and especially the resentment of not being compensated generously enough for one's talents. "Faculty members believe, on the basis of their mastery of an academic specialty, that they are superior people," writes Jeffrey Hart, a nationally syndicated columnist and longtime member of the faculty of Dartmouth College. "They are contemptuous of the world outside the academy, and resentful of its power."[2]

This intoxicating sense of intellectual superiority, if combined with a little contempt and a dash of resentment, can easily turn into something ugly—an arrogant conviction that one is above the rules and ethics that govern ordinary people, a conviction that because one is special, one need not live by the rules of the game. As R. Edward Freeman, director of the University of Virginia's Olsson Center for Applied Ethics, observed in 1991, "Academics believe that their pursuit of truth and knowledge is so important that they can bend the rules."[3]

While elitism, snobbery, and contempt are defining characteristics of many intellectuals, not much attention has been paid— almost as if the subject were taboo. But we do hear from the occasional iconoclast.

In May 1990, Nicholas Lemann, a well-known professional intellectual—contributing editor of the *Washington Monthly* and a national correspondent of *The Atlantic*—had the audacity, and some would say imprudence, to address the issue directly. In an article analyzing the popularity of H. L. Mencken among intellectuals, Lemann argued that Mencken's popularity stemmed from the fact that he was an elitist. Mencken, wrote Lemann, "considered the great mass of people to be inherently inferior . . . was full of ethnic prejudices . . . belonged to a tradition of complete uninterest in common people . . . the real common ground between him and the intellectuals was an antidemocratic spirit. It is no secret that Mencken disliked democracy . . . [and] antidemocracy has always been the secret vice of the intellectuals."[4]

Lemann concluded that he found it "amazing that at this late date intellectuals are willing to renounce racism but not snobbery," and that what remains as "an impetus to put down the common people is the need to feel superior . . . a base motive that thinking people ought to rid themselves of."[5]

The intellectual hubris that pervades the intellectual world is carefully nurtured and passed on from generation to generation. Usually it is done subtly and no fingerprints are left, but occasionally an older intellectual will just blurt things out to the younger ones. In June 1989, William Chace, president of Wesleyan University, spoke to Stanford's newly elected members of Phi Beta Kappa, the scholastic honor society formed in 1776. He gave them some advice and told them a secret.

The *Stanford Observer* reported Chace's speech in an article entitled "Be a Teacher." According to the *Observer,* Chace first noted that after graduation most of them would go through a "period of 'estrangement' as they try to readjust to life outside," and compared them to "soldiers stuck behind enemy lines." Then he invited them to become professors, saying, " 'Stay behind the enemy lines. You have done well there. Stay put. You have lost your intellectual innocence and any return to what you once knew is doubtful now.' " But he cautioned them about what awaited them if they "enter[ed] the intelligentsia."

"As a group," he lamented, "it has been impugned; it has been called 'the eggheads'; it has also been described as pointy-headed. But take heed," Chace counseled as he let them in on the secret, "it has been scorned precisely because it does have power and privilege. So join it. Become at one with the teachers who are there already and who are proud of you this evening . . . your talents make such a choice appropriate; your country needs you; and you will enjoy the life of secrecy, power, and detachment that all teachers, I can now tell you, relish."[6]

Many intellectuals seem to have a barely concealed lust for power, a lust which is rarely sated, a constant source of longing and frustration. It is as if the possession of superior intelligence somehow brings along with it the natural right to rule. Most of us think of education as thinking and studying and learning. But intellectuals often think about it in terms of power. Harvey Kaye, professor of social change and development at the University of Wisconsin, describes his "democratic vision of education" as one in which "the student is seen, in the words of the Italian political theorist Antonio Gramsci, 'as a person capable of thinking, studying, and ruling— or controlling those who rule.' "[7]

Intellectual elitism can begin early. A 1990 survey conducted by the American Council on Education and UCLA's Higher Education Research Institute revealed that "more than 99 percent of

Stanford's current freshmen rated themselves as above average."[8] And a good part of the remaining 1 percent probably thought so, but retained a bit of modesty from their early upbringing.

By the time most academic intellectuals have attained faculty status they have become discreet enough to mute any overt displays of hubris. But sometimes their unspoken thoughts come tumbling out of the mouths and pens of students. Here are a couple of examples. A Stanford student, Joseph Edozien, wrote in 1986: "A university with pretensions to excellence should not be in the business of producing obedient workers and job seekers. That is the job of factory schools, trade schools and polytechnical institutes. . . . Stanford's duty is to be educating thinkers, creators, planners and leaders. . . . We should be the visionaries who write the script for the new century. This is what it ought to mean to be a graduate of a top world university. This is what it ought to mean to hold a degree from Stanford. . . . This is why I am here."[9]

Another student, Lorne Needle, displaying a bit of incipient megalomania, declared: "When I came to Stanford I carried a bright, burning torch. It was the light of Truth and Justice, and I held it aloft before me as the symbol of what I would accomplish. . . . The poor and oppressed would flock to me as I wielded my diploma: slaying brutal dictators, driving corrupt, manipulative multinationals to their bloated knees, dispensing food, human rights, political power, equitable distributions of income and minimum standards of living to all who had awaited them so long. . . . We at universities may care, and may think about solutions to the world problems, but the vast majority of people do not and will not consider anything but how to get richer and keep my stinking hands off what is rightfully theirs."[10]

When the novelist F. Scott Fitzgerald once remarked to Ernest Hemingway, "The rich are different from us," Hemingway replied, "Yes, they have more money." Well, intellectuals are different from other people because they are smarter. That would not be a problem if they would let it go at that and be grateful for their genetic gifts. But too many of them move too easily from knowing they are smarter to believing they are better, to thinking they are an elite that is

bounded only by what they themselves believe is right and important, unfettered by the moral constraints that bind ordinary mortals.
Basically, they believe that the rules that govern others do not and
should not apply to them.

It is not that they have lost their values, although it may be
easy enough to draw this conclusion when you step back and look
at some of the things they have done. No, they have values, often
strong, deeply held values. The problem is that they see their values
as superior ones, of a higher order than the values of ordinary people.
And, if there is ever a clash between their values and the more
common values of society, they will follow their own without blink-
ing, without a trace of remorse.

It is possible for them to commit acts that, cumulatively, most
people would see as a loss of integrity but which they see as entirely
justified and moral within their system of higher-order values. The
reasoning goes like this: I am smarter, therefore I am better, what
I believe is right is right. Not all intellectuals look down on others
with contempt, but many of them do. If we keep this proclivity in
mind, then the spectacle of what they often do and say and write
will make more sense. And it will be much clearer as to what must
be done to deal with the problem.

While the most serious violations of integrity in the university
world—the neglect of teaching and the honoring of spurious research and writing—go largely unremarked in the national media,
other, less serious scandals are covered regularly. The public's concern has been centered on the more titillating scandals—on cases
of plagiarism and sexual harassment, on the necessity of being "politically correct," on the assaults on free speech and academic freedom, on financial fraud and corruption.

These ugly incidents are bewildering. With so much talent,
with so much going for them, with so much to lose if they get
caught and punished appropriately, it is difficult to understand why
men and women brazenly violate the unspoken oath of their chosen
profession, why they value their integrity so little.

On the other hand, perhaps it is not so surprising that these
petty, squalid scandals spot the university world like an acute case

of measles. When an institution has lost much of its primary integrity, when its soul is scarred by the neglect and abandonment of its primary responsibilities—teaching and important research—then perhaps we should not be too surprised that the same folks who brought us this intellectual corruption will, from time to time, commit other offenses.

When one encounters the abuses and scandals that are ever present on our university campuses today, it is all too easy to dismiss them as isolated incidents, with no common thread, with no larger meaning. True, each incident may be an isolated case, unlikely to be repeated in exactly the same way. It is also true that only a small number of people actively perpetrate these abuses. But that isn't what is important, for the same sort of thing happens in every profession, in every large organization.

What is important is how the academic intellectual community reacts, as a community, to the individual transgressions.

We'll start with a hypothetical analogy. Let's say a man murders a friend, chops him up into small pieces, and disposes of the remains in the corner sewer. Let's also assume that the society in which he lives has no strong reaction against what he has done. In fact, the people of the community hardly notice this brutal murder, focusing instead on the fact that the killer is normally polite, even jovial and friendly. There is no investigation by the police, no trial, no conviction and punishment. The only thing that happens is that a few weeks later some of the killer's friends give a party in his honor and he gets a nice write-up the next day in the newspaper's social section.

Is the murder an isolated incident? Yes, it is something that happens very rarely in the society. But that is not the point. What is of overwhelming importance is the reaction of the community, of the men and women in the important social institutions. What should we think of a community of rational adults that condoned such an atrocity?

That is the real import of the stories and incidents we will now examine. For the most part they are "isolated instances," some of them perhaps unique, never to happen again. What I think you will find striking, maybe alarming, is the extraordinary reaction of the academic intellectual community to these situations. We can tolerate isolated instances of corrupt, unethical behavior by individuals in the society. But we cannot accept institutions that tolerate corrupt, unethical behavior.

The ways in which academic intellectuals violate their professional integrity are rather limited. They almost never cheat or steal for personal monetary gain; they're not likely to embezzle money or even pad expense accounts. In this regard they are almost universally, scrupulously honest. They rarely commit the most egregious crimes; your typical professor is not a murderer, a rapist, or even a burglar. By and large, professors are peaceful, law-abiding members of society.

Their corruption is more subtle. While they won't violate professional and ethical standards for personal monetary gain, they will violate them for other baubles. The things that academic intellectuals have such rapacity for seem to fall into three categories. The first and foremost is personal prestige and reputation, something which can only be gained by research and writing, something they will figuratively kill for. This leads to what we might call professional corruption, breaking the rules for personal prestige and reputation. We have seen how they will shirk their teaching responsibilities to get more time for research and writing. We have seen how they will go to great lengths to inflate citation counts to gain recognition for their published work. Some become desperate enough to go further. If they can't think of something worthy of publication they will plagiarize, steal the words of someone else. A few won't even bother to steal, they will simply engage in fraud, making up whatever they need.

Of almost equal priority after prestige and reputation are the academic intellectual community's political values. Many professors, especially those in the humanities and social sciences, feel strongly about political issues, everything from welfare and medical care to taxation and defense spending. They feel so strongly and so righteous in their convictions that they see nothing wrong with using their positions to further the political ends they value, even if, in some cases, it means violating the integrity of their work. Call this political corruption.

Academic intellectuals are not supposed to consider political affiliations when hiring or promoting. They do. They are not supposed to consider political implications when they design courses and assign readings. They do. They are not supposed to judge students according to their political views. They do. And when they do, they are led down the path of academically suspect courses, of "political correctness," and finally into the violation of the most sacred tenets of their profession—free speech and academic freedom.

Academic intellectuals sometimes abuse their positions of authority by taking advantage of lower-ranked colleagues and students, a form of personal corruption. This largely takes the form of sexual harassment and abuse. While the actual number of such instances is low, what is noteworthy is the tepid reaction to these cases, and the light punishments levied for such transgressions.

Finally, there is a type of corruption that is limited to the administrators, the managers and trustees of our universities. Financial cheating on behalf of the university, or what we might call institutional corruption, is the corruption of choice for the administrators as opposed to the more personal, non-monetary corruptions of the faculty. And, like faculty, they don't steal for themselves. They connive and cheat for the university as an institution, something which they see of such transcendent value that it fully justifies their actions. This is the prime motivation behind the financial scandals that plague our universities and colleges today.

In sum, there are four basic types of corruption that pervade the academic intellectual world today. The first three—professional, political, and personal corruption—afflict the faculty. The fourth, institutional corruption, afflicts the administrators and trustees.

Professional Corruption

Sometimes academic intellectuals become so consumed in their quest for scholarly reputation that they cross the line between professional and unprofessional conduct. The badlands of academe are plagiarism and fraud. Why they do it, whether out of arrogance or stupidity, is difficult to know. What we do know is that such intellectual dishonesty occurs all too frequently, another portent of the death of integrity. For intellectual dishonesty is the cardinal sin of an intellectual.

Plagiarism and fraud are two very different kinds of intellectual dishonesty, and it is debatable which is worse. Both involve taking credit for something that is not yours. Plagiarism, which involves taking another person's words and ideas and affixing your name to them, at least has virtue in that most plagiarized material is of value. For if an intellectual is going to steal something he generally has the sense to steal something good. Here the essential ethical question is one of authorship, not the intrinsic worth of the work itself.

Intellectual fraud is a more serious matter, for the central issue is not authorship, but validity. Faked research data, fabricated facts, and phony statistics can have a far-reaching impact if they are acted upon by others. Until recently, raw intellectual fraud was a relatively rare phenomenon. Research done by academic intellectuals, especially in the sciences, may not have been overly exciting or interesting, but it did have a reputation for rock-hard integrity. No longer. Today, intellectual fraud is common, and spreading. If it were a disease, it might well be classified an epidemic.

In recent years there have been numerous cases of documented fraud in some of our best academic institutions, including Tufts University Medical School, the University of California at San Francisco, Harvard University Medical School, and Northwestern University.[11] The situation had gotten so far out of hand, and efforts at self-policing were so feeble, that the federal government found it necessary to establish a special office in March 1989 to investigate misconduct on the part of those receiving federal grants or contracts. A division of the National Institutes of Health, this special office has the Orwellian title "Office of Scientific Integrity" and is referred to by some as the "science police." It has an annual budget of $1 million, nine investigators, and seven staff workers. During its first two years of operation, it examined 174 allegations of misconduct. Actual misconduct was found in 19 out of 118 completed cases, and 56 investigations were still under way. [12]

There is probably no ranker humiliation for an intellectual than to have a government bureaucrat checking on his or her integrity. Yet this is the sorry state that American intellectuals seem to have single-handedly carved out for themselves. The Office of Scientific Integrity is not something some self-aggrandizing bureaucrat thought up to enhance his or her power. It was created in response to a perceived decline in intellectual integrity.

In 1988 the Acadia Institute, a center for the study of medicine, science, and society, surveyed 259 deans of major institutions of higher education, all of them members of the Council of Graduate Schools. Their conclusions? "Overall, 40% of the deans surveyed had received reports of possible faculty research misconduct during the previous five years, while only 2% (six) had received more than five reports." The Acadia Institute generously concluded that their survey results suggest that "research misconduct is not rampant in higher education."[13] I guess we should all be thankful that it is not "rampant."

But research misconduct, this most basic violation of intellectual integrity, is rampant enough that the National Academy of Sciences established a special study panel on scientific conduct in early 1991 to "assess mechanisms for encouraging integrity in research."[14] Headed by Edward E. David, who was science adviser to President Nixon, the twenty-five-member panel is a virtual "Who's Who" of distinguished academics. As the *New York Times* described the panel, it was set up "in an attempt to invigorate the ethical standards in science and forestall more outside investigations of misconduct."[15]

According to the panel's chairman, Dr. David, "It is terribly important for the country that the science community keep its ability to self-govern. That is what is being called into question now—the ability of universities and laboratories to govern themselves. And if we don't perform well to maintain that, we are in trouble. We must assure the people who pay for the work, such as Congress, that there is some reason to believe we are doing things right, and that we are not cheating." Dr. Rosemary Chalk, the top staff person for the panel, noted that "it was not known how much misconduct existed in science because no group was responsible for keeping such data or helping to set such standards." Dr. David concluded that many universities "simply cannot vouch for the honesty of the research process at their institutions."[16]

That, by itself, is a powerful indictment of their integrity. But what is perhaps worse is the collective yawn in response to the panel's charges. Where are the cries of alarm? Where are the proposals for reform?

Perhaps we should not be too surprised, given the reaction of the academic intellectual community to one of the most notorious allegations of intellectual fraud in this century—the recent case of David Baltimore. Dr. Baltimore, a Nobel laureate and the former president of Rockefeller University, was a professor at the Massachusetts Institute of Technology when the fraud occurred. What he did or didn't do will probably be argued about for years to come, but the critical part of the scandal is not so much the truth or falsity of the charge of research fraud, but the reaction of Dr. Baltimore and many of his colleagues to that charge, a reaction that casts severe doubt on the integrity of the academic intellectual community's leadership.

The Baltimore case was summed up on March 26, 1991, in the lead editorial of the *New York Times,* entitled "A Scientific Watergate?"

> Five years after disturbing questions were raised about a research paper written in part by the Nobel laureate David Baltimore, the celebrated case is finally moving toward a verdict. Federal investigators have concluded, in a draft report, that the paper contained fraudulent data and did not accurately reflect the

laboratory experiments on which it was supposedly based. Worse yet, data subsequently published by the Baltimore group to amend and justify its original paper were almost certainly fabricated.

The verdict may well destroy the career of the scientist accused of the misrepresentations and fabrications, Dr. Thereza Imanishi-Kari. But the most damning indictment should be lodged against the scientific community's weak-kneed mechanisms for investigating fraud. Faced with stonewalling by Dr. Baltimore, one of the nation's most prominent scientists, several investigative panels seemed more intent on smothering bad publicity than digging out the truth.

In this respect, the Baltimore case is reminiscent of the Watergate scandal. Just as Watergate started with a "third-rate burglary" and ended in a huge cover-up, so the Baltimore case started with apparent fraud by a single scientist and soon led to a widespread denial of wrongdoing by almost everyone in a position to right the wrong.

Eight months later, on December 2, Dr. Baltimore resigned from his position as president of Rockefeller University, after belatedly conceding that fraud might have been involved, and that he erred in failing to heed initial warnings and was "too willing to accept Dr. Imanishi-Kari's explanations and to excuse discrepancies as mere sloppiness."[17]

The rising incidence of research fraud in academe is a telling commentary on the state of integrity there. But what is even more telling is the ho-hum reaction of the academic community to these blatant intellectual crimes. Alarm bells should be going off all over the place. Administrators and faculty should be calling for the heads of those perpetrators of fraud. But they aren't. And that tells us more about the current state of integrity in academe than anything.

Plagiarism, while less serious than research fraud, is more widespread. The phenomenon is so common that it now has its own 300-page book, *Stolen Words: Forays into the Origins and Ravages of Plagiarism* by Thomas Mallon, a young lecturer in English at Vassar College.[18] No one even tries to count the instances of plagiarism that are detected, let alone estimate those that go undetected. What is striking about plagiarism in America is not that it occurs, but what is done about it when it does occur. In his research for *Stolen Words,* Mallon notes that he was appalled "by the victims [of plagiarism] I learned of, by the audacity of their predators, by the excuses made for the latter. The inability of the literary and academic worlds adequately to define, much less reasonably punish, instances of plagiarism was something I observed again and again."[19]

In a world of hundreds of thousands of academics, instances of plagiarism are bound to occur. But what is not bound to happen is the consistently light punishment meted out for such infractions, or the surprising defenses put forth for those who are caught plagiarizing. For example, in 1988 Dr. Shervert Frazier, a sixty-seven-year-old professor at Harvard Medical School, resigned in disgrace after admitting plagiarism. It seemed a reasonable thing to do; if you commit plagiarism and get caught, you resign or get fired. But a number of Frazier's colleagues objected heatedly. According to interviews with "more than a dozen medical leaders, many said they believed Dr. Frazier's downfall and disgrace amounted to far stiffer punishment than he deserved . . . one said he planned to offer him a temporary teaching post."[20] Dr. Alan A. Stone, "a member of the faculty of Harvard's medical and law schools . . . said Dr. Frazier's punishment was 'inappropriate' and 'unreasonable' considering his record."[21]

Every instance of plagiarism that is condoned, or excused, or only lightly punished rips out of academe one more piece of institutional integrity. As the first sentence of *Stolen Words* says, "No, it isn't murder. And as larceny goes it's usually more distasteful than grand. But it is a bad thing."[22]

Political Corruption

The most striking characteristic of America's academic intellectuals is the extent to which they subscribe to liberal, left-wing, or radical political views. The overwhelming majority of America's professoriate is politically left, and they have been that way for a long time.

Back in 1963, Richard Hofstadter described it this way in his classic book, *Anti-intellectualism in American Life:*

> At least from the Progressive era onward, the political commitment of the majority of the intellectual leadership in the United States has been to causes that might be variously described as liberal (in the American use of that word), progressive, or radical. . . . I am not denying that we have had a number of conservative intellectuals . . . but if there is anything that could be called an intellectual establishment in America, this establishment has been . . . on the left side of center.[23]

During the last thirty years or so the concentration of left-wing intellectuals on the faculties of our colleges and universities has increased steadily, inexorably, to the point where they now constitute a virtual monopoly in many departments of our elite colleges and universities.

The definitive study of politics in the American professoriate was conducted by two highly regarded political scientists—Everett Carll Ladd, Jr., and Seymour Martin Lipset—in 1975. It was based on an exhaustive survey, a sample of 111 colleges and universities chosen scientifically from the total of 2,827, and included responses from 4,081 professors, an unusually high response rate of 52 percent. Ladd and Lipset concluded that:

> Academe constitutes a massive force in favor of liberal domestic, pacifist, and antimilitarist policies. . . . The weight of academe, particularly as reflected within the major universities and among the most politically active, is preponderantly far to the left of the American public. . . . Compared to other groups in the U.S., the disproportionate liberalism of academics stands out. No other large occupational cohort is as supportive of liberal and equalitarian values. Professors have delivered majorities to Democratic nominees in every presidential election since the Great Depression. . . . The relative liberalism of professors can be seen not only in voting, of course, but in their positions on the entire range of social and economic issues.[24]

The Ladd-Lipset study found that "only 12 percent of all professors think of themselves as Republicans." In certain important areas the situation was even more unbalanced. For example, among social science and humanities professors at the major research-oriented colleges and universities, they found that 80 percent "regularly vote Democratic," compared to 5 percent who "regularly vote Republican." Even at "the least scholarly prestigious, least affluent, teaching-oriented colleges," more than 75 percent of them regularly voted Democratic in 1975.[25]

More recent studies have confirmed the path-breaking work of Ladd and Lipset in the mid-1970s. In August 1987 a professor of political science at Northeastern University in Boston decided to take the analytical tools that political scientists regularly use to study various segments of the American public and turn them on political scientists themselves. He mailed his questionnaire to approximately 700 experts in the field of American politics, those considered to be congressional and presidential scholars, and 361 of them returned the questionnaire. Eighty-seven percent of the respondents were affiliated with institutions of higher learning.[26]

Those who rated themselves "somewhat liberal," "very liberal," or beyond accounted for over 68 percent of the total responses. Only 16.1 percent admitted to being registered Republicans, and a tiny 8.2 percent said they voted a straight Republican ticket in elections. In the 1984 presidential election those voting favored Walter Mondale over President Reagan by 77.1 percent to 21.1 percent, with the remaining 1.8 percent going to minor party candidates.[27]

Even in some of the more traditional, conservative areas of the United States we find these politically lopsided faculties. In the spring of 1987 the *Colorado Review,* the campus publication of the University of Colorado, published the results of a survey of the political party affiliations of the faculty:

Out of 602 professors less than 7 percent of the faculty in the College of Arts and Sciences are Republicans . . . in the last ten years no Republican has been hired and . . . the average age of those Republican professors is 55. . . . The president of the university is unaffiliated and four of his top associates are Democrats;

the chancellor and four of his top associates are Democrats; the dean of the College of Arts and Sciences, his four top assistants, the dean and associate dean of the Law School are all Democrats, as are the deans of a number of other colleges. . . . Out of 33 departments in the College of Arts and Sciences, only one, which has five professors, is chaired by a Republican and 11, including the 57-member English Department, have no Republicans at all.[28]

Because of the advanced age of the dwindling band of Republicans remaining on the arts and sciences faculty of the University of Colorado, and the apparent de facto ban on hiring any more, the heavy imbalance may be headed for total conformity. The author of the study, Patrick Taylor, ruefully concluded, "Unless something is done now, there will be a one-party system at Colorado University, similar to the universities in the Soviet Union, Fascist Italy or Nazi Germany."[29]

That same year, 1987, a similar survey was done of the Stanford University faculty by a colleague of mine, George Marotta, a research fellow of the Hoover Institution. Marotta did the unthinkable. Applying some of the research methodology of the social sciences, he went to the public record and checked the political registration of Stanford professors, proceeding on the assumption that it is sometimes better to analyze what people do rather than what they say they do. Of the 262 Stanford professors surveyed, 218 were registered voters. One can only guess what the political predilections might be of those forty-four professors who do not vote. The table below shows the political affiliations of the professors who were registered. With the exception of the law school and the economics department, where, though outnumbered by more than 3 to 1, the Republicans were a substantial minority bloc, Republican professors were virtually nonexistent.

Only two places at Stanford University showed a degree of balance in the political registration of its staff and faculty. Both the Hoover Institution (fifty fellows) and the Graduate School of Business (forty-four professors) showed 48 percent registered as Democrat or independent and 52 percent as Republican.[30]

SCHOOL OR DEPARTMENT	NUMBER OF PROFESSORS REGISTERED TO VOTE	NUMBER REGISTERED AS		
		DEMOCRAT	INDEPENDENT	REPUBLICAN
Economics	21	15	1	5
Law School	36	23	5	8
Philosophy	13	10	1	2
Education	35	27	5	3
Political Science	26	22	2	2
Anthropology	15	13	1	1
English	29	27	1	1
History	26	22	3	1
Sociology	17	15	2	0
Total	218	174	21	23

The Stanford academic community apparently votes the way it registers. In the presidential election of 1984, 71 percent of the Stanford precinct voters supported Walter Mondale over President Reagan.[31] In 1988, they tightened up a bit and 78 percent sided with Michael Dukakis over George Bush.[32]

The most recent survey of the politics of professors was done for the Carnegie Foundation for the Advancement of Teaching in 1989. Fifty-six percent classified themselves as either liberal or moderately liberal. In our liberal arts colleges and major research universities the tally rose to 70 percent, high enough to be considered a landslide by normal political standards. In these same liberal arts colleges and major universities only 3 or 4 percent identified themselves as conservatives, and another 12 or 15 percent as "moderate" conservatives.

The ideology of professors by their field of study was equally striking. In economics, 63 percent called themselves liberals; in political science, sociology, and anthropology, 72 percent; in history, philosophy, and ethnic studies, 76 percent; in public affairs, 88 percent, while 12 percent considered themselves "middle of the road," leaving not enough conservatives to even show in the final poll results.[33]

Writing in the Spring 1991 issue of *The Public Interest,* David Bryden, a professor of law at the University of Minnesota, observed that "most of our universities are essentially one-party institutions, even more so than if they were owned by the Democratic party. For if they were owned by the Democratic party, their liberalism would be moderated by the worldly cynicism and maturity of politicians, as well as by the attitudes of average American voters. As it is, universities bear less resemblance to the Democratic party than to a seminary for party ideologues."[34]

What Professor Bryden says is outrageous, unbelievable—and true. All the evidence—national surveys, university studies—proves beyond a doubt what anyone who has spent a little time in academe knows: the college and university faculties of America have been politicized. Major chunks of the faculty and administration, especially in the social sciences and humanities, are rock-solid left in their political views. It is no longer a question of whether there is a tendency or a tilt to the left; the faculties of American universities and colleges are overwhelmingly leftist.

The most disturbing part of the left-liberal faculty phenomenon is the reaction of the academic community. There is not the slightest bit of curiosity on the part of most faculty or administrators as to how this massive political bias came to be. The fact that major segments of the university are often staffed with upwards of 90 percent Democrats is greeted with a figurative shrug. National studies document the extent of the imbalance. What happens? Nothing. Stories run in the newspapers. What happens? Same thing. Nobody in academia publicly defends the idea of faculties having almost as high a percentage of Democrats as the Democratic National Committee; the issue is simply not discussed at all.

A typical reaction is that of Professor Stephen Krasner, chairman of the department of political science at Stanford University. Addressing the charge of ideological imbalance, Krasner simply denied that there was any bias in the selection of professors: "If you look at our appointments in the last decade, they are extremely heterogeneous. There are people who would be considered quite conservative, and people who would be considered quite far left. I don't even know whether I can characterize them in terms of where the center is." When asked directly whether or not "ideology plays any role in the appointment of political science professors," Professor Krasner replied airily, "I think it's fairly limited."[35]

Remember, a recent check of Krasner's department revealed that of twenty-seven professors, twenty-two were registered Democrats, two were Republicans, two were independents, and one was not registered.[36] I suppose one should take some comfort in the idea that ideological bias plays only a "fairly limited" role in the selection process; if it were greater there would probably not even be two token Republicans.

It's bad enough when senior professors at our finest universities allow politics to intrude in their professional judgments, but when the political biases are plainly signaled by top university authorities, those in charge of hiring and firing, and of making policy, then the atmosphere becomes intimidating, diffuse, and stifling like a poison gas, and the accepted boundaries of intellectual discourse are made crystal clear. For example, on October 26, 1988, sixty-five American intellectuals paid for a full-page advertisement in the *New York Times*, trying to affect the outcome of the presidential election, which was thirteen days away. (Such ads are not cheap; in 1991 the cost of one would be $47,855.) The ad was basically an attack on George Bush's criticism of liberals and liberalism, but it also spelled out what the signers of the ad felt was acceptable discourse:

> We speak as American citizens who wish to reaffirm America's liberal tradition . . . one of our oldest and noblest traditions. . . . The President of the United States has . . . made sport of "the dreaded L-word" and continues to make "liberal" and "liberalism" terms of opprobrium. . . . Extremists of the right and left have long attacked liberalism as their greatest enemy. In our own time liberal democracies have been crushed by such extremists. . . . We feel obliged to speak out. We hope that others will do so as well.

Well, nothing wrong with some intellectuals exercising the rights of free speech and a free press to defend their political views. But what about the ten academic administrators who endorsed the ad? Signing boldly and proudly were: Derek Bok, president of Harvard University; Guido Calabresi, dean of the Yale Law School;

Elizabeth Coleman, president of Bennington College; Marvin Goldberger, director of the Institute for Advanced Study at Princeton; Sheldon Hackney, president of the University of Pennsylvania; Ira Michael Heyman, chancellor of the University of California at Berkeley; Thomas Hughes, president of the Carnegie Endowment for International Peace; Donald Kennedy, president of Stanford University; Steven Muller, president of Johns Hopkins University; and Donna Shalala, chancellor of the University of Wisconsin at Madison.[37]

When some of the biggest names in higher education in America sign such a public petition it sends a powerful signal to the entire intellectual community. The signers obviously felt that big stakes were involved ("liberal democracies have been crushed by [those who have] attacked liberalism.") How do you think a young faculty member at any of these august institutions, an assistant professor, say, without the protection of tenure, might feel if he or she had concluded that George Bush would make a dandy president? Would anyone in that position speak out publicly in support of Bush? Most of them would be silent. The chances of professional retaliation for their political views would be too great to risk a little freedom of speech. In fact, in some quarters this blatant political prejudice has become an accepted fact of academic life. As one reporter described the "dominance of liberals on college faculties across the country," it is "something old—one of the oldest puzzles of American academic life."[38]

The puzzle that few want to address is how this imbalance came to be. Every left-liberal professor I have discussed this with assures me that it is in the natural order of things. Men and women with left-leaning political views just naturally gravitate to the universities, especially to certain fields, they claim. The high percentages are nothing more than a reflection of that part of the population from which professors are drawn.

All right, I could accept that if we were talking about a slight imbalance, a small tilt to the left. But when the imbalance hits the range of 70, 80, or 90 percent, I have to part company. There is nothing in the natural order of things that would dictate such a small representation of Republicans and conservatives in these intellectual fields. There is not a shred of evidence to support the contention that Democrats prefer social science and humanities studies by a ratio of 9 or 10 to 1 over Republicans. No more evidence than when some in the South argued that blacks preferred to sit in the back of the bus or drink at separate water fountains.

Prejudice is prejudice, whether it is racist, sexist, or political. The evidence of political discrimination in the academic world is clear and stark, a prima facie case. If God did not cause it by his natural ordering of things, then it had to be caused by bias in the appointment and promotion of faculty. There is no other way. It is easy to understand why so many faculty and administrators are reluctant to discuss it. For, to the extent this discrimination exists, we have unprofessional conduct on the part of professors and administrators.

Theoretically, a politically unbalanced faculty does not mean there has to be a problem. If all professors acted professionally, and kept their political views from influencing their teaching, their research, and their selection of other professors, there would be no problem. But there is. The percentage of professors with left-liberal views has become so great that it has created a monolithic mindset, a pervasive form of group thinking. In some departments, the leftist political views of the faculty are so widespread that one rarely hears anything else. If day after day their political preferences are reflected back from colleagues in myriad ways, soon professors may come to believe their world is the real world. Powerful codes of politically correct thinking have become so entrenched that to violate them can be a gaffe of serious proportions. Where there should be a competition of ideas, a diversity of views and a tolerance of them, there is instead a desert of conformity.

That intellectual desert has overtaken campus after campus. Like grains of sand, the instances of intellectual prejudice and narrow-mindedness, each one small and insignificant in itself, pile up until the sum total is suffocating. To cite one example: When in 1989 the Hoover Institution sponsored a national conference on the controversial issue of national service, the coordinator, Williamson

Evers, was especially careful to invite roughly the same number of the most articulate and expert people he could find on both sides of the issue. The idea was to provide a forum in which the arguments for and against national service could be discussed frankly and fully.

On the second day of the conference I took a short walk on the Stanford campus during one of the coffee breaks. I encountered a Stanford professor I knew, and he noticed the conference name tag pinned on my coat.

"Hey, what are you doing?" he said.

I replied, "We're having a conference at Hoover this weekend."

"Oh? What's it on?"

"National service."

"Hey, that sounds interesting."

"Why don't you come join us?"

"Can't, I'm busy. But, say, who do you have at the conference?"

"Lots of people. Some of the top experts in the country. We have Charles Moskos, Donald Eberly, Congressman David Mc-Curdy, Milton Friedman . . ."

The professor interrupted me. "Milton Friedman? But isn't he against the idea of national service?"

"Yes, he is. We're having a debate at the conference. You know—different points of view."

"Oh," he said. A puzzled look briefly crossed his face, and then he said good-bye and walked away.

The root of the widely publicized problems with the issue of "political correctness" can be found in the political makeup of the faculties, something which did not happen by accident. When you have so many people of like political minds controlling the agenda of our campuses, men and women who feel so strongly about their political views, it is not surprising when they exercise their power to do what they believe is right. What is surprising is that the administrators and trustees have allowed this political bias to flourish with little heed for the consequences. And the consequences can be serious. When a professor's political views affect his hiring and promotion decisions, the reading assignments in courses, and sometimes even the grades given to students, there is a chill cast on free speech and academic freedom.

In the fall of 1987, Stephan Thernstrom, a professor at Harvard University for twenty-five years, was denounced as a racist. Couldn't be, I thought when I heard it. I had known Thernstrom many years ago and there wasn't a racist thought in his brain—left-liberal political thoughts aplenty, but not racist ones. Several 1987 articles in the *Harvard Crimson* had accused him of racial insensitivity in the teaching of one of his courses. His crime? Well, he "had used the word *Indians* instead of *Native Americans.*" Moreover, he had used the "word *Oriental,* with its imperialist overtones," in referring to an Oriental religion. But his worst transgressions were that he had assigned a book to the class "that mentioned that some people regarded affirmative action as preferential treatment," and had actually "endorsed, in class, Patrick Moynihan's emphasis on the breakup of the black family as a cause of persistent black poverty." All these were considered racist ideas.

Professor Thernstrom, one of the most honorable, decent scholars in America, tried to explain—but to no avail. "It's like being called a Commie in the fifties," he says. "Whatever explanation you offer, once accused, you're always suspect."[39] But the worst part for Thernstrom was the reaction of the Harvard intellectual community, which, instead of defending him, fell silent or issued official statements such as a letter from Fred Jewett, dean of the college, to the entire Harvard community saying that "recent events" compelled him to "speak out loudly and forcefully against all kinds of prejudice, harassment and discrimination."

"I felt like a rape victim," said Thernstrom, "and yet the silence of the administration seemed to give the benefit of the doubt to the students who attacked me. Maybe I was naïve, but I expected the university to come to my defense. I mean, that's what academic freedom is about, isn't it?"[40]

Thernstrom decided it just wasn't worth fighting any more. He gave up. The course is no longer given by him.[41]

At Smith College in 1990, the administrators issued a handout to all students explaining that many people were oppressed but just didn't know it. One section of the handout said, "As groups of people begin the process of realizing that they are oppressed, and why, new words tend to be created to express the concepts that the existing language cannot." The handout went on to list various categories of oppression. One was "ableism," defined as "oppression of the differently abled by the temporarily abled." Another was "lookism," defined as "the construction of a standard for beauty/ attractiveness; and oppression through stereotypes and generalizations of both those who do not fit that standard and those who do."[42]

An intense debate is now under way in our universities on the teaching of the so-called Great Books of literature and history. A small but influential number of faculty want to strip the curriculum of many of the great works of Western literature, most of them written by, as they put it, "dead white men," and to replace them with lesser-known works by authors of different racial backgrounds, authors from third world countries, and female authors. At one point in 1988, Stanford's courses in Western civilization were rearranged so that, as a *Wall Street Journal* editorial described it, "Of the 15 great works previously required, only six remain. . . . Dante's 'Inferno' is out . . . but 'I . . . Rigoberta Menchu' is in. . . . Aquinas and Thomas More are out, but 'Their Eyes Were Watching God' by feminist Zora Neale Hurston is in. . . . Locke and Mill go down the memory hole, replaced by such as the U.N. Declaration of Human Rights and Rastafarian poetry. . . . Virgil, Cicero and Tacitus give way to Frantz Fanon. . . . Martin Luther and Galileo are out, but such timeless notables as Juan Rulfo ('The Burning Plain') and Sandra Cisneros ('The House on Mango Street') are in. And so on."[43]

A valid argument can be made for expanding the horizons of students beyond the canon of great Western works, but why not keep all the great works and add to them? Surely our students are not that overburdened. Why must one acknowledged great work be banished for every new one that is added? The only answer is that a political agenda, not a desire to improve the education of young minds, is behind the drive to eliminate the great works of Western civilization.

A few professors have gone beyond criticizing the great works of Western literature, arguing that the English language itself conveys a cultural, political, and gender prejudice. The school of thought called "deconstruction" holds the view "that language is always so compromised by metaphor and ulterior motives that a text never means what it appears to mean." As one of the early pioneers of this grotesque reasoning explained it, "The relationship between truth and error that prevails in literature cannot be represented genetically since truth and error exist simultaneously, thus preventing the favoring of one over the other."[44]

Some of the core beliefs of those who adhere to the deconstructionist school are: (1) language itself is contradictory, if not empty; (2) meaning does not reside in a text or in an author's intent but in a reader's response; (3) the reader is the equal of, and perhaps superior to, the author; (4) literary influence—the accumulated insights of previous ages—can be harmful, not helpful; (5) no form of discourse (folk tale, video, novel, sonnet) is superior to any other; (6) the "classic books" approach to literary study is bankrupt—multiculturism is essential; and (7) all literary works must be viewed in a political context, as instruments of exclusion, oppression, or liberation on the issues of race, class, and gender.[45]

"Deconstruction" is a convenient framework for those with a political agenda. When words no longer have any meaning, anything goes. Many of today's professors take these notions seriously, teaching them to their students. To illustrate how far this nonsense of deconstructionism has gone, listen to a couple of arguments made in 1989 by one of its leading exponents, Professor Stanley Fish, chairman of Duke University's English department. In his 613-page tome, *Doing What Comes Naturally,* Fish sets forth his thesis "that the meaning of a sentence is *not* a function of the meaning of its constituent parts . . . that meaning cannot be formally calculated, derived from the shape of marks on a page; or to put it in the most direct way possible, that there is no such thing as literal meaning." Then, to ensure no one misunderstands him, he drives home the point: "It might seem that the thesis that there is no such thing as literal meaning is a limited one . . . but in fact it is a thesis whose implications are almost boundless, for they extend to the very underpinnings of the universe." Further on, Fish caps his bizarre philosophy: "I want to argue, in short, that there is no such thing as intrinsic merit."[46]

Do you suppose Professor Fish would be offended if we agreed with his nutty theses and pointed out that what he wrote confirms that his words have no literal meaning and no intrinsic merit?

Almost no device is overlooked in the rush to introduce politically correct forms of thinking. Beginning students at the University of Texas no longer will read the classics in their introductory writing class. Replacing the classics will be court decisions on affirmative action and civil rights cases. Now, the issue of civil rights is important, and worthy of college study. But as a vehicle for teaching freshman composition? Have court opinions become that eloquent?

At least one man at the University of Texas thinks not. Professor Alan Gribben of the English department says, "You cannot tell me that students will not inevitably be graded on politically correct thinking in these classes."[47]

At Haverford College in Pennsylvania, students must now fulfill a "social justice requirement" in order to graduate. That means they must take at least "one course in subjects like 'Postcolonial Women Writers,' 'Psychological Issues of Lesbians and Gay Males,' or 'Feminist Political Theory.' "[48] Again, interesting issues worthy of study. But required for graduation?

At the University of Pennsylvania, a student serving on a committee to examine "diversity in education" wrote a memo in which she referred to her regard for the individual. The memo landed in the lap of an indignant administrator, who returned the memo with the word "individual" circled. The University of Pennsylvania official warned the student that the word "individual" was "a red flag phrase today which is considered by many to be racist."[49]

Many of the incidents falling under the general heading of "political correctness" are so bizarre that it is difficult to believe that things like that really do happen at our universities. Dinesh D'Souza's 1991 book, *Illiberal Education,*[50] is one of the most comprehensive studies of how hubris and political bias have combined to create an atmosphere on our campuses that has been wickedly characterized by civil rights scholar Abigail Thernstrom as "an island of repression in a sea of freedom."[51] D'Souza tells story after story about the politics of race and sex occurring on the campuses of the University of California at Berkeley, Stanford, Howard, Michigan, Duke, and Harvard, detailing the strange things that go on in these places today.

Being a fellow of the Hoover Institution at Stanford University for twenty years has given me a catbird seat to observe the fog of politically correct thinking that has spread over our universities and colleges. Hoover has been an intellectual West Berlin, smack in the middle of a hostile ideological environment, the object of ostracism, ridicule, and verbal abuse. The non–politically correct thinking of many of the Hoover fellows so infuriated some of the Stanford faculty that they once even attempted to take control of the institution. In October 1988 a letter drafted by political science professor Alexander George and signed by seventeen more of Stanford University's most distinguished professors, demanded that the Hoover Institution be placed under the "normal academic governance" of the university. "Normal academic governance" is a euphemism for faculty control. The letter-writers demanded that Hoover become "a major research division of the university, complete with normal provisions of academic freedom and control." Hoover fellows were assured by all the left-wing professors who signed the letter that such a move "does not mean tight central control and the loss of proper academic independence." No one defined "tight" or "proper."

At the same time, fifty-seven Stanford professors signed a petition demanding that the university either exercise control over Hoover or "sever it from the university." The message was clear. Enough of this independent thinking and writing, submit to the control of the Stanford faculty or leave the campus.

These assaults on academic freedom were serious enough to attract the attention of the American Association of University Professors. In May 1988, John Rosenfeld, chairman of the Committee on Academic Freedom, reported: "There is concern that opposition to the presence of the Hoover Institution on the Stanford campus appears to be politically motivated and representative of an intolerance that is not compatible with a proper concern for academic freedom. Intolerance of 'conservatives' today could be just as easily transformed into intolerance of 'liberals' tomorrow. Both kinds of intolerance are reprehensible on a university campus."[52]

Alexander George and his cohorts failed. Led by its director, W. Glenn Campbell, the Hoover Institution defended itself vigorously and won, although the 18-15 vote of Stanford's faculty senate against the takeover was less than inspiring.[53] Today the Hoover Institution is thriving, stronger than ever. In January 1992 *The Economist* undertook a survey of the world's major think tanks. The Hoover Institution was ranked number one.[54]

But a disturbing thought lingers on. One can perhaps understand the unprofessional actions of a small number of professors overcome by political zeal, but what of their colleagues? Where oh where were the voices of the rest of the almost fourteen hundred Stanford faculty when this assault on academic freedom was taking place? Where was the rush of administrators and trustees to defend academic freedom? Barely a murmur. I can count on the fingers of one hand the Stanford professors who openly opposed this flagrant abuse of academic freedom.

Then there was the attempt to bring the Reagan Presidential Library to Stanford University in the mid-1980s. That was a serious mistake. For more than three years I was President Reagan's personal representative on the campus, taking part in an increasingly bitter round of negotiations. It seemed like a good idea when I first proposed locating the library on the Stanford campus. Stanford would acquire, free, a $50 million library and archival facility that would significantly enhance its intellectual resources, providing research opportunities not only to visiting presidential scholars from around the world, but also to all Stanford faculty and students. The scholars who used the library would, in turn, have access to Stanford's facilities. No one disputed the intellectual value of this resource.

But none of us supporting the library had reckoned on the

deep animosity that many of the Stanford faculty felt toward the policies and person of President Reagan. They made no pretense of their hatred. From the very first day the idea was proposed, there was a steady drumbeat of criticism—some of it direct and candid, most of it disingenuous. Finally, after several years of acrimonious debate, the Stanford trustees painted themselves into a corner, for they could not openly reject the Reagan library without exposing themselves to the charge of political bias. So the trustees reluctantly voted to approve the library—part of it. Stanford would accept the library and a small exhibit area, but it would not allow the construction of a center for public affairs, as was the custom in other presidential libraries. President Reagan surprised the Stanford trustees by agreeing to the indignity of a stripped-down library, and the plans proceeded.

Many of the Stanford faculty were incensed by the trustees' decision. The faculty's criticism of the Reagan library increased, including personal insults to the president, to the point where it became political harassment, creating a hostile, uncivil environment. The trustees and administration stood mute while a minority of Stanford faculty continued their savaging, until finally President Reagan said in effect that "life is too short for this kind of abuse" and ordered the trustees of the Reagan Foundation to withdraw the presidential library from the Stanford campus.

Today, the Reagan Presidential Library, complete with a center for public affairs, sits majestically on a high hill on a hundred unspoiled acres an hour's drive north of Los Angeles—far from any college or university. And Stanford remains politically unsullied—except of course for the Hoover Institution.

Politically correct thinking works in many different ways. In the spring of 1990, Linda Chavez, a former high-ranking official of the Reagan administration, was invited to give the commencement address at the University of Northern Colorado. An invitation to give the commencement address is one of the highest honors a university can bestow, and the administrators apparently "thought that inviting a successful female Hispanic would go down well with the 'cultural diversity' movement on campus." While qualifying unquestionably by ethnicity and gender, Linda Chavez had a political problem. Besides being a Republican and having worked for President Reagan, she also opposed the idea of "affirmative action and thinks Hispanic immigrants should learn English as quickly as possible." Obviously politically incorrect. When these heresies were discovered, the college withdrew the invitation.

To cap off the incident, the president of the University of Northern Colorado "apologized for appearing 'grossly insensitive' and said it was 'obviously wrong' to think that Chavez was a proper role model for Hispanic women."[55] As far as I know, the trustees of the university remained mute.

America's entrance into the Persian Gulf War in 1991 was vigorously opposed by almost all the political left in the country, and support for it soon appeared on the proscribed list of politically incorrect thinking on campuses. The thoroughness with which even the slightest deviation from the "correct" political view of the war was handled is exemplified in a story related in early 1991 by Lynne Cheney, chairman of the National Endowment for the Humanities.

A few students at the University of Maryland were openly displaying an American flag from their windows on campus. The university ordered them to take the flags down, "lest they offend someone in the 'diverse' campus community." The students resisted and the university, probably realizing the impossible position they had put themselves in, relented, and the flags blazed forth as the United States and its allies fought and defeated Iraq.[56]

Some scholars openly brag of what they are doing. Andrew Ross is a professor at Princeton University, a thirty-four-year-old Marxist scholar of American popular culture who was recently recommended for tenure. There is no doubt about his intentions. "I teach in the Ivy League in order to have direct access to the minds of the children of the ruling classes," says Professor Ross. "Whoever the politically correct are, it's about time some of them were in the universities."[57]

Some of them now are in our universities. As Jay Parini, a professor of English at Middlebury College, explained it in December 1988: "After the Vietnam war, a lot of us didn't just crawl back into our library cubicles; we stepped into academic positions. . . . Now we have tenure, and the hard work of reshaping the universities has begun in earnest."[58]

Listening to Annette Kolodny, "a former Berkeley radical and now the dean of the humanities faculty at the University of Arizona," one hears the message just as clearly. "I see my scholarship as an extension of my political activism," she asserts.[59] Or to Dale Bauer, a professor of English at the University of Wisconsin, who says proudly, "I definitely bring politics into the classroom, but I would argue that everybody does."[60]

Sometimes students may be saying what their professors are thinking. Reacting to implied criticism of political bias in the Stanford faculty in 1985, Jim Naureckas, a senior majoring in political science and columnist for the student paper, explained it this way: "You won't find a lot of Reaganites in the Political Science Department at Stanford. Some claim this as evidence of bias, but I think it indicates that to some extent the University is acting the way it is supposed to: In the 'free market' of ideas, those that are not credible are eventually junked."[61] Perhaps not as eloquent as his mentors, but at least he is more forthright.

The informal constitution that is supposed to guide the academic intellectual community is the "1940 Statement of Principles on Academic Freedom and Tenure." First set forth in 1925, it was restated in 1940 and has been endorsed by every major intellectual association in the United States. It is what all professors agree to abide by. Here is what it says about academic freedom:

> (a) Teachers are entitled to full freedom in research and in the publication of the results. . . .
> (b) Teachers are entitled to freedom in the classroom in discussing the subject, but they should be careful not to introduce into their teaching controversial matter which has no relation to their subject. . . .
> (c) College and university teachers are citizens, members of a learned profession, and officers of an educational institution.

When they speak or write as citizens, they should be free from
institutional censorship or discipline. [62]

That statement of academic freedom is infringed every day on
campuses across the country. And barely a finger is raised in protest,
either by faculty, administrators, or trustees. But that may soon
change, in the face of a nascent resistance movement.

The most important resistance group is the fledgling National
Association of Scholars. Founded in 1986 to further "reasoned
scholarship in a free society," this group of professors, while still
small, is growing rapidly. In December 1988, NAS had 500 members. By October 1991 its rolls had swelled to 2,500, with twenty
chapters on college and university campuses and twenty-two state
affiliates. [63] The aims of the National Association of Scholars include:

- Resisting the ideological misuse of teaching and scholarship
- Maintaining rigorous standards in research, teaching, and
academic self-governance
- Encouraging intellectual balance and realism in campus
debate on contemporary issues
- Preserving academic freedom and the free exchange of ideas
on and off the campus. [64]

Most of the members of NAS are professors with conservative
political views who have experienced the sting of prejudice on their
campuses. But an increasing number of professors with liberal political views are also joining. For example, James David Barber, a
well-known left-liberal political scientist, joined the Duke University
chapter because "its aims address exactly what concerns me, which
is that what's going on in universities now threatens everything that
a university is supposed to be about. It is about scholarship. Students'
minds are supposed to be trained, not converted politically."[65]

But the new resistance forces defending academic freedom have
a long way to go. The situation was aptly summed up in the fall of
1990 by Harvey C. Mansfield, Jr., professor of government at Harvard University:

In American universities now . . . the evil is politicization, an
ugly word for deliberate, organized bias. . . . Professors regarded

as reactionary are isolated, their views dismissed disrespectfully, and their students shut out of academia. So far the evil is concentrated in the humanities, but it is also felt very strongly in the social sciences. . . . Politicization comes from the Left . . . the present assault on the universities comes from within.[66]

Personal Corruption

Besides breaking the ethical rules that govern intellectual life to advance their scholarly reputations or further their political agenda, a distressingly large number of academic intellectuals break the rules for personal behavior, pursuing sexual pleasure where they should not. It is an age-old problem, the problem of sexual attraction between professor and student, between mentor and apprentice.

The problem is both delicate and difficult because it mixes two emotional, powerful issues—sexual attraction and abuse of authority. The problem is not sexual attraction. There are many examples of professors falling in love with students and vice versa. All of the professors are over twenty-one years old, and so are many of the students, especially the graduate students. On occasion students will initiate advances toward professors rather than the reverse. Handled properly, there is theoretically no cause for alarm. But unfortunately the situation is rarely handled properly, and some will argue it cannot be.

The reason is the power relationship between teacher and student. The average professor, and even the average teaching assistant, wields enormous power over his or her students. Sexual harassment by academic intellectuals is flagrant abuse of their authority, using the power they wield over students to coerce sexual favors.

The power a professor holds over a student, especially a graduate student pursuing an advanced degree, can be difficult to imagine for anyone who has not been in that position. Depending on how badly the student wants a grade or a degree in order to pursue a lifelong dream, the professor's power can approach that exercised by a warden over a prisoner, by a master over a slave. Nothing so gross as a physical threat or force is necessary; the threat to one's career carries the equivalent weight.

During a recent case involving sexual harassment of students at Yale University, the Dean's Advisory Committee on Grievance Procedure published a report which summed up the problem:

> Though sexual harassment in any situation is reprehensible, it must be a matter of particularly deep concern to an academic community in which students and faculty are related by strong bonds of intellectual dependence and trust. Further, the vulnerability of undergraduates to such harassment is particularly great and the potential impact upon them is particularly severe. Not only does sexual harassment betray the special bond between teacher and student, but it also exploits unfairly the power inherent in an instructor's relationship to his or her student. Through grades, recommendations, research appointments, or job referrals, an instructor can have a decisive influence on a student's academic success and future career. If this influence should be used overtly or implicitly in an attempt to exact sexual favors, a situation is created that may have devastating implications for individual students and for the academic community as a whole. Through fear of academic reprisal, a student may be forced to comply with sexual demands at the price of a debilitating personal anguish, or to withdraw from a course, a major, or even a career, and thus is forced to change plans for a life's work.[67]

The idea of holding a young student's career hostage to a demand for sex is so repugnant that it is difficult to conceive of such a thing taking place in these temples of integrity, our colleges and universities. But it does and, as with other breaches of integrity in the academic world, what is of particular concern beyond the incidents themselves is the reaction of the intellectual community.

For a long time the problem of sex between professors and students was known only by rumor and innuendo, by cryptic remarks and jokes. It was a subject cloaked by the embarrassment of the victims and the guilt of the predators. There was no hard information on which to judge the extent of the problem, just the occasional sensational newspaper story.

That is no longer the case. One consequence of the feminist movement is the analysis and study of some subjects that previously suffered from neglect. The early reports are not encouraging. In fact, they indicate a deep breach of the integrity that must exist between student and teacher. Like plagiarism, the subject of sexual harassment now has its own books, including *The Lecherous Professor* (1984) by Billie Wright Dzeich and Linda Weiner and *Ivory Power: Sexual Harassment on Campus* (1990), edited by Michele Paludi. What is notable is how little note has been taken of these books, especially *Ivory Power*, which is a collection containing more than a dozen articles and a comprehensive bibliography listing fifty works published since 1980.

Studies more than confirm what has long been suspected. In the university world dominated and controlled by males, the female student is substantially at risk. I am sure that someone somewhere will find a female professor who has taken sexual advantage of a student, but that will be a rare exception. Here are some survey results: A 1983 study conducted at Harvard University concluded "that 15 percent of the graduate students and 12 percent of the undergraduate students who had been harassed by their professors changed their major or educational program because of the harassment."[68] In a paper entitled "Tarnishing the Ivory Tower," presented to the American Psychological Association in 1985, the authors reported that "of 246 women graduate students in their sample, 12.7 percent indicated they had been sexually harassed, 21 percent had not enrolled in a course to avoid such behavior . . . 2.6 percent dropped a course because of it, and 15.9 percent indicated they had been directly assaulted."[69]

The most damning evidence comes from a 1988 study conducted by Louise Fitzgerald, a professor at the University of Illinois, and several associates. Instead of surveying the victims, they surveyed potential perpetrators: "235 male academics employed at a prestigious research-oriented university." In a virtuoso display of hubris, 37 percent of those proud professors said that they had at one time or another "attempted to initiate a personal friendship with a student (e.g., asking for a date, suggesting you get together for a drink, etc.)" and 26 percent admitted they had "had a sexual encounter or relationship with a student."[70]

It can be argued that some of this sexual activity between professor and student not only may have been consented to by the student, but may indeed have been initiated by the student. In fact, 14 percent of those surveyed asserted that a student had implied or offered "sexual favors or cooperation in return for some reward (e.g., grade, assistantship, etc.)," and there was a significant degree of overlap between those who received offers and those who indulged.[71] But, as the authors note, the data are based on those faculty who were willing to report on their sexual behavior and thus the results are a "lower bound estimate on the number of faculty members who become sexually involved with students."[72]

One might expect the academic community to be up in arms over these recurring reports of flagrant abuse of authority. But except for a brief flurry of indignation when an incident surfaces publicly, little if anything is done. And the incidents continue. In March 1991 the Emory University law school opened an investigation "into the conduct of a law professor who has been charged with sexual harassment by more than a dozen female law students."[73] In June 1991 a professor at the Stanford University medical school was charged with making "inappropriate sexual remarks to one student," and denying "a teaching assistant position to another because she refused to have a sexual relationship with him." The accused professor strongly denied the charges.[74]

Not all cases of sexual abuse involve female students. In February 1991 a long-festering saga of sexual abuse at Middlebury College in the mountains of Vermont burst into print in *Boston Magazine* with ugly charges against one of the school's most distinguished professors. Four young men who attended Middlebury during the 1980s charged that "they had been sexually abused by Paul Cubeta, a Shakespeare scholar and director of the college's prestigious graduate-level Bread Loaf School of English." Each claimed Professor Cubeta "had made unwanted sexual advances after trying to get him drunk, often repeating the overtures despite the student's objections."

Years earlier, in 1977, two senior English professors—Robert Hill and David Littlefield—had reportedly gone personally to Olin Robison, the president of Middlebury, and told him of two allegations of sexual harassment by Cubeta. Robison dismissed their complaints without investigation. As Hill said later, there was "no further inquiry, nothing." In October 1988, the four young men testified against Cubeta. There might have been at least one other accuser, a young man, but he had committed suicide in 1986.[75] Although there was no official finding of guilt and Cubeta continued to deny the charges, the hearing conducted by the administrators of Middlebury College concluded that Cubeta was unfit to teach.

His punishment? It was announced that Professor Cubeta had requested "early retirement" and that it had been granted, although it was stated that he would "continue a limited role in fund-raising activities." Further, Robison created a new administrative job in Middlebury's school of English, "director of development, raising funds and administering scholarships," and appointed Cubeta to it. The appointment was withdrawn in the face of continued protests from the Bread Loaf staff. The students were not ignored. Middlebury offered them "10 hours of free psychological counseling." One of the student victims wrote back to Robison and suggested that he "give my 10 hours to Mr. Cubeta."[76]

The essence of the Middlebury scandal was succinctly stated by Margaret Doody, a former professor of English at Princeton University, who left Princeton in 1989 because of the way a similar, though more violent, case was handled by the administrators. "The interest of the institution is to bury it in-house. Administrators have their first loyalty—mistakenly—to the institution, instead of to the students and the integrity of the academic environment."[77] Earlier, commenting on that Princeton University sex scandal, in which a twenty-four-year-old graduate student claimed that he had been sexually attacked by an English professor, Thomas McFarland, Doody explained the mind-set that seems to exist on that campus, a description that is probably not unique to Princeton:

> What we are talking about here is violence. It does not matter what the gender preference is. It's true that some professors for a very long time have seen students as a box of chocolates for their delectation. . . . It's true that fifteen years ago a man or woman to whom this happened would have slunk back to the dormitory and said nothing. That's why the perpetrators are conditioned to the notion that this is normal. . . . The issue . . . is a violent assault upon a student. Teaching is a responsibility. A human being has been put in your charge. You have the utmost responsibility not to damage him. . . . Physical violence of any kind by a professor against a student should be, in itself, enough to get you thrown out of your job—let's start with that. I think a lot of Princeton parents would be very surprised that that does not obtain now.[78]

Sometimes professors even prey on their colleagues, especially the younger, more vulnerable ones—usually defined as those without tenure. One of the most notorious cases in recent years occurred at Harvard University and involved a young female professor, Terry Karl, and an older male professor, Jorge Dominguez, both on the faculty of the government department. The case was simple and perhaps classic. She had no tenure and was struggling to establish an academic career; he was a tenured, senior member of her department, a person to whom others in her profession would turn for evaluations of her work. According to press reports, the incidents of sexual harassment occured over a two-year period, between 1981 and 1983, and, Karl claimed, included his inviting her to his home when his wife and children were away, introducing her at a party as "my slave," threats of rape, and finally assault.[79]

The classic part was the implication that Professor Karl would have to trade sexual favors in order to prevent her career from being damaged. "During that period," she recalled, "I was afraid, not just for my physical safety but also for my career. After working so hard to earn my doctorate degree and achieve a major academic position, I was forced to choose between pleasing this man or losing everything

I had worked for." So Karl, fearing for her job and her career, made repeated complaints for two years, beginning in 1981, until she reached Henry Rosovsky, Harvard's dean of the entire faculty of arts and sciences. By this time, there reportedly were other sexual harassment complaints pending about Professor Dominguez involving several students. Harvard agreed to investigate the charges.[80]

The verdict was clear. The Harvard officials concluded that Professor Dominguez had abused his authority as charged. Confirming this, Dean Rosovsky wrote a letter to Professor Karl which included the admission that "the repeated sexual advances and certain other deprecating actions constituted a serious abuse of authority."[81]

We all know what should happen now. Founded in 1636, Harvard is considered by many to be the most prestigious university in the world. Its academic leaders have built over the centuries a towering reputation for integrity. As Henry Rosovsky himself once approvingly quoted the medieval history scholar E.K. Kantorowicz: "There are three professions which are entitled to wear the gown: the judge, the priest, and the scholar. This garment stands for its bearer's maturity of mind, his independence of judgment, and his direct responsibility to his conscience and his god."[82] Naturally one assumes that Jorge Dominguez was summarily fired, and that Terry Karl was consoled and comforted and today is a happy, tenured professor at Harvard.

Wrong. This is what happened.

According to Professor Karl, after the case was resolved in her favor, Dean Rosovsky talked to her and indicated that Karl, not Professor Dominguez, should be the one to leave the university. The reason given was that Jorge Dominguez had tenure and she did not. Actually, Rosovsky did ask Dominguez to leave Harvard— but only temporarily. He was given a year's leave with pay. So, in effect, Harvard solved one of its sexual harassment problems by suggesting that the victim go away, and by giving the alleged perpetrator a year's paid vacation.[83] Terry Karl later joked about it, saying, "I refer to it as the Guggenheim for sexual harassment."[84]

Frustrated by Harvard's brand of justice, Karl filed a formal complaint with the Equal Employment Opportunity Commission, which took the case and began to investigate. Harvard then seemed to take Karl's charges somewhat more seriously. She even met personally with President Derek Bok to discuss the matter. But little happened. According to Karl, Harvard continued to stonewall on Dominguez and refused to take any serious disciplinary action against him. They did, however, bend to Professor Karl's demand that the university's policy on sexual harassment be improved, and in 1985 adopted a strong official policy against sexual harassment. But even after this victory Karl concluded she would be better off leaving Harvard, explaining that "I did not want to continue working in a hostile environment."[85]

Before she left, Karl says, Henry Rosovsky tried to persuade her to sign a binding legal agreement which would prevent her from ever discussing the case publicly. Karl refused, although she did sign an agreement, on the advice of her lawyer, to the effect that she would not mention Dominguez's name publicly and, in return, he could not mention hers. Harvard feels keenly about keeping its secrets from the public, having a policy of not releasing any information—especially the names of the parties concerned—about any investigation of sexual harassment or the resolution of those cases.[86]

Harvard's desire for secrecy is well founded, for Professor Karl's case was not that unusual. Partly as a result of her charges, an extensive survey of the Harvard academic community was conducted in the spring of 1983. The results were unexpected: 34 percent of female undergraduates, 41 percent of female graduate students, and 49 percent of the nontenured women on the faculty reported experiencing some form of sexual harassment. It was an epidemic of abuse. Seventeen percent of nontenured female faculty—in the same position as Professor Karl—reported what they described as serious harassment.[87]

Today Harvard's secrets seem to be safe. Jorge Dominguez stayed at Harvard and, in the spring of 1991, was awarded the prestigious Levinson Prize for excellence in undergraduate teaching.[88] Terry Karl left Harvard and eventually became an associate professor at Stanford, with tenure. Henry Rosovsky, no longer dean, was accorded the high honor of being named a fellow of the Harvard Corporation. Derek Bok retired with full honors and is now ensconced at the Center for Advanced Study in the Behavioral Sciences in the sylvan hills of Palo Alto, California. Here is the hubris of academic intellectuals at full flower, an unfortunate example of the brand of justice that too often reigns in the American university.

There is a small epilogue to the Karl–Dominguez–Rosovsky–Bok affair at Harvard. In 1990 Henry Rosovsky's book *The University: An Owner's Manual* was published. Interesting book. Toward the end Rosovsky describes in some detail how, in the early 1980s, while he was the dean of Harvard, circumstances required him to become familiar with the problem of sexual harassment and what he had done about it:

> Amorous relationships that might be appropriate in other circumstances are always wrong when they occur between any teacher and any student for whom he or she has a professional responsibility. . . . It is incumbent upon those with authority not to abuse, nor seem to abuse, the power with which they are entrusted.
>
> Members of the teaching staff should be aware that any romantic involvement with their students makes them liable for formal action against them if a complaint is initiated by a student. *Even when both parties have consented to the development of such a relationship, it is the officer or instructor who, by virtue of his or her special relationship, will be held accountable for unprofessional behavior.* . . .
>
> In my opinion, these principles apply equally to relations between tenured and non-tenured faculty members. Opportunities for the abuse of power are just as common, and for all these transgressions, I urged clear procedures and stern punishment.[89]

I suppose that for those who read only Rosovsky's version of his conduct at Harvard, the judgment of history will be that he was more than fit to wear the scholar's robe, but I can't help wondering if Harvard's "stern punishment" for sexual harassment is still a year's paid vacation.

One might also wonder where the distinguished overseers of Harvard were when the scandals erupted in their university. Did they know? Did they read the newspapers? What did they do?

But perhaps we worry too much. In the fall of 1991 the current chairman of the government department at Harvard, Robert O. Keohane (who is also the Stanfield Professor of International Peace), was asked about changes in attitude about sexual harassment. "Most of us are aware now that this is an abuse of power, not an issue of sexuality," he said. "We are much more aware of the debilitating effect on victims. We didn't know that 10 years ago."[90]

Well, at least Harvard is learning.

Stung by the accumulating charges of notorious sexual abuse by faculty members, the academic establishment has begun to respond to these aspersions on its integrity. New guidelines dealing with how professors deal with students? Perhaps a ban on all sexual fraternization between teacher and student? Not quite.

In June 1991 the American Association of University Professors issued a formal statement on sexual harassment complaints that expressed concern over whether safeguards of academic due process *for faculty* were being disregarded in dealing with such complaints. While noting that they did not condone sexual harassment, they emphasized that strong "protections of academic due process are necessary for the individual, for the institution, and for the principles of academic freedom and tenure."[91]

Somehow during the past few decades many of our university communities have drifted into condoning sexual relationships between teacher and student. The issue is not whether the student is underage or over twenty-one, the issue is not the sexual relationship, the issue is the abuse of authority and the violation of the integrity of the teaching process. The potential for abuse of authority, of creating situations of favoritism that cause resentment among other students, is so great that the practice should be stopped. In the few instances of incipient young love between professor and student, there would still be numerous options: the student could leave school, the professor could leave, or—heresy—they both could wait until the student graduates. In any event there should be a firm policy prohibiting any sexual relationship between faculty and students.

Institutional Corruption

Now let us move to an area where the rules are broken and integrity cast aside, not for personal prestige or political ends, but for financial gain for the institution itself. For more than a century, intellectuals have led the attack on big business, condemning monopoly and conspiratorial practices such as price-fixing. Intellectuals were a major force behind the passage of the Sherman Anti-Trust Act in 1890 outlawing such practices. So it was a bit of a surprise when, in the fall of 1989, the Justice Department announced it was investigating whether a large number of our elite colleges and universities had deliberately violated federal antitrust laws by conspiring to fix tuition fees and the level of financial aid.

By the spring of 1991 the investigation was complete. Under a consent decree signed on May 22, 1991, eight of our most distinguished colleges and universities—Brown, Columbia, Cornell, Dartmouth, Harvard, Princeton, Pennsylvania, and Yale—denied any wrongdoing but agreed to stop holding the meetings at which they and "15 other prestigious northeastern institutions jointly discussed the financial aid applications of some 10,000 students who had been accepted to more than one institution in the group . . . to agree to uniform financial aid offers."[92]

Together, all the schools in the alleged conspiracy were known as the "Overlap Group." The ones that were not covered by the consent decree but had participated in the meetings were Amherst, Barnard, Bowdoin, Bryn Mawr, Colby, M.I.T., Middlebury, Mount Holyoke, Smith, Trinity, Tufts, Vassar, Wellesley, Wesleyan, and Williams.

Attorney General Richard Thornburgh, a 1954 Yale graduate himself, declared that "this collegiate cartel denied [students and their families] the right to compare prices and discounts among schools, just as they would in shopping for any other service. . . .

The revered stature of these institutions of higher learning in our society does not insulate them from the requirements of the antitrust laws."[93]

Of the nine schools named in the government's lawsuit, only the Massachusetts Institute of Technology decided to fight the charges. The chairman of M.I.T., Paul Gray, later argued that the Sherman Anti-Trust Act was never intended to apply to college financial aid and that, besides, "the issue is not price-fixing. There is no personal gain or profit motive involved here."[94] Attorney General Thornburgh saw it differently: "Federal prosecutors will take M.I.T. to trial on federal antitrust charges."[95]

One of the striking aspects of the 1991 price-fixing scandal is how so many college and university leaders could allegedly collude in price-rigging for some thirty-five years in violation of our antitrust laws. Didn't they know what they were doing? And after being asked to cease and desist, none of them apologized, in fact, their reaction was one of indignation rather than remorse. Perhaps they felt the laws of business did not apply to them, that their actions should not be bound by the same legal and moral constraints binding other organizations in our society. If so it's another bad case of twentieth-century hubris.

A few of the elite universities retained enough integrity to resist, demonstrating that some people in the higher reaches of academe did believe that the Overlap Group's activities were wrong. Stanford University was one that did not join the gang, even though invited. According to Stanford's general counsel John Schwartz, Stanford "explicitly refused" to join the Overlap Group, saying that the university had a policy "that forbids the sharing of information with other schools before prices are set."[96]

The price-fixing scandal of 1991 was just a warm-up for the major financial corruption scandal that engulfed the world of higher education that same year. By the middle of 1991 a large number of our most distinguished universities found themselves under investigation by the federal government, accused of claiming fraudulent expenses for government-sponsored research projects, their administrators under the threat of criminal prosecution. From coast to coast, universities were accused of stealing the taxpayers blind—to the tune of millions of dollars a year.

Those caught in the widening web of the government's investigation of financial corruption included California (Berkeley), the California Institute of Technology, Carnegie-Mellon, Chicago, Columbia, Cornell, Dartmouth, Duke, Emory, Harvard Medical School, Hawaii, Johns Hopkins, M.I.T., Pennsylvania, Pittsburgh, Rutgers, Southern California, Stanford, Washington, and Yale.

Six institutions earned the questionable distinction of getting tangled up in both of the 1991 corruption scandals: Columbia, Cornell, Dartmouth, M.I.T., Pennsylvania, and Yale. But the university that suffered the most, the one that was in the forefront of the corruption scandal, was Stanford. Ironically, just after it had congratulated itself on its integrity by avoiding the price-fixing scandal that swallowed up many of its elite sisters, Stanford fell headlong into a much deeper tar pit of financial corruption.

It all began in 1990 when federal auditors, led by Paul Biddle, a former bank auditor and financial consultant from the Office of Naval Research, began to question hundreds of millions of dollars of overhead charges for research conducted by Stanford University scholars.

For decades the U.S. government had poured billions of dollars into our universities to support a wide array of basic and applied research. For every dollar a university received for research, it was also entitled to receive an additional amount for overhead expenses—electricity, heat, building upkeep, etc.—that were incurred in the course of conducting the research. No one seems to have checked the universities' accounting books very carefully. There was a deep feeling of trust and, essentially, the government accepted whatever amount the universities claimed as research overhead charges. The feeling seemed to be that if you can't trust Yale and Berkeley and M.I.T., whom can you trust?

In their defense, the university administrators faced temptations that would probably have fatally seduced a saint and, not being saints, some of them succumbed. Billion-dollar businesses like universities must raise billions of dollars to stay in business. Tuition revenue from their main product, teaching, only brings in, on average, about 23 percent of their annual revenues. The biggest slug of their money, about 45 percent, comes from government—federal, state, and local.[97] Like any business, universities are under intense pressure to meet constantly rising costs and demands from their staff and faculty for more money. Apparently when they realized that the federal government wasn't watching the books very closely, and that classifying questionable items as bona fide research expenses could bring in millions of dollars—well, they just couldn't resist.

What auditor Biddle found when he began to pore over Stanford's financial records turned out to be highly embarrassing to all, shocking to many—and perhaps criminal as well. Stanford had one of the highest overhead rates in the business; for every dollar it received in federal funds, it tacked on an additional 74 cents for "overhead." During the 1980s Stanford received hundreds of millions of dollars from the federal government for research. At the end of 1991, after a lengthy examination of the books, Biddle estimated that the university may have overcharged taxpayers a staggering $480 million for research costs during the 1980s.[98]

It is difficult to appreciate the audacity of what was done without examining some of the specific charges. Remember, it wasn't just that money was spent on these items, it was that the university administrators claimed that the items were legitimate research expenses, qualifying for federal reimbursement at certain agreed-upon rates. The following expenses charged by Stanford University to the federal government are a partial list of those uncovered in the early phases of the investigation. Some of these charges were fully reimbursed by the government; others went into a general pool of expenses and were reimbursed at the rate of 23 percent.

The "research" expense that gained the most notoriety was $184,286 in depreciation charges, primarily for a 72-foot yacht, the *Victoria*. In December 1987 a "donor" sold the yacht to Stanford University for $100,000, a price well below its appraised value, which was approximately $475,000. Stanford did not sell the yacht to recoup its investment and make a large profit, which could have funded a lot of scholarships for needy students. No, it kept the yacht, obtained a nice slip for it at a marina in Alameda—about forty miles north of the campus on San Francisco Bay—and spruced it up. It was a handsome yacht—a Herreshoff sailing ketch—with wood-paneled cabins, marble counters, two wood-burning fireplaces, and a Jacuzzi. It was used on weekends by members of the Stanford Sailing Association, which included faculty, staff, and alumni.[99]

When the question of Stanford's "research" yacht was first raised by Leila Kahn, a staff member of the congressional subcommittee investigating the charges of financial corruption, Stanford denied everything. Larry Horton, associate vice president for public affairs, wrote the subcommittee on October 25, 1990, saying the *Victoria* did not "affect charges to the government in any way."[100] Further government prodding forced Stanford to reverse its position five weeks later. In a letter dated November 29, Horton admitted that the information provided earlier "was in error," and sent the government a check for $184,286 to cover the spurious depreciation charges on the *Victoria* and some other incidental items that were "inadvertently included in the equipment depreciation pool."[101]

That was just the beginning. The government's suspicions were aroused. If Stanford would use $100,000 of its resources to buy a yacht, pay for its dockage and upkeep, use it for recreation on weekends, and then charge it to the U.S. taxpayers as "research," what else might it have done? Soon a large team of tough federal auditors—at one point there were thirty of them—descended on the Stanford campus and began to scrutinize the financial records. What they found was astonishing.

Some of the charges for which Stanford was fully or partially reimbursed by the federal government included: $218,230 in operating expenses for a privately owned chancellor's residence from 1986 to 1990 (the chancellor died in 1985), $707,737 for the administrative costs of running a commercial shopping center for profit, $2,164 to send a public affairs official to Paris for an alumni conference, $2,000 for alcoholic beverages served at a pre–football game party for selected faculty,[102] $17,500 for a wedding reception for the president of the university and his new wife, $3,000 for stereo systems, soft drinks, and rock bands to entertain students,[103] $400 for a floral arrangement for the dedication of the Stanford stables,[104] and one plum for the board of trustees of Stanford: $45,250 for a retreat at Lake Tahoe.[105]

Of special interest to the government auditors were "research" expenses pertaining to the household of Stanford's president, Donald Kennedy. The residence, Hoover House, is owned by the university. The charges included $750 to a woodworking company to enlarge his bed, $1,610 to install a shower curtain and two window shades in his bathroom, $184 for bedsheets from Neiman-Marcus, $2,500 for fabric for a bedspread and draperies in the master bedroom, $2,910 for a pair of antique Voltaire chairs from Pierre Deux, $1,200 for a nineteenth-century Italian fruitwood commode,[106] $4,000 paid to Edible Art (a catering firm), $2,500 to refurbish the downstairs piano, $3,000 to line the bedroom closet with cedar, and $2,000 a month for fresh flowers.[107] These disclosures seemed especially annoying to Kennedy. Speaking to the Stanford faculty on April 4, 1991, he complained that "one aspect of the hearing and press coverage has been especially disturbing; it is the ugly and erroneous implication that as president of Stanford University I have somehow been living extravagantly, partly at public expense."[108]

By mid-May 1991 the federal government had notified 250 universities and colleges that the charges they had chalked up to academic research over the years were subject to audit and investigation. So Stanford University was by no means alone in its arrogant exploitation of the public purse, although it had gained the lion's share of the probing and publicity, partly because of its haughty response to the initial inquiry. As the tide of financial scandal inundated Stanford and stained its reputation for integrity, the country was treated to the spectacle of preemptive confessions as university officials scurried to pay back any overcharges before the government auditors got to them.

Of fourteen additional universities whose financial records had been checked, all "so far had charged inappropriate costs to the government," according to Kevin Moley, budget director of the Department of Health and Human Services.[109] Some of the gleanings from the early returns of the government investigators are enlightening. It should be noted that most of the fraudulent charges were voluntarily retracted by the universities, obviously in the hope of avoiding a more intensive inquiry, and in fact did not come under the kind of scrutiny Stanford's books received.

The California Institute of Technology, for example, retracted a $20,000 charge for "a three-day meeting by the board of trustees at the Smoke Tree Ranch in Palm Springs." Nearly $8,500 was for a dinner party for the trustees during that trip, including "ten $4 cigars, $120 for parking, $375 for musicians and $167 for the dance floor."[110] The University of Texas charged off "a dozen engraved crystal decanters from Neiman-Marcus" as a research expense.[111] The president of the University of Pittsburgh charged off his golf club membership, opera tickets, a trip his wife took to Grand Cayman, and travel expenses to "football matches in Dublin."[112]

The University of Michigan withdrew $5.9 million of spurious research charges in the wake of the investigation. Among other things, Michigan had charged off the cost of decorations for the Christmas tree in the president's office and an excursion to the 1989 Rose Bowl game, "including $4,329 for the university's director of communications and his wife to fly to Pasadena to attend the football game and the Tournament of Roses Parade." Michigan defended charging the expenses of Martin Luther King Day celebrations on campus because "they involved discussions of research on racism."[113]

Cornell University agreed to repay the federal government $319,541 for inappropriate research expenses, including $12,000 to Taughannock Aviation for a private chartered plane used by Cornell president Francis T. Rhodes, $442 for college hockey playoff tickets, $75 for a speech writer for the president, and the payment of his library fines. They also threw in some Steuben wine glasses, and part of the costs of construction of a new alumni club in New York City.[114] The University of Pennsylvania had $1.3 million in questionable charges, including $98,891 spent to run the chaplain's office, $58,994 to maintain the president's house, and entertainment bills totaling $22,713 for items such as a $723 outing for the wives of the university trustees.[115] Harvard Medical School withdrew approximately $500,000 in "research" charges, including a $7,500 contribution to the Boston public schools, $1,800 of a $3,100 retirement reception for a senior dean, and $140,000 for the president's house and the office of the dean of the medical school.[116]

M.I.T., the fourth-largest recipient of federal funds ($236 million in 1989), gave back over $778,000, saying, "We're not embarrassed, because we're voluntarily cleaning up the last five years." The research charges about which M.I.T. was not embarrassed included $75,000 in salary and benefits for the president's cook, more than $12,000 in travel expenses to Beijing, London, Rome, and Barbados, almost $20,000 for flowers, $10,000 worth of gifts and memorabilia, and a $13,751 reception for the board of trustees. M.I.T. had earlier repaid $23,317 used "to pay a law firm that lobbied Congress." But the most notable charge that M.I.T. laid on U.S. taxpayers during the 1980s was some $68,000 for legal expenses incurred in defending David Baltimore—who was at M.I.T. before becoming president of Rockefeller University— against charges of scientific fraud.[117]

Dartmouth College, while not making the list of the top one hundred colleges and universities in the amount of federal funds received, agreed to retract a whopping $746,031 of research charges. The pulled expenses included $20,490 for a chauffeur used by Dartmouth president James Freedman and his wife, $46,500 for parties at the president's house, $12,134 for the study of "the College's investments in South Africa," $60,343 for expenses "connected to laying off employees," and $55,470 in legal fees to defend the college against a civil rights lawsuit brought by a student newspaper, the *Dartmouth Review*.[118]

Perhaps the most interesting lesson of the research overhead scandal is what it tells us about the attitude of many of our leading academic intellectuals. The statements that Stanford faculty, administrators, and their critics made as the scandal unfolded are instructive. When the story broke in 1990, Stanford's response was calm and confident. President Kennedy conceded that it would require a "lot of explanation" to make the public understand the accounting process that made such charges as the piano and flowers reasonable, and said that although he was prepared to eliminate those charges, he found "nothing improper in their inclusion."[119] Kennedy denied that the university had done anything wrong.[120]

At times Kennedy even got a mite testy. "I don't care whether it's flowers, or dinners and receptions, or whether it's washing the table linen after it's been used, or buying an antique here or there, or refinishing a piano when its finish gets crappy, or repairing a closet and refinishing it," said Kennedy. "All those are investments in a University facility."[121]

A couple of Stanford faculty and staff decided to attack the messenger, federal auditor Paul Biddle. Janet Sweet, assistant controller, told the press that Biddle was "full of venom . . . does not communicate well," and that some of the positions he has taken are "crazy."[122] When Biddle was so indiscreet as to remark that Stanford did not "have a corner on intelligence," Professor J. Martin Brown of the medical school attacked him for making a "reckless, arrogant statement," suggesting darkly that Biddle had another "agenda."[123]

In the middle of the investigation of financial corruption, William F. Massy, chief financial officer of Stanford University since 1977, suddenly resigned. President Kennedy praised Massy as "a marvelous asset to this University in a number of roles—as vice provost for research, as vice president for business and finance and, later, finance," and asserted that his "national leadership in higher education finance and policy had served Stanford well." The same day, it was reported that Stanford's Institute for Higher Education, headed by Professor Massy, had been given a $1 million research grant by the U.S. Department of Education, and that Massy expected to do research on the financing of higher education.[124]

As the investigation continued, Stanford seemed to become more aggrieved and its protestations of innocence escalated. After Congressman John Dingell (D.–Mich.) announced his investigation of Stanford's research bills, the president of Stanford's board of trustees, James Gaither, and three former presidents of the board, including Warren Christopher, former deputy secretary of state for President Carter, sent Dingell a letter defending the practice of charging the upkeep of the president's house as research overhead. "Our view has been . . . that the Hoover House expenditures are important, reasonable and appropriate,"[125] they wrote. Professor James Collman of the Stanford chemistry department went after Congressman Dingell directly, impugning both his character and motives, charging that "many scientists compare him to Joe McCarthy. . . . He has a kind of vendetta against science. . . . They [Dingell's committee] have a history of McCarthyism in regard to science."[126] Robert C. Byer, the Stanford dean of research, took a more positive approach, arguing that "we are as open and as honest and as straightforward with the federal government as we can be."[127] President Kennedy argued that charging expenses for such items as the party introducing his new wife were in his judgment "allowable," the problem being that "they just don't appear reasonable to most people."[128]

Others had a different view. In January 1991 one lonely Stanford professor, William Spicer in the department of electrical engineering, did speak out, publicly charging that "the Stanford administration is losing much more than dollars in the overhead fight. It is losing integrity."[129] In March, at the congressional hearings in Washington, Dingell lambasted Stanford for excess and arrogance, accusing it of exhibiting "a brazen 'catch me if you can' attitude similar to that found in the defense industry." Congressman Ron Wyden (D.–Oreg.), a 1971 graduate of Stanford, said the hearing marked "a very sad day for one of the world's greatest universities." Congressman John Bryant (D.–Texas) accused Kennedy of "stonewalling this committee like a common politician."[130]

Throughout, most of the Stanford administrators appeared more hurt and shocked than venal. As the hearings approached, Kennedy observed that in the past "we were seen as special, now we're going to be held to a much higher standard—and it's going to be expensive."[131] A few weeks after the hearings Kennedy said, "We thought we had earned society's respect, and now we discover that we didn't have nearly as much of it as we thought and that's a shock."[137]

And that may be the key to the scandal that shattered Stanford's integrity: that absolute conviction of being special, revered by all of society, incapable of doing wrong. Perhaps Paul Biddle was right when, after months of investigation, he concluded that "the general crux of the problem is that Stanford felt it had the right to taxpayer money, and [its claims] were associated with the nobility of purpose."[133]

Even after the investigation, after the congressional hearings, after the scalding blast of national publicity, most members of the Stanford intellectual community did not seem to comprehend what had happened. Robert Freelen, vice president for public affairs, asserted confidently that "this is an institution that has manifested very high integrity in all of its dealings, whether it's admissions or athletics or research, for a long period of time. I don't think one particular controversy is going to erode decades of having done business with high integrity."[134] A staff member, Stephanie Stockbridge, wrote that it was "about time somebody stood up and asked not, 'What has Stanford *taken* from the government?' but 'What has Stanford *given* to the government, the country, and the world?' . . . [Stanford] has changed our planet for the better . . . an institution which makes America a leader in research and development, in business and world politics. . . . There is no price too high for an enlightened mind and dreams fulfilled."[135] As late as mid-May 1991 most of the Stanford faculty seemed content with the leadership. A poll of the professors revealed that 71 percent of them seemed to feel comfortable with President Kennedy: 51 percent did not want him to resign, 20 percent had "no opinion" one way or the other. [136]

Finally, one Stanford professor stood up and publicly called for Kennedy's head. John Manley, a member of the political science department, charged that on Kennedy's "watch—abetted by the Stanford Board of Trustees—Stanford was corrupted." Manley pressed his point relentlessly: "Congress knows it. Columnists know it. Editorial boards know it. Stanford graduates know it. The attentive American public knows it. And people in other countries know it. The one who seems not to know it, who claims the scandal will fade away, is Kennedy."[137]

The pressures on Stanford mounted rapidly. The government's rate of reimbursement for research overhead expenses was cut dramatically. The result was that Stanford's budget was suddenly short a total of $95 million for the next two years, forcing serious cutbacks in its activities. The cost of outside lawyers (in addition to its own staff of twenty-five lawyers, perhaps the largest of any university in the U.S.) and outside accountants was running at about $600,000 a month. The Internal Revenue Service announced its own separate investigation of research universities to see whether or not they "have been claiming as deductions the same items that have been improperly included as indirect costs of research."[138] A pall settled over the Stanford community.

Suddenly, unexpectedly, on July 30, 1991, the president of Stanford announced that he would resign at the end of the *next* academic year—the fall of 1992. Later it was also announced that after Kennedy served as president for another year or so at full pay, he would revert to his old job as tenured professor and immediately take a year's sabbatical (academese for a year off with pay). At least for Stanford the end of the research overhead scandal was in sight.[139] On March 19, 1992, Gerhard Casper, the provost of the University of Chicago, was named the ninth president of Stanford University.

One footnote: Five weeks after Kennedy announced his resignation, another fraudulent charge was unearthed. The remains of Leland Stanford, the university's founder, and those of his wife and son lie entombed on the campus grounds in a stately granite mausoleum watched over by a massive sphinx sculpture. The annual upkeep of the tomb is about $1,300, and during the 1980s Stanford administrators charged it regularly to the taxpayers as one of their "research" expenses.[140]

Looking back at the scandal, at how it developed, and its sad ending, we can discern similarities to a Greek tragedy. As Sheldon Steinbach, general counsel for the American Council on Education, warned his colleagues just one month before Kennedy resigned the presidency of Stanford: "Colleges need to respond to a growing public perception about the 'hubris of higher education.' "[141]

The Greeks believed that each man had a fate (*moira*) "assigned to him and marked clearly by boundaries that should never be crossed," that he should bear the limits of his human condition "with style, pride, and dignity, gaining as much fame as he can within the boundaries of his *moira*." And, if he should be "induced by Folly to commit an excess (*hybris*) with regard to his *moira,* he will be punished without fail by the divine vengeance personified as Nemesis."[142] Perhaps someday we shall see a play written about how some of the gifted intellectuals of our time who crossed the boundaries of their *moira* were brought down by a nemesis named Biddle.

The third great financial corruption scandal that afflicts American colleges and universities in the 1990s is big-time college athletics. Under-the-table deals in the recruitment of student athletes is nothing new. Everyone knows how admission, eligibility, and graduation rules have been bent and twisted to accommodate student athletes. But for a long time it was pretty much nickel-and-dime corruption, done as much to boost the spirits of the school's alumni and students as it was to raise money. Like prostitution and gambling, it was always with us, but it was controlled, mostly out of sight.

As early as the 1920s student athletes were a cause of concern, giving rise to the fear that the integrity of higher education was being undermined. In 1929 the Carnegie Foundation for the Advancement of Teaching issued a report that charged our colleges and universities with recruiting athletes, paying them, and subverting academic standards. Some of the specific points made then would apply today. For example, the Carnegie report stated that: "(1) commercialization had caused abandonment of the game for the game's sake; (2) one-seventh of all athletes and from 25 to 50 percent of football players were subsidized; (3) many officials were guilty of evading regulations regarding recruiting; and (4) college heads evaded responsibility for commercialization."

At the time, few bothered to deny the charges. "For years," admitted William H. Nichols, acting chancellor of New York University in 1929, "some colleges, it is well known, have gone into the business of shopping around for athletes. It has been the dark spot on university sports."[143]

That dark spot has now grown into a black smear on the integrity of American higher education. The driving force behind this particular corruption is money. It is not only to satisfy the wishes of alumni and students that professional-level teams are recruited by our universities; it is to make money for the university. At a time when a five-year television contract between the College Football Association and Capital Cities/ABC Television is worth a cool $300 million, all other considerations, including academic standards, take a back seat—way back.[144]

In 1989 the trustees of the Knight Foundation, concerned that "abuses in athletics had reached proportions threatening the very integrity of higher education," created a commission to propose a reform agenda for intercollegiate athletics. The twenty-two-member commission included some of America's top university educators and college sports experts, among them Lamar Alexander, who went on to become secretary of education under President Bush. The chairman of the Knight Commission on Intercollegiate Athletics was the Rev. Theodore Hesburgh, president emeritus of the University of Notre Dame. When the commission finished its deliberations and submitted its reports in March 1991, the findings were clear.

The Knight Commission found "disturbing patterns of abuse," stating that on too many campuses "big-time revenue sports are out of control," and that "within the last decade, big-time athletics programs have taken on all of the trappings of a major entertainment enterprise."[145] The commission found that the problems of college athletics were so serious and systematic that they could "no longer be swept under the rug or kept under control by tinkering around the edges." The chairman felt strongly about the findings. "We wanted a report that would make a difference," Hesburgh said. "We would love to put the sleaziness of college sports to rest."[146]

Normally, our big universities and colleges would politely ignore such lectures, and focus their attention on nailing down a winning football and basketball team for the coming season. But not this time. A few weeks after the Knight Commission report hit the streets, the Federal Trade Commission subpoenaed the last ten years of financial records of 106 universities that play big-time football, attempting to prove that the sport has primarily "commercial, not educational, objectives." In a related move, the Internal Revenue Service "ruled that Ohio State University must pay taxes on the $1 million it receives each year from companies that advertise in its football stadium and basketball arena," a decision that, if upheld, "could have huge financial ramifications for the scores of institutions that have increasingly turned to corporate sponsorship to raise money."[147]

Hit from one side by a national commission and from the other by two federal agencies, perhaps now our universities will answer the key question posed by the Knight Commission: "If the university is not itself a model of ethical behavior, why should we expect such behavior from students or from the larger society?"[148]

The problem with college sports is not the hundreds of millions of dollars in revenues the colleges and universities receive from their sports programs. The problem is not the granting of special scholarships to student athletes. The problem is that many of the student athletes do not meet minimum academic standards. They have no business in the university.

The only reason these academically unqualified athletes are in our universities is that administrators and professors cheat. Administrators cheat when they enroll an athlete who doesn't have the intellectual capacity to complete and pass his courses. Professors cheat when they give a passing grade to a student athlete who has not earned it. And every time they cheat they compromise their own integrity, and the integrity of the university.

One of the few people who knew both the world of higher education and professional sports was A. Bartlett Giamatti, who left the presidency of Yale to assume the presidency of baseball's National League. He had no doubts as to who was responsible for the student-athlete corruption in America's universities. In his book *A Free and Ordered Space: The Real World of the University*, Giamatti wrote:

> I blame those responsible for running the offending colleges or universities that a number of institutions are the minor-league clubs for the NFL and the NBA; that there is a scandalous set of arrangements everyone knows about whereby young people are given money—regardless of whether they need it—to attend some school for the sole purpose of playing a sport for the commercial gain of the institution. The blame lies with the academic leadership, not with evil external forces.
>
> It is *their* students who are often segregated in separate but equal or better housing; who have often special academic tutors and programs of study; who may lose their scholarship or grant-in-aid if they are injured and therefore unable to play; who are expected to fulfill four years of eligibility (often taking five years in the practice called red-shirting) but not four years of course work; who are recruited specially; who are often admitted outside the normal admissions process. These students are not subjected to the same norms, expectations, and academic requirements as other students. They have perpetrated upon them—by the very educational institution that makes money off them, increases its fame because of them, and does not educate them or give them the space and time to educate themselves—a cruel hoax; they are called students, meant to receive an education, when whey are in reality mercenaries.[149]

One exception worth noting is that athletic corruption does not seem to have touched baseball. Ever heard of a college or university being criticized for its recruitment efforts concerning baseball players? No, it's largely football and basketball that cause the problems. The prime reason is that neither football nor basketball has the comprehensive farm team system that is the foundation of professional baseball. Consequently, a young man who dreams of playing professional football or basketball is faced with a stark fact when he graduates from high school: either get admitted to a college or university with a nationally prominent team or forget about playing pro ball. These young men have no choice but to play the university's game.

A university is not supposed to be a farm team for turning out professional football and basketball players, or any other kind of professional athletes. As Donna Shalala, chancellor of the University of Wisconsin at Madison, recently stated, "The tragedy is that we've become minor-league training camps for the pros, a place for young people to build up their strength and experience."[150] Not one college or university in America openly says that its purpose is to train athletes. Athletics is an extracurricular activity; teaching is the business of the university, which is concerned with the mind, not the body. In fact, some of America's top universities—M.I.T., for example—have managed to survive nicely without a football team.

The major corrupting impact of big-time university athletics has been on academic integrity. For example, Stanford University now grants academic credit to its football players *for playing football.* In response to the unrelenting pressure to squeeze unqualified young men through the doors of higher education, Stanford now allows up to twelve full units of academic credit—7 percent of the total units required for the undergraduate degree—for playing ball. Perhaps so as not to appear too blatant, the university has magnanimously extended this privilege to a number of other athletic activities in which many of its less talented students engage.

At Stanford a student can earn one unit of academic credit for the following courses of "study": golf (fundamentals of golf swing, use of various clubs, golf etiquette); tennis (fundamental strokes: forehand, backhand, service, and net play; rules and scoring); badminton (fundamental strokes and rules, introduction of round-the-head shot); horsemanship (walk, trot, and canter); posture clinic (individual posture evaluation, exercises for proper body alignment emphasizing flexibility and balance of muscle strength); self-defense (practical self-defense methods against single and multiple attackers); and wilderness skills (introduction to living and traveling in the wilderness; emphasis on interpersonal relations; camping, first aid, nutrition, baking, astronomy, group dynamics, tracking, environmental issues, and tree hugging).

At a higher level—varsity sports—a student can earn as many as two units of academic credit for playing basketball, golf, tennis, baseball, field hockey, soccer, volleyball, water polo, and, of course, football, or by participating in gymnastics, track and field, cross-country, fencing, wrestling, swimming, diving, sailing, and crew. If a student can play a musical instrument, he or she can earn one unit of academic credit by playing in the football marching band. Young women who make Stanford's cheerleading team, called "Dollies," earn one unit of academic credit for their exertions. [151]

Giving academic credit to students for athletic play is wrong. Football and backpacking and cheerleading are great extracurricular activities, lots of fun, fine to note in your résumé. But when a university, especially one with the academic reputation of Stanford, gives degree credit for play, it corrupts the essence of higher education. In the end it is mostly the students who lose, it is their degree that is cheapened and stripped of dignity. Of course, as in all matters of corruption, there are those who gain—the athletes who, but for the grace of no-brainer courses, could never receive a degree. But perhaps the biggest winners in this academic scam are the faculty. To the extent that students earn academic credit for athletics, the overall teaching responsibility in real courses is reduced. The more academic credit students receive for play, the less professors have to teach.

One striking example of the perversion of priorities that afflicts big-time athletics is the compensation paid to coaches, particularly football and basketball coaches. Usually a tightly guarded secret, these salaries are often among the highest in our colleges and universities.

In January 1992, when Stanford University was experiencing draconian budget cuts as a direct result of the research overhead scandal—eliminating faculty, raising tuition, shortening library hours, dropping a doctoral course in music, increasing the use of graduate students as teachers[152]—it was reported that they had just signed a new five-year contract with a football coach for $350,000 a year. [153] The Stanford administrators saw nothing wrong with their spending priorities. In fact, they were a bit indignant at the criticism that surfaced. Ted Leland, director of the athletic department, said it was a "great day for Stanford," that the football coach was "not being paid an extraordinarily high salary," and that salary figures being reported were "incorrect and simply speculation by uninformed people."

Leland did, however, refuse to divulge the "correct" salary, declaring loftily that "the financial arrangements must remain between Bill [the new coach] and ourselves."[154]

In the land of academic Oz, these bizarre priorities are, for the most part, calmly accepted. That same month it was also reported that the public employee in the state of California with the highest annual salary was not the governor ($120,000), not the president of the University of California ($243,500), but rather Terry Donahue, the UCLA football coach ($359,000).[155] Moreover, the football coach at the University of California at Berkeley, Stanford's archrival, had just left to take on the coaching duties at another taxpayer-supported school, Arizona State University, for a reported $600,000 a year.[156]

Obviously a winning football team is valued more highly than a few pesky doctoral students in music or long library hours. But at least the policy seems to work. During the 1991–1992 football season the Stanford offensive line *averaged* 6 foot 6 inches in height and 300 pounds in weight, causing a few people to marvel at how big some young scholars are these days. The new coach, Bill Walsh, is the legendary former coach of pro football's Super Bowl champion San Francisco Forty Niners. Stanford's football team is now an odds-on favorite to be nationally ranked and to play in post-season Bowl games for some time to come.

None of this means that we should banish college sports. The positive aspects of sports are many, and college sports are so beloved—especially by alumni—that any serious effort to ban them would inevitably fail.

Perhaps the answer is to resort to that last refuge of scoundrels— the truth. Truth One: almost everyone loves college sports, the excitement of the amateur games. Truth Two: many of the students playing in those games are not intellectually qualified to earn a college degree, and have had but a passing acquaintance with the classroom. What we need to do is legitimize them.

What if we just said that a student athlete is a student athlete, that he doesn't have to pass the same academic hurdles as regular students. If he wants to spend four years at a college or university just to play ball—well, fine. At the end of the four years he will have earned what we might call an "affiliate degree," a degree certifying that he was there, played ball, and took a course or two. At the same time, any student athlete could take the regular academic course of study, pass the qualifying examinations, and receive the normal academic degree.

The recruiting rules, the questions of eligibility and subsidization, and even paying student athletes are of minor consequence compared to the question of meeting academic standards. The violation of academic standards is what compromises the integrity of our institutions of higher learning. If we can fix that, we can probably live with the rest.

The academic community is fully aware that college sports are riddled with dishonesty and deceit. Some would say they are out of control, but the reality is that those who do control them know exactly what they are doing, and they do it for good reasons— primarily money and acclaim. In early 1991 a Louis Harris poll asked a large sample of college presidents, trustees, faculty, and coaches, congressmen, and the general public for their "views on the state of college sports and what should be done about it."

Almost everyone—except for college coaches—agreed with the statement "In too many universities with big-time athletics programs the academic mission has not been given proper priority over the athletics program." When asked if they agreed with the statement "Students who play intercollegiate sports should graduate in the same proportion as the rest of the student body, and their academic performance should be measured by the same criteria that are applied to other students," 96 percent of the college presidents said yes, 91 percent of the trustees said yes, 92 percent of the faculty said yes, and 93 percent of the general public said yes. Even 82 percent of the coaches and 59 percent of congressmen said yes.[157]

It's time to eradicate at least one stain on the intellectual integrity of America's colleges and universities. And if they can stop pretending and lying about their student athletes, perhaps it will give them the heart to restore integrity in other, more important areas as well.

These, then, are the four common kinds of corruption—professional, political, personal, and institutional—that afflict the university today. While each instance of corruption is serious in itself, a more global concern is the response of the university community, a response that often reflects a pervasive hubris, a deep conviction that the regular rules of society do not apply to academic intellectuals and the conduct of their universities.

Sometimes a story can capture the essence of a problem better than a recitation of facts and explanatory theories. I think the Allan Cox story is one of those. It tells us how, from the heights of hubris, one can tumble into the depths of depravity.

Allan Cox was a sixty-year-old Stanford professor. A world-renowned scientist, a former dean of the School of Earth Sciences, he had just been named acting associate provost and dean of all research activities at Stanford. Considered one of the best teachers on the campus, he had close relationships with his students, even living for a time in a student dormitory as a resident adviser. Cox was a tall, slender bachelor in splendid physical condition. He lived alone near the campus. In a densely wooded canyon high in the hills to the west of Stanford, he also owned a redwood log cabin, complete with a hot tub that was sometimes used as a social center by his students.[158]

On Tuesday, January 27, 1987, Cox apparently set out on one of his regular early morning bicycle rides. Soon he was whistling down a steep hill near the Stanford campus. Leaning forward in the cool morning air, the bike in the highest-speed 15th gear, he pushed hard on the pedals, his tight muscles straining as he raced down the smooth black surface faster and faster. Suddenly the road curved sharply, but he kept going straight—straight off the road, plowing about twenty feet through the moist dirt, through a barbed-wire fence, hurtling up over the handlebars head first into a big California redwood tree. Cox wore no helmet and his skull shattered against the rough bark. Hours later, at 1:35 P.M., he was found dead about a hundred feet from the tree.

When word of his death reached the campus there was intense, widespread grief. Professor George Thompson called Cox's death "an enormous loss to undergraduate students."[159] With great sorrow spreading across the campus, plans were made for the funeral. That was on Wednesday.

On Thursday, the scandal broke. His death was not an accident. Mike Dirickson, one of the detectives who investigated Cox's death, said, "I'm convinced it was a suicide, a staged accident."[160] Six weeks later Dirickson's judgment was confirmed by county coroner Paul Jensen after three of Cox's close friends came forward and told investigators that he had revealed his suicide plans to them the day before he killed himself.[161]

The learned professor had reason to kill himself. According to the local sheriff's department, they had just received a complaint from Bellingham, Washington, alleging that "Cox had molested a 19-year-old youth from the time he was 14." The boy whom Professor Cox had seduced was the son of a Stanford Ph.D. student whose work Cox was supervising.

Early in December 1986 the boy "told his parents that Cox had been molesting him for five years," and that "the acts occurred both in the Bay area and in Bellingham." One newspaper account described Cox as being especially close to the victim's parents and their "mentally disturbed" son.[162] Dirickson said that "the teenager's father called Cox and confronted him with the claim. Cox allegedly admitted the acts and offered to help pay for the boy's counseling." Then, three days before his death, Cox learned that "the parents and the youth had given Bellingham police signed statements accusing the professor of molestation,"[163] a felony offense.

The Stanford academic community was stunned. First, Professor Cox was guilty of a shameful abuse of authority. There were plenty of adult males around Stanford on whom Cox could have plied his attentions. There were even teenage male prostitutes available on the streets of San Francisco if he had been willing to pay to satisfy his special lust. But he chose to force his attentions on a child whose father, had he found out, would have faced a terrible dilemma—to choose between protecting his son and jeopardizing his own academic career.

Second, the person Cox seduced was underage. Pedophiles have a preference for sexual relations with children. They are almost always men, and although their behavior rarely involves a physical attack it usually involves "fondling the child or persuading the child to manipulate his genitals or engage in some degree of oral or anal sodomy."[164] They are usually fixated on children of a particular age and appearance, and as the child grows and matures he or she no longer appeals to the pedophile, who must then look for fresh conquests. Pedophiles frequently associate with others of like mind, exchanging information and sometimes swapping their young victims in the murky underworld they inhabit.

True, Allan Cox was never tried by a jury and proven guilty of the charges leveled against him. But his suicide seemed to be far more eloquent and convincing evidence of his guilt than the judgment of any jury could be. If the professor had had the courage to live, and if he had been convicted of these sensational charges, he most certainly would have gone to jail. But he killed himself.

I wondered how Cox's colleagues would react to the discovery that one of their best and brightest had been a moral monster. Would they wonder if there had been a pattern of such sexual abuse? Had Cox used his position to force his sexual attentions on other children, on his students? Was he alone in his depravity? I did not envy the administrators the unpleasant investigation that their duty demanded of them.

I was mistaken in my concern. The administrators and faculty of Stanford absorbed this tragedy in the blink of an eye, and quickly turned a terrible scandal into a celebration of Cox's character.

Ray Bacchetti, vice provost of Stanford and a close friend of Cox's, extolled him in a newspaper account. Speaking of a recent dinner to which Cox had invited a grieving widow, Bacchetti emphasized that "it was a lovely, warm evening full of affection. That's the kind of respect Allan had for people." Bacchetti also spoke sorrowfully of his last meeting with Cox the day before he died, when they made arrangements to attend a performance of the American Ballet Theater: "He loved the arts, and said he was looking forward to it." Bacchetti was almost wistful about the unfolding tragedy, saying, "I wish a novelist could have been with Allan these past weeks. The complexity of human nature wrapped up in all of this we will never have any way of knowing."[165]

There was not a single word of regret or sympathy reported for the boy or his parents, nor one word censuring Professor Cox. There was no word of an investigation of whether or not there were other instances of this kind of authority rape, whether the professor had indulged his proclivities while he lived with students in their dormitories, or when he invited them to share weekends with him at his cabin in the woods.

At four o'clock on Tuesday, February 3, 1987—just one week after Cox's suicide—a capacity crowd of one thousand jammed into Memorial Church on the Stanford campus and heard university leaders praise him.[166] The president of Stanford declared that Cox was "the very ideal of the teacher-scholar," lauded his "respect for people," and with great emotion mourned his loss, saying, "Those of us who knew him know his fineness, know his compassion and commitment to others, and know that a generous and sensitive regard permeated all his human relationships. We loved him; we trusted him; and we still do. Most of all, we wish he were here so we could show him."[167]

Albert Hastorf, former provost of Stanford and a professor of psychology, stood in the pulpit of that beautiful old church with its magnificent stained-glass windows and eulogized Allan Cox as a "decent and thoughtful man," with "an abiding warmth and sensitivity." The students of Stanford, he said, "have lost a mentor in every sense of the word."[168]

Not a word about the sickening charges, not a word about suicide, not a word about any investigation, not a hint of disapproval of the professor's conduct.

Then, not content with simply covering up the black deeds of their colleague, the faculty and administration went further and glorified him, making him a permanent hero of the Stanford academic community.

First, the Stanford faculty honored Cox. On April 2, 1987, the faculty senate, chaired by economist Kenneth J. Arrow, with forty-nine members present, passed by unanimous consent a formal memorial resolution. Anyone reading it would learn only that the professor died "in a bicycle accident near his home," that he was a "mentor to many students," and that he "holds a place of respect and admiration in our hearts and those of many of our alumni. . . . The essence of Allan Cox is a rare quality—the ability and determination to bring out the very best in others."[169]

Then the Stanford administration bestowed a final honor on Allan Cox, a rare accolade: the minting of a Stanford medal. On June 13, 1987—less than five months after Cox's suicide—Norman K. Wessels, dean of humanities and sciences, announced the establishment of the Allan V. Cox Medal. To be presented annually, it was inscribed with the words FOR FACULTY EXCELLENCE FOSTERING UNDERGRADUATE RESEARCH AT STANFORD UNIVERSITY. The first person to get the Cox Medal was the dean of undergraduate studies, Carolyn Lougee.[170]

It is a handsome medal, three inches in diameter, made of heavy bronze. In the center is a striking profile of Professor Cox with the words ALLAN V. COX MEDAL below.

The announcement of the medal in 1987 stressed that it "honors Cox's vision of the potential for faculty–student partnership."[171] A letter circulated to Stanford faculty on April 28, 1988, by Tom Wasow, the new dean of undergraduate studies, asking for nominations for the Cox Medal listed as one of the criteria for selection: "creative work with students."[172] In 1990 the official announcement from Dean Wasow calling for nominations stressed that Allan Cox was "a friend and leader of undergraduates . . . and a gentle and humane person who was a teacher to students, faculty and administrators."

Throughout this whole affair there was no protest. Not a peep from the trustees of Stanford, not a tweet from the faculty, not a

chirp from the alumni. Just an all-pervasive, condoning silence.

Oh, there was one exception. An outraged professor of radiology at Stanford's school of medicine penned a short protest to the editor of the university newspaper after a laudatory biographical article on Cox ran in October 1987. Professor Michael Goris wrote: "It is sad to find a panegyric to a child molester in the *Campus Report*. . . . The piece by Joel Shurkin wants us to admire a man who committed suicide to avoid the consequences of a grievous act, the molestation of a . . . child. We have had Gay Awareness Week, Safe Sex Week; should we now expect Child Molestation Week?"[173]

John Ruskin, the great nineteenth-century writer and critic, once wrote that "the essence of lying is in deception, not in words; a lie may be told by silence, by equivocation, by the accent on a syllable, by a glance of the eyes attaching a peculiar significance to a sentence; and all these kinds of lies are worse and baser by many degrees than a lie plainly worded."[174]

The very existence of the Cox Medal proclaims to the world that this was a good man who cared for his students. And that is a lie, a lie perpetrated by a community whose most fundamental and sacred rule should be truth. That is the importance of the Cox Medal at Stanford. It is an institutional lie, and its existence tells us a great deal about the nature of the academic intellectual community we must deal with in the 1990s.

The cost of preparing the die for the Cox Medal was estimated to be $1,800. I could not bring myself to call Stanford's accounting office to find out whether or not the cost of minting the medal had been charged to the U.S. taxpayers as a "research" expense.

When one reviews the corruption that pervades the American academic intellectual world in the 1990s—the corruption of teaching and research, the political corruption, the personal corruption, the institutional financial corruption—it is difficult not to believe in a destructive force at work, a fatal hubris. The one thread that seems to link all these corruptions is the intellectual arrogance of the players, their sense of being superior, their tendency to view others with disdain.

That thread is a shameless breaking of the ordinary rules of society, as if, somehow, the breakers of the rules were earthly gods, incapable of being called to account. The tragic hero of ancient Greek drama was a man "born with a flaw that prevents his attaining the happiness he wants, a flaw as real to the sensitive Greek as the flaw of original sin to the sensitive Christian"—the flaw of hubris. [175] Perhaps the Greeks were right, at least insofar as it concerns today's academic intellectuals.

CHAPTER SIX

CULPRITS
AND SOLUTIONS

THERE ARE PLENTY of people who can be blamed for the decline of the American university. But there is one group who, far more than any other, bears the chief responsibility for the current sorry state of affairs. This is the group of men and women who constitute the governing boards of our universities and colleges—the trustees, the overseers, the regents.

We could blame the professors. There is no question that academic intellectuals have, as a group, conducted themselves badly. The list of their transgressions is long and growing. Unfortunately, self-policing has failed miserably in the past, and there is no reason, given their personal hubris and their strong vested interest in the status quo, to expect professors to clean their own house. True, some are trying, such as those who recently founded the National Association of Scholars, but their numbers are still small and their influence even smaller.

We could blame the administrators, especially the presidents of the colleges and universities. But, in truth, they have little power to change fundamentally what must be changed. They have little real authority over professors, particularly the tenured ones, who in effect run their own little fiefdoms. There is little a president of a university can command; he must cajole and persuade. In most matters concerning teaching and research, the professorial dukes of academia treat the administrators with amused disdain, for they know better than anyone the near invulnerability of their tenured posts.

We could blame the students for allowing themselves to be treated with such callous contempt. But that would truly be blaming the chief victims of the intellectual decay in academe. For students have even less power to affect the behavior of their professors than university presidents.

We could blame our politicians for not taking decisive action, for not passing laws to correct the situation. We could, but we should strongly resist this temptation. The only thing guaranteed to make matters worse would be expanded government interference in the running of our colleges and universities. And, besides, even if elected officials knew what to do, which they do not, there is no way one can legislate integrity and intellectual distinction. There is nothing the schools are doing badly now—with the exception of illegal matters such as financial corruption—that government intervention would not aggravate.

Given the way our universities and colleges are organized, the unique autonomy they enjoy in our society, the hundreds of years of tradition and history that went into their making, and the powerful vested interests of the millions of people—alumni, students, administrators, and faculty—associated with them, there is no realistic way of imposing radical change from the outside.

We have no choice but to work from within.

Let us begin with the men and women who control the universities and colleges. We usually call them trustees, some we call regents or overseers. They are the ones who are responsible for the death of integrity in the world of higher education. We should not blame those who play by the rules laid down or condoned by the trustees of the universities. We should blame those who make the rules, for they are the ultimate governing bodies, they are the ones who bear the guilt and the shame.

These governing boards, not the presidents or the faculty, are primarily responsible for the scandals of recent decades. When Stanford was casting out of its curriculum some of the canons of Western civilization and cheating the taxpayer with phony research charges, it was James Gaither who was chairing the board of trustees, not president Donald Kennedy. When Harvard was violating the nation's antitrust laws by price-rigging of tuition fees and financial aid, it was Samuel Butler, not president Derek Bok, who was overseeing the overseers. When Dartmouth was infringing on the academic freedom of a student newspaper, the *Dartmouth Review,* it was George Monroe, not president James Freedman, who headed the trustees. When the University of California was substituting students for professors to teach its freshmen and sophomores, it was Roy Brophy, not president David Gardner, who chaired the board of regents.

The reason why we must blame the governing boards is three-fold: (1) they are the only people with both the responsibility and the authority to take decisive, effective action, (2) by the very nature of the autonomy of most universities and colleges they are the only people, barring some unlikely radical change in our entire system of higher education, who in the foreseeable future are going to have the power to do something, and (3) they have been derelict in their duties as trustees; it is they who have presided over the decline of the American university.

The trustees are the invisible men and women of American higher education. We may have heard of presidents Kennedy, Freedman, Gardner, and Bok—but who among us knows Messrs. Gaither, Monroe, Brophy, and Butler? Yet it is these men, and all their colleagues on the governing boards of our colleges and universities, who presided over the scandals and corruption of the late 1980s.

There are a lot of trustees. A survey conducted by the Association of Governing Boards of Universities and Colleges in 1985 estimated there were 48,000 trustees and regents governing some 3,200 institutions of higher education. Most of the trustees, 86 percent, governed private schools, while the remaining 14 percent were on boards governing public universities. The governing boards of private colleges and universities had an average of twenty-eight actively voting trustees, whereas the boards of public universities averaged nine trustees.[1]

The key to the power of the trustees is the organizational structure of our colleges and universities. The public universities are government entities, run with the same élan and dispatch as other government businesses, for example, the U.S. postal service. Approximately 75 percent of the trustees of public universities are "appointed by public officials, most often by the governor with the consent of at least one house of the legislature." The remainder are either elected by the citizens, attain their position by virtue of holding some other public office, or, in a very few cases, are selected by existing trustees.[2] The political spoils system gives trustees their position, much like appointed judges in the court system, and once appointed they are independent, immune from any controls, political or otherwise.

There is a thin thread of responsibility in the governing of our public colleges and universities, since most of the trustees are picked by a government official who is elected by the people. If the people become upset enough they can elect another governor, who might make better selections in future years. But even that slender thread is missing in much of higher education, our private colleges and universities. The typical private college or university surpasses even the government in inefficiency and unresponsiveness, being, in effect, responsible only to itself.

Home base for the academic intellectual is, in certain key aspects, about as close as you can get to socialism in this country, and many of the same problems that plague any socialist society afflict colleges and universities. As Milton Friedman observed, universities "are inefficient for the same reason that governmental enterprises are. They are not dependent on a market test, because they have sources of funds, like government grants and faithful alumni, that are not really affected by markets."[3]

First and foremost is the fundamental question of ownership and control: Who owns a private university? Who owns Harvard? Dartmouth? Stanford? In effect, nobody. There are no shareholders. There is no discipline that flows from ownership; there are no owners to answer to. At least when there is state ownership, there is public accountability, a bow to the political will of the people. But the assets of these often huge, multibillion-dollar "private" organizations are subject only to the control of a small group of trustees.

Who selects the rulers of these private institutions? In effect, they select themselves. The trustees of most private colleges and universities are self-perpetuating. New trustees are elected by old trustees in a sort of ultimate old-boy (and a few old girls these days) network. The trustees do not really answer to anyone. A few are elected by alumni, and some are appointed because of their position in the university. But the overwhelming majority are selected in much the same manner that fraternities select new members: they choose people who look and speak and think like themselves. Trustees might listen to the alumni and faculty, but when they exercise power we are likely to see a demonstration of group-think.

The result of this incestuous selection system is that the typical trustee is an old white male, a businessman who holds no advanced academic degree, a nonintellectual. Look at the demographics. Based on an exhaustive survey in 1985 of the governing boards of more than 1,000 colleges and universities we learned that: 80 percent of trustees were men; 90 percent were white; only 11 percent had earned a doctoral degree; and 70 percent were more than fifty years old. By occupation 42 percent of the trustees were business executives; another 10 percent were either lawyers or doctors. Only 3 percent were honest-to-goodness academic intellectuals—practicing members of college or university faculties—and another 3 percent were administrators in higher education.[4]

The composition of our boards of trustees is a recipe for disaster, a witch's brew of incompetence, timidity, and neglect. Because the trustees are remiss—guilty of a dereliction of responsibility on a grand scale—today's colleges and universities are a workers' paradise where the workers, the professors and the administrators, are in effect the management, deciding whom to hire and whom to promote, how much to increase salaries, and what is to be taught and how. The practical power of the faculty and administrators is theirs largely by default, the trustees having abdicated. Usually the trustees, and they alone, hire and fire the president. They have fiduciary responsibility. They have the authority to set policies that deal with teaching and with research and publication. But they rarely use that authority; they do not exercise leadership.

Trustees love being trustees. They love the prestige, strolling into the monthly board meetings, gossiping with their fellow trustees, basking in the glow of being a trustee. They just don't like to do what should be their main business. In 1984 the Association of Governing Boards of Universities and Colleges surveyed 549 college and university trustees on the extent of their involvement in crucial academic decisions. The percentage of the boards of trustees who did *not* have anything to do with decisions on important academic issues is revealing: 73 percent had nothing to do with the "initial appointment of faculty to tenure-track positions"; 99 percent had nothing to do with "evaluating the performance of individual faculty members"; 53 percent had nothing to do with "establishing faculty compensation policies"; 91 percent had nothing to do with "establishing faculty work loads"; and 89 percent had nothing to do with "establishing academic program requirements."

On the other hand, most boards (78 percent) did take responsibility for appointing the president and administrators, and for evaluating their performance (66 percent). Of course, another way to look at these statistics is to conclude that one in five boards did not appoint the president and administrators, and one in three did not even evaluate them.[5]

Given who the trustees are, this aloofness from the central academic concerns of the university is not surprising. Most of the trustees are unqualified for the positions they hold. Yes, they are by and large intelligent, talented people, often distinguished in their own fields of business or law or medicine. But that is not the business of the university; its business is teaching and scholarly research. And in these areas of intellectual endeavor most trustees are babes in the woods.

Compare them, for example, to the board of directors of any major corporation. No corporate board is dominated by men and women who are academic intellectuals. And for good reason. Professors don't know much about manufacturing automobiles or drilling for oil or building computers and thus could not, in good conscience, discharge their fiduciary responsibilities. Plus, the shareowners would not elect them. Having one or two token academic intellectuals on a corporate board could add diversity and strengthen the board, but no one would ever dream of letting them run the store.

If you examine the background of university trustees you will find very few who know the profession for which they have accepted fiduciary responsibility. They will know people with high political connections, they will know other board members, and quite often they will know how to give money to the university. Many of them, in effect, buy their seats on university boards, just as they're accustomed to acquiring other assets.

Moreover, trustees as a rule are not paid. The honor bestowed upon them by asking them to serve is considered to be more than just compensation, although it would be unthinkable to ask a man or woman to serve on the board of a multibillion-dollar company, to devote weeks or months of one's time to overseeing its affairs, to expose oneself to the liability of lawsuits, without reasonable monetary compensation. One result of not being paid is a lack of any feeling of obligation to work hard, or to explore new issues and ask tough questions.

Another factor that tends to keep trustees docile is their fear of losing the job. For many, being a trustee is the zenith of their ambitions, the height of community prestige. In board meetings they are loath to ask incisive questions that might prove embarrassing or, at the least, incur the displeasure of the other trustees who will one day vote on their reappointment. The typical trustee remains quiet and goes along to get along.

Finally, there is a tradition in America that holds that trustees should not meddle in the intellectual affairs of the university. Rather, they are looked upon condescendingly as so many golden geese, whose prime function is to raise money for the university. An official report of the Association of Governing Boards of Universities and Colleges minces no words in this regard: "Academic affairs are by definition the central concern of an educational institution. . . . For the last hundred years administrators and faculty have been left very largely in charge of internal academic matters, while trustees have concentrated on external questions such as buildings and grounds, fund raising, and public and governmental relations. As volunteer lay men and women who are not professional educators, they were warned, quite properly, not to meddle in courses of instruction."[6]

Rare is the trustee who would dare question the judgment of the faculty on matters of teaching or research, on details of course development or the criteria for the promotion of faculty, on whether or not a professor's publications were relevant or important. Generally speaking, trustees are terrified of the faculties they oversee. The faculties know this, delight in it, and largely ignore these wealthy, distinguished "overseers."

There are trustees who are exceptions to these gray, timid ranks. I have known a few of them over the years who have served on the governing boards of Dartmouth, Harvard, California, and Stanford. They are aware of much of what is wrong, but they are lonely voices and accept the futility and powerlessness of their position. Every now and then they may win a small point, but the tradition bound fraternity that is the typical university board pays them little attention. The timid derelicts far outnumber the men and women with vision and responsibility.

Perhaps the first fundamental change that should be made is to add more intellectuals to the governing boards, men and women who understand the business they agree to oversee. Think of the possibilities: Milton Friedman an overseer of Harvard, Jacques Barzun a trustee of Stanford, Allan Bloom a trustee of Dartmouth, Thomas Sowell a trustee of Yale, William Bennett a regent of the University of California. No timid, uncertain voices here.

There is one remaining problem, a big one. How do you persuade a small, powerful, entrenched group of men and women to act, and more important, to act wisely, even if against their own perceived self-interest? At first, the task may seem quite hopeless. But there are ways. The struggle with the governing boards is, in its broadest sense, a political problem, susceptible to pressures from interested members of society—especially those who are professional intellectuals or other hardy souls who have both a keen interest in the future of American education and the talents and resources to further that interest.

The men and women who today govern our universities are not fools. They are usually highly accomplished people who simply do not feel comfortable and confident where they are—sort of like fish out of water. Most of them, if pressed, have the ability to redress their untenable situation. They have, for example, the intelligence and wit to institute policies that would require courses to be taught and graded by professors, or to add more intellectuals to their board to enable them to evaluate the quality of faculty research. But they must be prodded into it, until they feel more uncomfortable not doing it than doing it.

So we shall have to spur on our trustees and overseers and regents by making them uncomfortable. For those of us who happen to know one or two personally, we can talk to them, ask them why they have not done certain things, why they have apparently condoned so much of what has occurred. But personal lobbying is generally of limited effect.

A far more effective way to move America's college and university trustees to action is to turn the hot beam of the public spotlight on them. Trustees need, and deserve, a merciless scrutiny. We need to ask who they are, what their qualifications are for the job, what actions they have taken or not taken, how they voted on issues that came before their governing boards. We need to make them as accountable to us as the most public of public figures. We need photographs of them and stories about them in the newspapers; we need to hear them on radio and see them on television. We need to know them well enough so we can write them and telephone them, and personally tell them how we feel about their performance. We need to praise them when they do well, and we need to punish them when they are negligent. They need a lot of tough, loving attention.

The single group in our society with the power to bring the university trustees out into the sunlight are the professional intellectuals in the press and the media. If they devoted some of their investigative energies to probing the workings of governing boards, it would be only a short time indeed before we saw some dramatic changes in the way our universities and colleges are governed. Of all the things I have learned and observed during my many years in the intellectual world, there are few I am more certain of than this: most trustees dread the prospect of public examination; they are usually not only highly successful but very private people, not at all comfortable dealing with inquisitive writers or reporters.

We could also try a few other things. We could begin to treat the job of trustee of a multibillion-dollar university as seriously as the job of director of a multibillion-dollar corporation. Among other things, that would mean overturning hundreds of years of tradition and paying trustees adequately for the work they are supposed to do, and then demanding that they earn their pay. Some will protest that trustees don't do it for the money, that they do it for the honor or to give public service, and that they are usually so wealthy that money doesn't make any difference. Maybe, but many of these same men and women serve on corporate boards and readily accept director's fees of $25,000, $35,000, $50,000 a year. They may not need the money, but they will take it. The reason corporations pay their directors is that it adds a note of seriousness and earnestness to their work on the board. So, let's try paying our university trustees fees comparable to what the directors of a comparably sized company would receive. It could be the best investment our colleges and universities ever made.

We may have to go further in some cases. If private pressure or the glare of intense publicity or fat fees fail to flush them out, we may have to resort to the ultimate weapon: lawsuits. Trustees are people who are not used to being bothered, and many will be particularly sensitive if their financial assets are threatened in any way. But the time may be nigh when the only way to get their undivided attention will be a lawsuit, when interested parties—be they alumni, faculty, or even students—sue university trustees for breach of their fiduciary responsibilities.

Finally, certain hardy souls could take a political plunge and attempt to gain a seat on a governing board of a university or college.

For even if there were only a handful of tough, new members on a board they could accomplish a great deal. Just asking the right questions, thoughtfully and persistently, could force many boards to begin to change their ways. But running for board membership is not for the faint of heart; it's probably easier to get elected to the U.S. Senate than to the governing board of an elite American university.

And there may be a shortcut to making university trustees more responsible. Trying to influence some 48,000 trustees directly is a Herculean job. Only a relatively small number of schools, however, occupy a leadership position of immense influence. What the elite schools do, the others are likely to follow.

So, let's begin with ten of the best colleges and universities in the United States. The argument over which ten are the best is a never-ending one, but it is possible to put together a list of ten that many people will agree on. The list of the top ten schools would include Harvard, Princeton, Stanford, Yale, M.I.T., California (Berkeley), Columbia, Dartmouth, Chicago, and Michigan.

These ten schools are at the heart of our intellectual life. They are the intellectual engine of America. They are our teachers. Where they lead most of us follow, knowingly or not. If we are to resurrect the integrity of academe, here is where we must begin. For if these ten schools were to fully reclaim their honor by wiping away the personal and institutional corruption that now stains them, it will not be long before the others will do so as well.

These ten schools at the top of America's higher education pyramid are controlled by 299 governing trustees. It's quite an interesting group, even more tightly packed with people who don't know the governance business than the average university or college governing board. Almost all of them are successful men and women, wealthy and powerful in their own fields. Eighty-two percent are men. Fully 68 percent are in business or finance or law; adding in those from government, they total 74 percent of the governing boards of our ten best schools. Only 5 percent are teaching faculty at the university or college level. Even adding together all those who would be considered "intellectuals"—journalists, authors, editors, fellows, academic administrators, and students—one still ends up with less than 17 percent of the members of those governing boards.

If we were to try to invent a governing structure for the preeminent institutions of our intellectual life, it is difficult to think of one more certain to guarantee irresponsible, incompetent leadership than the one we now have—not necessarily because of the organizational structure, but because of those whom we have allowed to hold positions in that structure. The typical trustee of our finest schools comes to the task with an extensive background in business, law, or government service and, thus lightly equipped, attempts to govern an institution predicated on scholarship and academic excellence—in his spare time. It is not working.

Looked at school by school, the percentage of the governing board composed of people from business, finance, law, and government is even more striking. From the lowest or "best" to the highest or "worst," they are: Harvard (59 percent), Stanford (65 percent), Yale (67 percent), California (68 percent), M.I.T. (72 percent), Princeton (73 percent), Dartmouth (75 percent), Chicago (90 percent), Columbia (95 percent), and Michigan (100 percent). Bona fide intellectuals who actually teach students are scarce on the governing boards. Most boards have one or two token professors, although Chicago, Columbia, and Michigan don't have any.

If one were asked to assign guilt for the sorry state of our universities and colleges, the list of those responsible would have to include these 299 men and women first. (See Appendix for a list of trustees of the ten universities and colleges.) If you wished to narrow the list to the "Ten Most Wanted," the heads of these ten governing boards would do nicely. In the 1990s the destiny of American education lies largely in the hands of these elite trustees. Perhaps it is time we all got to know them better.

Any thorough, extensive look at how the world of higher education works today is bound to be depressing. So much is wrong in so many places, and everything is so tightly controlled by men and women who don't believe anything is seriously amiss, that it is difficult to see a way out of this deep dark hole that is the American academy. Many intellectuals seem to share the view that was expressed by Allan Bloom in the closing words of his powerful 1987 book, *The Closing of the American Mind.*

Bloom warned Americans that "this is the American moment in history, the one for which we shall forever be judged. Just as in politics the responsibility for the fate of freedom in the world has devolved upon our regime, so the fate of philosophy in the world has devolved upon our universities, and the two are related as they have never been before." And then he ended on this pessimistic note: "The gravity of our given task is great, and it is very much in doubt how the future will judge our stewardship."[7]

There is no question about the importance of what is involved and the difficulty of resurrecting the integrity of the academic intellectual world. But there is no justification for the deep pessimism that seems to pervade the intellectual ranks today. Much that should be done can be done.

The agenda for reform is not long, the changes proposed are simple in concept, and all the changes are entirely within the existing authority of the governing boards of our universities and colleges. We know what is wrong, and we know what must be done to correct it. The crucial question is whether the only people with the power to do something about it—the governing boards of academe—will have the wit to see what is wrong, the wisdom to figure out what should be done, and the courage to do it.

To sum up, there are ten critical points that must be addressed if we are to restore the integrity of the academic intellectual world and make it a place of teaching and learning of which we can all be proud.

1. Prohibit student teaching

There is no other single change that could have as drastic and far-reaching effects as prohibiting teaching by students. In one thrust we would free tens of thousands of graduate students from the teaching duties that so prolong their quest for the Ph.D., thus accelerating the production of new professors and at the same time making it necessary for current professors to do what they were hired to do. The biggest winners of all would be the undergraduates who once again would be taught, graded, and counseled by mature, learned adults.

2. STOP REWARDING SPURIOUS RESEARCH AND WRITING

Only if and when our universities and colleges stop playing the glass bead game and begin to base academic promotions and salary increases solely on the quality of research and writing, instead of the quantity, will the mindless scramble for worthless publication cease. Most professors will breathe a deep sigh of relief, for they never cared much for the game in the first place. But the real winners will be the best and brightest of our scholars, who can concentrate on truly important research subjects and forget about how many pieces they publish in their careers. There will be losers—those academic intellectuals who have mastered the glass bead game and play it well—but perhaps society will be better off if they find something else to do with their time; some might even become better teachers.

3. CHANGE THE PH.D. DEGREE PROCESS

As long as we insist that university teachers have a Ph.D., and that one must prove one can research and write a lengthy document in order to earn one, we will discourage many qualified men and women from concentrating on what might be their best capability: teaching. By giving one variety of the Ph.D. solely for mastery of a field of study, we could greatly expand the ranks of top-flight university teachers. And we won't cut down one bit on the number of people who are truly capable of producing original, important research and writing. The big winners will be the learned, natural teachers whose talents do not lie in research and writing, and all the students who will have the pleasure of their company.

4. END FACULTY TENURE

Whatever tenuous justification existed for establishing tenure some fifty years ago is gone, and the corrupting influence of a guaranteed job for life far outweighs any arguments in support of the idea. Governing boards can easily establish policies that will protect against arbitrary dismissal for unpopular political or social views, or anything else that is deemed worth protecting, but which will allow dismissal for such things as incompetence or neglect. Perhaps professors who already have tenure will have to be "grandfathered" and allowed to keep their sinecure, but the future of American education belongs to those who are good enough to keep their jobs on the basis of performance.

5. REORGANIZE FACULTY TITLES AND RESPONSIBILITIES

We need to reconcile the organization of academe with what it is supposed to do. We need an organizational structure that we can all understand. Let us call university teachers "teachers," pay them the highest salaries, and grant them the respect and honor they will deserve if they do what their calling requires. For those who play an important role in the university solely through their research and writing efforts, similar to what the fellows do at our think tanks, let us call them "fellows," pay them according to the quality of their work, and grant them the respect and honor appropriate to what they do. Sure, some university teachers will produce important research and writing, and some fellows may even teach a bit, but at least it will be clear to all what their chief responsibilities are and we can then judge them accordingly.

6. RETURN TO THE FOUR-YEAR BACHELOR'S DEGREE

Most people are unaware we have left the four-year college degree behind us. To accept five years as the normal amount of time spent in earning a college degree is unconscionable. To countenance taking six years or even longer is outrageous. Clear policies should be adopted to strongly encourage (except in cases of illness, financial hardship, or other serious problems) all students to complete their studies for the degree in the allotted four years. To take longer is simply a waste of the students' time and the parents' (or the taxpayers') money.

7. TAKE SEXUAL HARASSMENT SERIOUSLY

It is unacceptable for any college teacher to have a sexual relationship with his or her students. The enormous difference in authority between the two parties lends itself to sexual extortion on the teacher's part, or in the reverse instance, sexual bribery. To condone sexual relationships of this nature is inherently corrupting to the relationship of trust and fairness that must exist between teacher and student. Governing boards should insist on clear policies prohibiting such practices and enforce them rigorously.

8. BAN POLITICAL DISCRIMINATION

We don't allow discrimination on the basis of race, sex, religion, or sexual orientation in our universities, but political discrimination runs rampant. Today it is the political left that discriminates, tomorrow it may be the political right. The governing boards of universities should adopt policies that strictly forbid political bias in either teaching or faculty hiring and promotion. Our universities should be places where all political views can be examined and discussed; there are more than enough forums outside the university for real political action, for voting, patronage, and policymaking.

9. STOP ATHLETIC CORRUPTION

This is probably both the simplest and the hardest of all the reforms. The practice of giving unearned academic credit to student athletes deeply corrodes the integrity of the university. Most of us love the excitement of college football and basketball, but the governing boards must stop pretending that all those splendid young men and women who play so well meet the academic requirements for the degree. It's just a question of being honest.

10. CRACK DOWN ON INSTITUTIONAL CORRUPTION

Perhaps more than anything else, a university or college teaches values by example. When students view the sweeping corruption on the part of the university administrators—cheating the taxpayers by fraudulently charging up research expenses and conspiring secretly to fix tuition and financial aid—they take the lesson seriously. Of all the things wrong with our universities and colleges today, the issue of institutional financial corruption is one issue that governing boards should have no hesitancy in dealing with. As part of their fiduciary responsibilities they should constantly audit the financial probity of their schools, insist on scrupulous operations, and summarily fire—and/or prosecute—those who violate these standards.

If we made only some of these ten changes it would go a long way toward restoring integrity in America's academic world. If we could make all of them, and soon, why then, we might live to see our colleges and universities become the temples of integrity and learning they should be.

It is time to clean academic house in America; it is time to drive the impostors from the temple.

Appendix

Governing Boards of
Ten Selected Colleges and Universities
—1992—

HARVARD UNIVERSITY
Cambridge, Massachusetts 02138
(617) 495-1534

CHAIRMAN

FRANKLIN D. RAINES [investment banker], Lazard Freres & Company

MEMBERS [28]

JOHN A. ARMSTRONG [business executive], Vice President, IBM Corporation

STEVEN BALLMER [business executive] Microsoft Corporation

CHRISTOPHER T. BAYLEY [business executive], President, Glacier Park Company

ANDREW F. BRIMMER [business executive], President, Brimmer & Company, Inc.

MICHAEL CRICHTON [author]

ELIZABETH H. DOLE [public official], Director, American Red Cross

DUDLEY FISHBURN [public official], M.P., House of Commons

ALBERT GORE, JR. [public official], United States Senator

211

HANNA H. GRAY [academic administrator], President, University of Chicago

DEBORAH TEPPER HAIMO [professor], Mathematics and Computer Science, University of Missouri

ARTHUR A. HARTMAN [consultant], Apco Associates

BERNADINE P. HEALY [scientist], National Institutes of Health

THEODORE M. HESBURGH [academic administrator] University of Notre Dame

RENEE LANDERS [professor], Boston College Law School

ARTHUR L. LIMAN [lawyer], Paul, Weiss, Rifkind, Wharton & Garrison

JOHN LITHGOW [actor]

PETER L. MALKIN [lawyer], Wein, Malkin & Bettex

THOMAS S. MURPHY [business executive], Capital Cities/ABC, Inc.

THOMAS L. P. O'DONNELL [lawyer], Ropes and Gray

GAY W. SEIDMAN [graduate student] University of California (Berkeley)

RICHARD A. SMITH [business executive], Chairman, General Cinema Corporation

DESMOND M. TUTU [archbishop], Capetown, South Africa

HENRY G. VAN DER EB [business executive], retired CEO, Container Corporation of America

CONSUELA M. WASHINGTON [public official], Counsel, Committee on Energy and Commerce

JEROME B. WIESNER [academic administrator], President emeritus, M.I.T.

PETER H. WOOD [professor], Department of History, Duke University

K. TIM YEE [foundation executive], Queen Emma Foundation

RYA WEICKERT ZOBEL [judge], Federal District (Massachusetts)

PRINCETON UNIVERSITY
Princeton, New Jersey 08544
(609) 258-5560

CHAIRMAN

JAMES A. HENDERSON [business executive], President, Cummins Engine Co., Inc.

MEMBERS [36]

NORMAN R. AUGUSTINE [business executive], Chairman, Martin Marietta Corp.

212

Jon E. Barfield [business executive], President, Bartech

Thomas A. Barron [investment banker], President, Evergreen Management

John C. Beck [lawyer], Beck, Mack & Oliver

John E. Bjorkholm [scientist], Physicist, AT&T Bell Laboratories

Philip C. Bobbitt [public official], Counselor, Department of State

Julian T. Buxton, Jr. [professor], Medical University of South Carolina

Ronald E. Cape [business executive], Chairman, Cetus Corporation

W. Hodding Carter III [journalist]

Sung Hoon Cho [investment banker], Financial analyst, Morgan Stanley & Co., Inc.

Elgin R. Clemons, Jr. [student], New York University Law School

John C. Danforth [public official], United States Senator (Missouri)

Richard B. Fisher [investment banker], President, Morgan Stanley Group, Inc.

William H. Frist [doctor], Director, Vanderbilt Transplant Center

Wilbur H. Gantz [business executive], President, Baxter International

William R. Hambrecht [investment banker], President, Hambrecht & Quist

Robert P. Hauptfuhrer [business executive], Chairman, Oryx Energy

Patricia L. Irvin [lawyer], Milbank, Tweed, Hadley & McCloy

Juanita T. James [business executive], Vice President, Book-of-the-Month Club

Virginia A. Kamsky [business executive], President, Kamsky Associates

Richard W. Kazmaier [business executive], President, Kazmaier Associates

John C. Kenefick [business executive], retired Chairman, Union Pacific Railroad

Thomas W. Langfitt [foundation executive], President, Glenmede Trust

Marsha H. Levy-Warren [doctor], Psychoanalyst

Jason McManus [business executive], Editor-in-Chief, Time Warner

Robert H. Rawson, Jr. [lawyer], Jones, Day, Reavis & Pogue

W. Taylor Reveley, III [lawyer], Hunton & Williams

Cecilia Rey [student], Kennedy School of Government, Harvard University

John W. Rogers, Jr. [business executive], President, Ariel Capital Management

Susan Craig Scott [doctor]

John H. Scully [business executive], SPO Partners and Co.

JOHN J. F. SHERRERD [business executive], Miller, Anderson & Sherrerd

CHANG-LIN TIEN [academic administrator], Chancellor, University of California (Berkeley)

DANIEL R. TOLL [business executive], Chairman, Corona Corporation

JOHN L. WEINBERG [investment banker], Chairman, Goldman Sachs & Co.

MICHEL N. ZHUPARRIS [business executive], Douglas Friedman Associates

YALE UNIVERSITY
New Haven, Connecticut 06520
(203) 432-2311

CHAIRMAN

BENNO C. SCHMIDT, JR. [academic administrator], President, Yale University

MEMBERS [17]

SID R. BASS [business executive], President, Sid R. Bass

DAVID L. BOREN [public official], United States Senator (Oklahoma)

DIANA BROOKS [business executive], President, Sotheby's

JOSE A. CABRANES [judge], United States District Court

WILLIAM H. DRAPER [public official], Administrator, UN Development Programme

RICHARD J. FRANKE [business executive], President, John Nuveen & Co.

JOSEPH H. GALL [fellow], Staff Researcher, Carnegie Institution

WILLIAM L. KISSICK [professor], School of Public Health, University of Pennsylvania

LINDA K. LORIMER [academic administrator], President, Randolph-Macon College

VERNON R. LOUCKS, JR. [business executive], President, Baxter International

ROBERT W. LYNN [foundation executive], Vice President, Lilly Endowment, Inc.

ELLEN ASH PETERS [judge], Chief Justice, Connecticut Supreme Court

FREDERICK P. ROSE [business executive], Chairman, Rose Associates

HENRY B. SCHACHT [business executive], Chairman, Cummins Engine Co., Inc.

KURT L. SCHMOKE [public official], Mayor of Baltimore

Calvin M. Trillin [author]

Lowell Weicker, Jr. [public official], Governor of Connecticut

STANFORD UNIVERSITY
Stanford, California 94305
(415) 723-2483

CHAIRMAN

James C. Gaither [lawyer], Cooley, Godward, Castro, Huddleson & Tatum

MEMBERS [30]

Robert M. Bass [business executive], President, Robert M. Bass Group

Leonard C. Beckum [academic administrator], Vice President, Duke University

Peter S. Bing [philanthropist]

John E. Bryson [business executive], Chairman, Southern California Edison

Malin Burnham [business executive], Chairman, John Burnham & Co.

Cynthia C. Cannady [lawyer], Fenwick, Davis & West

Warren Christopher [lawyer], O'Melveny & Myers

Roger A. Clay, Jr. [lawyer], Goldfarb & Lipman

Irving C. Deal [business executive], Owner, I.C. Deal Investments

James F. Dickason [business executive], Chairman, Newhall Land and Farming Co.

Herbert M. Dwight, Jr. [business executive], President, Optical Coating Labs, Inc.

Bernadine Chuck Fong [academic administrator], Vice President, Foothill College

John Freidenrich [business executive], Bay Partners

Ruth L. Halperin [civil leader]

David A. Hamburg [foundation executive], President, Carnegie Corporation

George H. Hume [business executive], President, Basic American Foods

Gerhard Casper [academic administrator], President, Stanford University

John M. Lillie [business executive], President, American President Companies, Ltd.

John B. McCoy [investment banker], Chairman, Banc One Corp.

DOYLE McMANUS [journalist], *Los Angeles Times*

LINDA RANDALL MEIER [civic leader]

HENRY J. MULLER, JR. [business executive], *Time* magazine

WOODROW A. MYERS, JR. [doctor], New York City Health Department

LUIS G. NOGALES [business executive], Nogales Partners

CHARLES J. OGLETREE [professor], Harvard Law School

DENISE M. O'LEARY [investment banker], Menlo Ventures

SUSAN W. PRAGER [academic administrator], Dean, School of Law, University of California (Los Angeles)

J. F. SANDY SMITH [lawyer], Morris, Manning & Martin

JAMES R. UKROPINA [business executive], CEO, Pacific Enterprises

J. FRED WEINTZ, JR. [investment banker], Goldman Sachs Group

MASSACHUSETTS INSTITUTE OF TECHNOLOGY
Cambridge, Massachusetts 02139
(617) 253-5614

CHAIRMAN

PAUL E. GRAY [academic administrator]

MEMBERS [70]

KAREN W. ARENSON [business executive], Editor, *The New York Times*

W. GERALD AUSTEN [professor], Harvard Medical School

SAMUEL W. BODMAN [business executive], Chairman, Cabot Corporation

DANIS A. BOVIN [investment banker], Bear, Stearns and Co., Inc.

WILLIAM R. BRODY [professor], The Johns Hopkins University School of Medicine

LOUIS W. CABOT [business executive], retired Chairman, Cabot Corporation

FRANK T. CARY [business executive], retired Chairman, IBM Corporation

JOHN K. CASTLE [business executive], Chairman, Castle Harlan, Inc.

COLBY H. CHANDLER [business executive], retired Chairman, Eastman Kodak Company

ROBERT A. CHARPIE [business executive], Chairman, Ampersand Ventures

PAUL M. COOK [business executive], Chairman, Raychem Corporation

ALEXANDER V. D'ARBELOFF [business executive], Chairman, Teradyne, Inc.

EDWARD E. DAVID, JR. [business executive], retired President, Exxon Research and Engineering Company

HERBERT H. DOW [business executive], Vice President, Dow Chemical Company

ALEXANDER W. DREYFOOS, JR. [business executive], Chairman, Photo Electronics Corporation

GEORGE P. GARDNER [business executive], Advisory director, Paine Webber Inc.

JOSEPH G. GAVIN, JR. [business executive], former President, Grumman Corporation

JEROME H. GROSSMAN [professor], Tufts University Medical School

MARGARET COLEMAN HAAS [business executive], Treasurer, International Center of West Lafayette

JOHN M. HENNESSY [business executive], President, CS First Boston, Inc.

ROBERT B. HORTON [business executive], Chairman, British Petroleum

WALTER J. HUMANN [business executive], Chairman, Hunt Consolidated, Inc.

SHIRLEY A. JACKSON [professor], Department of Physics, Rutgers University

HOWARD W. JOHNSON [academic administrator], former Chairman of the M.I.T. Corporation

GEORGE M. KELLER [business executive], retired Chairman, Chevron Corporation

BREENE M. KERR [business executive], Chairman, Brookside Investments

DAVID H. KOCH [business executive], Vice President, Koch Industries, Inc.

MICHAEL M. KOERNER [business executive], President, Canada Overseas Investments, Ltd.

NORMAN B. LEVENTHAL [business executive], Chairman, The Beacon Companies

JAMES A. LEVITAN [lawyer], Skadden, Arps, Slate, Meagher & Flom

PAUL J. LIACOS [judge], Chief Justice, Massachusetts Supreme Court

EDWARD H. LINDE [business executive], President, Boston Properties

BERNARD LOYD [consultant], McKinsey & Company

JENNIFER L. LUND [student], University of Michigan

ANGUS MACDONALD [business executive], President, Angus MacDonald & Company, Inc.

CLAUDINE B. MALONE [business executive], President, Financial & Management Consulting

CHRISTIAN J. MATTHEW [foundation executive], retired Executive Vice President, St. Mary's Foundation

PATRICK J. MCGOVERN [business executive], Chairman, International Data Group, Inc.

F. RICHARD MEYER, III [consultant]

H. DUBOSE MONTGOMERY [investment banker], Menlo Ventures

CARL M. MUELLER [banker], retired Vice Chairman, Bankers Trust Company

ROBERT A. MUH [investment banker]

RITA A. O'BRIEN [business executive], President, H.O. Sports

KENNETH H. OLSEN [business executive], President, Digital Equipment Corporation

DUWAYNE J. PETERSON, JR. [business executive], President, DuWayne Peterson Associates

FRANK PRESS [academic administrator], President, National Academy of Sciences

JOHN S. REED [banker], Chairman, Citicorp/Citibank

PETER M. SAINT GERMAIN [investment banker], Advisory Director, Morgan Stanley & Co., Inc.

DAVID S. SAXON [academic administrator], President Emeritus, University of California

RICHARD P. SIMMONS [business executive], Chairman, Allegheny Ludlum Corporation

CONSTANTINE B. SIMONIDES [academic administrator], Vice President and Secretary of the Corporation, M.I.T.

MEGAN J. SMITH [engineer], General Magic, Inc.

CHARLES H. SPAULDING [business executive], President, Spaulding Investment Co.

MITCHELL W. SPELLMAN [academic administrator], Dean Emeritus, Harvard Medical School

RAYMOND S. STATA [business executive], Chairman, Analog Devices, Inc.

GLENN P. STREHLE [academic administrator], Vice President and Treasurer, M.I.T.

MORRIS TANENBAUM [business executive], retired Vice Chairman, AT&T

REGINALD D. TUCKER [engineer], Hewlett Packard

CHARLES M. VEST [academic administrator], President, M.I.T.

EDWARD O. VETTER [business executive], President, Vetter & Associates, Inc.

EMILY V. WADE [scientist], Vice Chairman, Manomet Bird Observatory

MARY FRANCES WAGLEY [academician], retired

ROBIN M. WAGNER [student], Johns Hopkins School of Hygiene and Public Health

D. REID WEEDON, JR. [business executive], Senior Vice President, Arthur D. Little, Inc.

HARRIS WEINSTEIN [lawyer], Department of the Treasury

WILLIAM J. WEISZ [business executive], retired CEO, Motorola, Inc.

WILLIAM F. WELD [public official], Governor of Massachusetts

DOLORES WHARTON [foundation executive], President, The Fund for Corporate Initiatives, Inc.

T. A. WILSON [business executive], Chairman Emeritus, The Boeing Company

FRANK S. WYLE [business executive], Founder Chairman, Wyle Laboratories

UNIVERSITY OF CHICAGO
Chicago, Illinois 60637
(312) 702-8808

CHAIRMAN

BARRY F. SULLIVAN [banker], Chairman, First Chicago Corporation

MEMBERS [39]

JOHN H. BRYAN, JR. [business executive], CEO, Sarah Lee Corporation

LAWRENCE B. BUTTENWIESER [lawyer], Rosenman & Colin

WESTON R. CHRISTOPHERSON [banker], retired Chairman, The Northern Trust Company

THEODORE COOPER [business executive], Chairman, The Upjohn Company

JAMES S. CROWN [business executive], Partner, Henry Crown and Company

ROBERT J. DARNALL [business executive], President, Inland Steel Company

KATHARINE P. DARROW [business executive], Vice President, The New York Times Company

WILLIE D. DAVIS [business executive], President, All Pro Broadcasting Co.

ROBERT FEITLER [business executive], President, Weyco Group, Inc.

RICHARD J. FRANKE [business executive], Chairman, John Noveen and Company, Inc.

James J. Glasser [business executive], Chairman, GATX Corporation

Stanford Goldblatt [lawyer], Hopkins & Sutter

Hanna H. Gray [academic administrator], President, The University of Chicago

Jay Parker Hall III [business executive], President Lincoln Capital Management Company

Robert M. Halperin [business executive], Vice Chairman, Raychem Corporation

King Harris [business executive], President, Pittway Corporation

Edgar D. Jannotta [lawyer], William Blair & Company

Ann Dibble Jordan [volunteer]

Arthur L. Kelly [business executive], Partner, KEL Enterprises, Ltd.

Reatha Clark King [foundation executive], President, General Mills Foundation

Michael L. Klowden [lawyer], Mogan, Lewis & Bockius

Howard G. Krane [lawyer], Kirkland and Ellis

John D. Mabie [business executive], President, Mid-Continent Capital, Inc.

Robert H. Malott [business executive], Chairman, FMC Corporation

Charles Marshall [business executive], former Chairman, AT&T

Richard M. Morrow [business executive], retired Chairman, Amoco Corporation

Kenneth Nebanzahl [business executive], President, Kenneth Nebenzahl, Inc.

Joseph Neubauer [business executive], President, ARA Services, Inc.

John D. Nichols [business executive], Chairman, Illinois Tool Works, Inc.

John D. Ong [business executive], Chairman, BFGoodrich Company

George A. Ranney, Jr. [lawyer], Mayer, Brown & Platt

James T. Rhind [lawyer], Bell, Boyde & Lloyd

Sharon Percy Rockefeller [business executive], President, WETA

Steven G. Rothmeier [business executive], President, IAI Capital Group

Robert G. Schloerb [lawyer], Peterson, Ross, Schloerb and Seidel

Nancy A. Stevenson [volunteer], former Chairman, Illinois Humanities Council

Richard P. Strubel [business executive], President, Microdot, Inc.

Ormond J. Wade [business executive], Vice Chairman, Ameritech

B. Kenneth West [banker], Chairman, Harris Bankcorp, Inc.

UNIVERSITY OF CALIFORNIA
Berkeley, California 94720
(510) 987-9220

CHAIRMAN

MEREDITH J. KHACHIGIAN [volunteer]

MEMBERS [27]

GAIL ANDERSON [public official], Superintendent of Schools, Piedmont School Unified School Districts

WILLIAM T. BAGLEY [lawyer], Nossaman, Guthner, Knox & Elliott

CARLTON BOVELL [professor], Department of Biology, University of California (Riverside)

ROY T. BROPHY [business executive], President, Roy T. Brophy Associates, Inc.

WILLIE L. BROWN, JR. [public official], Speaker of the Assembly

W. ELLIOT BROWNLEE [professor], Department of History, University of California (Santa Barbara)

CLAIR W. BURGENER [public official], former U.S. Congressman

YVONNE BRATHWAITE BURKE [lawyer], Jones, Day, Reavis and Pogue

W. GLENN CAMPBELL [academic administrator], Counsellor and former Director, Hoover Institution, Stanford University

FRANK W. CLARK, JR. [lawyer], Parker, Milliken, Clark, O'Hara & Samuelian

DIANA DARNELL [student], University of California (San Francisco)

TIRSO DEL JUNCO [doctor], surgeon

DAVID P. GARDNER [academic administrator], President of the University of California

ALICE J. GONZALES [public official], retired Director, State Employment Development Department

JEREMIAH F. HALLISEY [lawyer], Hallisey & Johnson

BILL HONIG [public official], State Superintendent of Public Instruction

SYLVIA SUE JOHNSON [foundation executive], President, Mission Inn Foundation

LEO S. KOLLIGIAN [lawyer], The Kolligian Group, Ltd.

HOWARD H. LEACH [business executive], President, Cypress Farms, Inc.

LEO T. McCARTHY [public official], Lieutenant Governor of California

S. STEPHEN NAKASHIMA [lawyer], Nakashima & Boynton

221

RALPH OCHOA [lawyer], Ochoa & Sillas

YORI WADA, retired Executive Director of Buchanan YMCA

DEAN A. WATKINS [business executive], Chairman, Watkins-Johnson Company

HAROLD M. WILLIAMS [lawyer], President, J. Paul Getty Museum

PETE WILSON [public official], Governor of California

JACQUES S. Yeager [business executive], Yeager Construction Co.

DARTMOUTH COLLEGE
Hanover, New Hampshire 03755
(603) 646-2582

CHAIRMAN

IRA M. HEYMAN [professor], University of California (Berkeley)

MEMBERS [15]

LISLE C. CARTER, JR. [lawyer], United Way of America

ROBERT A. DANZIGER [business executive], President, Northland Investment Corporation

ROBERT R. DOUGLASS [banker], Vice Chairman, Chase Manhattan Corporation

JAMES O. FREEDMAN [academic administrator], President, Dartmouth College

JUDD GREGG [public official], Governor of New Hampshire

ANN FRITZ HACKETT [consultant], former Vice President, Strategic Planning Associates

WILLIAM H. KING, JR. [lawyer], McGuire, Woods, Battle & Boothe

BARRY L. MACLEAN [business executive], President, MacLean-Fogg Company

JOSEPH D. MATHEWSON [banker], President, Mid-America National Bank of Chicago

RICHARD M. PAGE [business executive], retired Chairman, Sedgwick James Ltd.

ROBERT B. REICH [lecturer], John F. Kennedy School of Government, Harvard University

E. JOHN ROSENWALD, JR. [business executive], Vice Chairman, Bear Stearns Companies, Inc.

RONALD B. SCHRAM [lawyer], Ropes & Gray

ANDREW C. SIGLER [business executive], Chairman, Champion International Corporation

KATE STITH-CABRANES [professor], Yale Law School

COLUMBIA UNIVERSITY
New York, New York 10027
(212) 854-5017

CHAIRMAN

G. G. MICHELSON [business executive], Vice President, R. H. Macy & Co., Inc.

MEMBERS [20]

EDWARD BOTWINICK [business executive], Chairman, VideoServer, Inc.

WALTER BURKE [business executive], President, Sherman Fairchild Foundation

VINCENT A. CARROZZA [business executive], Carrozza Investments and Properties

EDWARD N. COSTIKYAN [lawyer], Paul, Weiss, Rifkind, Wharton & Garrison

JOHN J. CURLEY [business executive], President, Gannett Co., Inc.

STEPHEN FRIEDMAN [investment banker], Goldman, Sachs & Co.

HENRY L. KING [lawyer], Davis Polk & Wardwell

ROBERT K. KRAFT [business executive], President, International Forest Products Corp.

MARYLIN B. LEVITT [professor], University Hospital

ANNA K. LONGOBARDO [engineer], Unisys Defense Systems, Inc.

MARGARET E. MAHONEY [business executive], President, The Commonwealth Fund

ARCHIBALD R. MURRAY [lawyer], Executive Director, The Legal Aid Society

WARREN H. PHILLIPS [business executive], Director, Dow Jones & Company, Inc.

LIONEL I. PINCUS [investment banker], Chairman, E. M. Warburg, Pincus & Co., Inc.

ARNOLD S. RELMAN [professor], Harvard Medical School

EDWIN ROBBINS [lawyer], Skadden, Arps, Slate, Meagher & Flom

MAURICE V. RUSSELL [business executive], President, Kenworthy-Swift Foundation

JERRY I. SPEYER [business executive], President, Tishman Speyer Properties, Inc.

DAVID J. STERN [business executive], Commissioner, National Basketball Association

JOHN E. ZUCCOTTI [business executive], President, Olympia & York Companies (USA)

UNIVERSITY OF MICHIGAN
Ann Arbor, Michigan 48109
(313) 936-2255

No chairman, all Regents have equal status

MEMBERS [8]

DEANE BAKER [business executive], President, Ann Arbor Group

PAUL W. BROWN [lawyer], Marco, Litzenburger, Smith, Brown and Wynn

SHIRLEY M. McFEE [public official], Mayor of Battle Creek, Michigan

NEAL D. NEILSEN [lawyer], Neilsen and Plunkett

PHILIP H. POWER [business executive], Chairman, Suburban Communications Corporations

VERONICA LATTA SMITH [business executive], Manager of Latta Insurance Agency, retired

NELLIE M. VARNER [business executive], President, Primco Foods

JAMES L. WATERS [lawyer], James L. Waters Law Firm

Acknowledgments

I have been thinking about the subject of this book and gathering material on it for over thirty years, ever since I entered the graduate school of M.I.T. and began to discover that intellectual life in the higher realms of academe was not quite what it was supposed to be. I've known many intellectuals in the intervening years. Many of them were wise and learned men and women of integrity. But some—too many of them—were impostors, and this book is largely directed at them.

I am indebted to all the intellectuals I have encountered, whether in person or through their writings. They have, in their own way, some a little, some a lot, contributed to this work. I am especially indebted to my colleagues at the Hoover Institution who, in my judgment, are models of what intellectuals should be; most of them are honest, brilliant, and intrepid with a great talent for communicating their thinking to others.

Special thanks and acknowledgment must go to Brenda McLean, my assistant for many years at the Hoover Institution. She transferred each draft chapter onto the computer, and then edited it. Beyond that, she conducted many library searches, tracking down hundreds of books and manuscripts, of which bits and pieces are now part of this work. She also supervised the work of a succession of research assistants—J. Scott Johnson, John Reimers, Anurag Chandra, and Kristin Ryan—who at various stages carried out specific research tasks for the book.

Marie Arana-Ward, senior editor and vice president of Simon & Schuster, was very helpful, as always, in shaping my manuscript into a coherent story through incisive questions and skillful editing. She gets credit for contributing the title of the book. I am also appreciative of the superb copyediting that was done by Eileen Caughlin and the advice of counsel Leslie Jones. Jack McKeown, the publisher of Simon & Schuster, and Victoria Meyer, vice president for publicity, both provided suggestions that sharpened and focused the manuscript. My agent, Robert Gottlieb of the William Morris Agency, provided excellent strategic advice and encouragement throughout the entire project.

Finally, I want to thank especially a number of men and women who read all or parts of the manuscript, particularly my wife, Annelise, who is also a fellow of the Hoover Institution and read all the drafts. Their comments and criticisms improved the manuscript, and their words of encouragement inspired me. They are: Arnold Beichman, Mikhail Bernstam, John H. Bunzel, Angelo Codevilla, John Cogan, Robert Conquest, Williamson Evers, David Gress, Robert Hessen, Kevin Hopkins, Melvyn Krauss, Everett Carll Ladd, Thomas Moore, Gil Shelton, Judy Shelton, Thomas Sowell, Joan Kennedy Taylor, Darrell Trent, Judith Trent, and Deborah Ventura.

Sources

ONE: TWO INTELLECTUAL CLASSES

1 Samuel Johnson, *Rasselas*, XLI, 1759.
2 *Book Industry Trends 1991*, prepared for the Book Industry Study Group, Inc., pp. 2–4.
3 Nielsen Media Research, Season-to-date averages, September 1990–February 24, 1991.
4 Ibid.
5 Keiko Nakao and Judith Treas, "Computing 1989 Occupational Prestige Scores," 1990 study done for the University of Chicago's National Opinion Research Center.
6 A. Bartlett Giamatti, *A Free and Ordered Space: The Real World of the University* (W. W. Norton, 1988), p. 190.
7 Bruce Wilshire, *The Moral Collapse of the University: Professionalism, Purity, and Alienation* (State University of New York Press, 1990), p. 34.
8 Carol Innerst, "Conservative Warns Colleges: 'Go West,' " *Washington Times,* April 5, 1991.
9 Robert Skidelsky, *John Maynard Keynes, vol. 1: Hopes Betrayed 1883–1920* (Viking, 1986), p. 382.

TWO: ACADEME

1 *Statistical Abstract of the United States,* U.S. Department of Commerce, 1990, Table No. 208, "School Expenditures, by Type of Control and Level of Instruction, 1960 to 1989," p. 129.
2 *Fact Book on Higher Education, 1989–90,* American Council on Education, Table 96, "Current Fund Revenue of Public Institutions of Higher Education, Selected Fiscal Years, 1966–1986," pp. 148–49.

3 Ibid., Table 97, "Current Fund Revenue of Independent Institutions of Higher Education, Selected Fiscal Years, 1966–1986," pp. 150–51.

4 U.S. Department of Education, *National Center for Education Statistics, Survey Report,* March 1990, Table 2.5, "Faculty in Higher Education Institutions, 1988," p. 13.

5 *Historical Statistics of the United States, Colonial Times to 1957,* U.S. Department of Commerce, Series H316–326, "Institutions of Higher Education— Number, Faculty, and Enrollment: 1870 to 1956," pp. 210–11.

6 Ibid., and *Statistical Abstract of the United States,* 1975, Table No. 225, "Institutions of Higher Education—Faculty and Enrollment: 1940 to 1974," p. 136.

7 *Fact Book on Higher Education, 1989–90,* Table 45, "Enrollment by Level of Study, Selected Years, 1899–1900–1997," p. 70.

8 William Carrell, "American College Professors: 1750–1800," *History of Education Quarterly* 8, (1968), pp. 289–305; cited in Martin J. Finkelstein, *The American Academic Profession* (Ohio State University Press, 1984), p. 9.

9 *Historical Statistics of the United States: Colonial Times to 1957,* Series H316–326, p. 211.

10 Estimates of faculty/adult population ratio compiled from ibid., pp. 210– 11, and Series A71–85, "Population, by Age, Sex, Race, and Nativity: 1790 to 1950," p. 10; *Statistical Abstract of the United States, 1990,* Table No. 13, "Total Population, by Age and Sex: 1960 to 1988," p. 13; *Fact Book on Higher Education, 1989–90,* Table 105, "Faculty and Enrollment, Selected Years, 1959–1997," p. 167, and Table 108, "Women, as a Percentage of Instructional Faculty, by Rank, Selected Years, 1972–1985," p. 171.

11 *Chronicle of Higher Education,* April 3, 1991, pp. A15–A18, and May 22, 1991, p. A14.

12 *Stanford University Campus Report,* April 17, 1991, p. 18.

13 *Business Week,* August 21, 1989, p. 90.

14 Cited in *Harvard Magazine,* May–June 1991, p. 91; William Trombley, "UC Officials Among Elite in Pay," *Los Angeles Times,* September 16, 1991, p. A3.

15 Courtney Leatherman, "Salaries of Chief Executives in Higher Education Found to Have Grown by 6% a Year Since 1988," *Chronicle of Higher Education,* July 3, 1991, p. A11.

16 *Chronicle of Higher Education,* July 10, 1991, p. A11.

THREE: CHILDREN TEACHING CHILDREN

1 Ernest L. Boyer, *Scholarship Reconsidered: Priorities of the Professoriate,* Special Report of the Carnegie Foundation for the Advancement of Teaching, 1990, pp. xi–xii.

2 *Stanford University Campus Report,* "Kennedy Shares Vision of Stanford

in 2010 with Community," April 11, 1990, p. 17; *Stanford Observer,* "Kennedy's Vision," April–May 1990, p. 19.

3 James David Barber, letter to the editor, *Washington Monthly,* January 1990, p. 2.

4 Thomas J. DeLoughry, "Education Secretary Calls on Colleges to Hold Down Costs," *Chronicle of Higher Education,* December 5, 1990, p. A1.

5 Michael Novak, "Jefferson's People," *Washington Times,* April 30, 1984, p. 4B.

6 Carol Cartwright, vice chancellor for academic affairs, University of California at Davis. Keynote Address, University of California Conference on "Teaching Assistants and the University," sponsored by the President's Advisory Committee on Undergraduate Education, April 13–14, 1989, University of California at Davis.

7 "Report of the Committee on Graduate Student Instructors," University of California at Berkeley, October 1984, p. 1.

8 Theodore Ziolkowski, "The Ph.D. Squid," *American Scholar* 29, 2 (Spring 1990), p. 179.

9 Nancy Van Note Chism, general editor, *Institutional Responsibilities and Responses in the Employment and Education of Teaching Assistants,* Ohio State University Center for Teaching Excellence, March 1987, pp. v–vi.

10 Ibid., p. iv.

11 Ibid., p. v.

12 Ibid.

13 Ibid., p. 4.

14 Kenneth Eble, "Defending the Indefensible," in ibid., p. 8.

15 Ibid., pp. 9, 12.

16 Jody D. Nyquist and Donald H. Wilff, "The Training of Graduate Teaching Assistants at the University of Washington," in ibid., p. 144.

17 Including the University of Arizona, University of California–Berkeley, University of California–Los Angeles, University of Iowa, University of Michigan, University of Illinois–Champaign, University of North Carolina–Chapel Hill, and the University of Oregon.

18 Ibid., p. 144.

19 Ibid., pp. 160, 174, 230, 238, 251.

20 *Chronicle of Higher Education,* November 20, 1991. p. A4.

21 G. Roger Sell and Nancy V. Chism, "Teaching Associates," *Notes on Teaching* 6 (Autumn 1989), p. 1.

22 Ibid., p. 2.

23 "1975–76 Report of the Committee on Evaluation of Teaching," *Stanford University Campus Report,* September 29, 1976, p. 9.

24 Charles J. Sykes, *ProfScam: Professors and the Demise of Higher Education* (Regnery Gateway, 1988), p. 42.

25 Ibid., p. 43.

26 Ibid., p. 69.

27 "Report of the Committee on Graduate Student Instructors," p. 8.

28 Scott Heller, "Teaching Assistants Get Increased Training: Problems Arise

in Foreign-Student Programs," *Chronicle of Higher Education,* October 29, 1986, pp. 9, 12.

29 General Assembly of Pennsylvania, Senate Bill No. 539, as amended, February 7, 1990.

30 Scott Heller, "7,000 Students Protest Michigan State U. Decision to Offer Required History Course Using Television," *Chronicle of Higher Education,* October 16, 1991, p. A47.

31 Nancy Staab, "A Cure for Nostalgia: The Ultimate Comp Exam," *Dartmouth Alumni Magazine,* September 1989, p. 31.

32 Richard Sabot and John Wakeman-Linn, "Grade Inflation and Course Choice," *Journal of Economic Perspectives* 5, 1 (Winter 1991), pp. 160–62.

33 Oscar F. Porter, *Undergraduate Completion and Persistence at Four-Year Colleges and Universities: Detailed Findings,* National Institute of Independent Colleges and Universities, 1990, pp. 5, 14–15, 33, 42–43.

34 April Lynch, "It's Taking Longer to Get a Degree," *San Francisco Chronicle,* September 12, 1990, p. 1.

35 Ibid.

36 *Newsweek,* "Decade of the Student: Universities Are Rediscovering the Virtues of Undergraduate Teaching," December 10, 1990, p. 72.

37 University of California Task Force Report, "Lower Division Education in the University of California," June 1986, p. 15.

38 *Stanford University Campus Report,* April 3, 1991, p. 16.

39 James S. Craig, "University-Level Policies for TAs: Experience at the University of Wisconsin–Madison," in *Institutional Responsibilities and Responses in the Employment and Education of Teaching Assistants,* readings from a National Conference, Ohio State University Center for Teaching Excellence, March 1987, p. 38.

40 Jacques Barzun, "We Need Leaders Who Can Make Our Institutions Companies of Scholars, Not Corporations with Employees and Customers," *Chronicle of Higher Education,* March 20, 1991, p. B2.

41 Cited from the Ph.D. degree granted by M.I.T.

42 "Doctorate Recipients from United States Universities: Summary Report 1988," Office of Scientific and Engineering Personnel, National Research Council (National Academy Press, 1989), p. 2.

43 Stephen Jay Gould, *Wonderful Life* (W. W. Norton, 1989), p. 139–40.

44 Ibid., p. 139.

45 Ibid., p. 140.

46 New Encyclopaedia Britannica, Macropaedia, 15th ed., vol. 2, pp. 93–94.

47 Ibid., vol. 1, p. 1018.

48 Ibid., Table K, "Summary Report on Doctorates 1988, p. 26.

49 "Courses and Degrees 1989–90," Stanford University Bulletin, pp. 369, 564.

50 Ibid., Table K, "Summary Report on Doctorates 1988," p. 26.

51 Ibid.

52 Pauline Maier, review of *The Great Challenge: The Myth of Laissez-faire*

in the Early Republic by Frank Bourgin, in *New York Times Book Review,* July 30, 1989, p. 11.

53 "Doctorate Recipients from United States Universities: Summary Report 1988," Table 1, "Median Years to Degree for Doctorate Recipients, 1968–1988," p. 23.

54 Ibid., Table J, p. 24.

55 U.S. Department of Education, Office of Educational Research and Improvement, National Center for Education Statistics, Survey Report, "Faculty in Higher Education Institutions, 1988," March 1990, computer diskette.

56 Ziolkowski, "The Ph.D. Squid," p. 187.

57 Ibid., p. 190.

58 Ibid., p. 187.

59 Ibid., p. 186.

60 William G. Bowen and Neil L. Rudenstine, *In Pursuit of the PhD* (Princeton University Press, 1992), pp. 105, 108.

61 Ibid., p. 2.

62 Andrew Hacker, review of *Preferential Policies* by Thomas Sowell, *New York Times Book Review,* July 1, 1990, p. 7.

63 Ziolkowski, "Ph.D. Squid," p. 182.

64 William James, "The Ph.D. Octopus," from a collection of his writings 1902–1910, Library of America series.

FOUR: THE GLASS BEAD GAME

1 William J. Broad, "Science Can't Keep Up with Flood of New Journals," *New York Times,* February 16, 1988, p. C1.

2 Donald Kennedy, "Reward Research Quality," speech, pp. 16–17.

3 Ibid., p. 17.

4 Maurice Allais, "My Life Philosophy," *American Economist* 33, 2 (Fall 1989), p. 13.

5 Wassily Leontief, "Academic Economics," *Science* 217 (July 9, 1982), p. 104.

6 Derek Bok, *Universities and the Future of America* (Duke University Press, 1990), p. 105.

7 Robert W. Clower, "The State of Economics: Hopeless But Not Serious?" in *The Spread of Economic Ideas,* edited by David C. Colander and A. W. Coats (Cambridge University Press, 1989), p. 27.

8 J. A. Kregel, ed., *Recollections of Eminent Economists,* vol. 2 (New York University Press, 1989), p. 160.

9 Martin Anderson, "The Effect of a Customs Union on Direct Investment," May 1960, submitted for course in international economics taught by Charles P. Kindleberger at M.I.T.

10 W. Lee Hansen, "The AEA Commission of Graduate Education in Economics: Educating and Training New Economics Ph.D.s—How Good a Job Are We Doing?" *American Economic Review,* May 1990, p. 445. Papers and Pro-

ceedings of the 102nd Annual Meeting of the American Economic Association.

11 Arjo Klamer and David Colander, *The Making of an Economist* (Westview Press, 1990), pp. 18, 53.

12 Ibid., p. 15.

13 Ibid., p. 17.

14 Ibid., pp. 82, 83, 92, 132.

15 Ibid., p. 18.

16 Ibid., p. 184.

17 *American Economic Review,* March 1979.

18 Ibid., June 1979.

19 Ibid., June 1980.

20 Ibid., March 1981.

21 Ibid., December 1981.

22 Ibid., June 1982.

23 Ibid., December 1982.

24 Ibid., March 1984.

25 Ibid., December 1985.

26 Ibid., March 1986.

27 Ibid., September 1986.

28 Ibid., December 1987.

29 Ibid., March 1988.

30 Ibid., December 1988.

31 Ibid., June 1989.

32 Robert Alter, *The Pleasures of Reading in an Ideological Age* (Simon and Schuster, 1989), p. 9.

33 Ibid., pp. 10, 11.

34 Ibid., p. 11.

35 Ibid., p. 17.

36 Lynne V. Cheney, letter to the editor, *Chronicle of Higher Education,* July 17, 1991, p. B2.

37 David P. Hamilton, "Trivia Pursuit: Too Much of America's Research Money Goes to Studies Nobody Wants to Read," *Washington Monthly,* March 1991, p. 38.

38 Quoted in ibid., p. 38.

39 Quoted in ibid., pp. 38–39.

40 Ibid., p. 36.

41 David P. Hamilton, "Research Papers: Who's Uncited Now?" *Science,* January 4, 1991, p. 25; letter to the editor of *Science* from David P. Pendlebury, Research Department, Institute for Scientific Information, February 9, 1991.

42 John A. Byrne, "Is Research in the Ivory Tower 'Fuzzy, Irrelevant, Pretentious'?" *Business Week,* October 29, 1990, p. 62.

43 Ibid.

44 Quoted in ibid., p. 63.

45 Jacobs, quoted in ibid., p. 63.

46 Page Smith, *Killing the Spirit* (Viking Penguin, 1990), p. 7.

47 Sar A. Levitan, letter to Professor Robert Moffitt, March 20, 1989.

48 Robert Moffitt, letter to Professor Sar A. Levitan, April 11, 1989.

49 Sar Levitan, letter to Professor Robert Moffitt, May 1, 1989.

50 Armstrong, quoted in Hamilton, "Trivia Pursuit," p. 40.

51 Broad, "Science Can't Keep Up with Flood of New Journals," p. C1.

52 *New Encyclopaedia Britannica, Micropaedia,* 15th ed. vol. 8, p. 323.

53 Hesse, pp. 32–33, 37.

54 *Social Sciences Citation Index,* "Guide & Lists of Source Publications," 1989, p. 61.

55 *Stanford University Campus Report,* February 7, 1990, p. 2.

56 Ibid.

57 Steve Dowrick and Duc-Tho Nguyen, "OECD Comparative Economic Growth 1950–85: Catch-Up and Convergence," *The American Economic Review,* December 1989, p. 1010.

58 James N. Brown, "Why Do Wages Increase with Tenure? On-the-Job Training and Life-Cycle Wage Growth Observed Within Firms," *American Economic Review,* December 1989, p. 971.

59 Yoram Neumann and Lily Neumann, "Research Indicators and Departmental Outcomes: A Comparison of Four Academic Fields," *International Social Science Review,* Spring 1988, pp. 94–97.

60 *Social Sciences Citation Index,* pp. 60–61.

61 Byrne, "Is Research in the Ivory Tower," p. 63.

62 Samuel Johnson, *Boswell's Life,* April 5, 1776, cited in H. L. Mencken, *A New Dictionary of Quotations,* p. 1338.

63 Susan Wolfe, "Rapid Information Key to Economic Life," *Stanford University Campus Report,* September 26, 1990. p. 10.

64 Ernest L. Boyer, *Scholarship Reconsidered: Priorities of the Professoriate* (Carnegie Foundation for the Advancement of Teaching, 1990), Appendices A, B, C.

65 "Scholar or Teacher: The Debate Flares Anew on College Campuses," *Wall Street Journal,* February 6, 1990, p. 1.

66 Elizabeth Weiss, "Research Hampers Teaching Emphasis," *Stanford Daily,* April 20, 1990, p. 1.

67 Kenneth A. Feldman, "Research Productivity and Scholarly Accomplishment of College Teachers as Related to Their Instructional Effectiveness: A Review and Exploration," *Research in Higher Education* 26, 3 (1978) pp. 227–98.

FIVE: HUBRIS

1 *New Encyclopaedia Britannica, Micropaedia,* 15th ed. vol. 5, p. 179.

2 Jeffrey Hart, " 'Poisoned Ivy' Doesn't Affect Everyone the Same Way," *Washington Times,* November 21, 1984, p. 3C.

3 Claudia H. Deutsch, "Academia Fails the Ethics Test," *New York Times,* November 3, 1991, Sec. 4A, Education Life, pp. 26–28.

4 Nicholas Lemann, "Snob Rule," *Washington Monthly,* May 1990, pp. 55–56.

5 Ibid., pp. 56–57.

6 *Stanford Observer,* "Be a Teacher!" June 1989, p. 16.

7 Harvey J. Kaye, "Colleges Must Prepare the Next Generation of Public Intellectuals," *Chronicle of Higher Education,* June 12, 1991, p. A40.

8 Cecilia Tom, "Freshmen Rate Themselves Highly," *Stanford Daily,* January 23, 1990, p. 2.

9 Joseph Edozien, "Farm Must Regain Ideals," *Stanford Daily,* January 14, 1986.

10 Lorne Needle, "Idealists Must Retain Convictions," *Stanford Daily,* February 6, 1986.

11 David L. Wheeler, "U.S. Has Barred Grants to Six Scientists in Past Two Years," *Chronicle of Higher Education,* July 3, 1991, p. A7.

12 Warren E. Leary, "On the Trail of Misconduct in Science Where U.S. Billions Can Be at Stake," *New York Times,* March 25, 1991, p. A10; Wheeler, "U.S. Has Barred Grants," p. 1.

13 Judith P. Swazey, Karen Seashore Louis, and Melissa S. Anderson, "University Policies and Ethical Issues in Research and Graduate Education: Highlights of the CGS Deans' Survey," *CGS Communicator* 13, 3 (March 1989), p. 2.

14 Press Announcement, "New Panel on Scientific Conduct Formed," National Academy of Sciences, January 1991.

15 Philip J. Hilts, "Panel Urges Standards to Curb Science Fraud," *New York Times,* March 28, 1991, p. A12.

16 Ibid.

17 Philip J. Hilts, "Nobelist Caught Up in Fraud Case Resigns as Head of Rockefeller U.," *New York Times,* December 3, 1991, p. A1.

18 Thomas Mallon, *Stolen Words: Forays into the Origins and Ravages of Plagiarism* (Ticknor & Fields, 1989).

19 Ibid., p. xii.

20 Lawrence K. Altman, "Harvard Professor's Downfall Prompts Physicians' Protests," *New York Times,* December 2, 1988, p. A1.

21 Ibid.

22 Mallon, *Stolen Words,* p. xi.

23 Richard Hofstadter, *Anti-intellectualism in American Life* (Alfred A. Knopf, 1963), p. 39.

24 Everett Carll Ladd, Jr., and Seymour Martin Lipset, *Survey of the Social, Political, and Educational Perspectives of American College and University Faculty,* vol. 2, Final Report, National Institute of Education Project No. 3-3053, pp. 282, 361–62.

25 Ibid., Table 2, "Democratic and Republican Support, Faculty by Discipline and Type of Institution," p. 287.

26 Christopher J. Bosso, "Congressional and Presidential Scholars: Some Basic Traits," *PS: Political Science and Politics,* December 1989, pp. 839–48.

27 Ibid.

28 Steve Millard, "CU Faculty's Liberal Tilt the Norm in Academia," *Boulder Daily Camera,* August 23, 1987, p. 1.

29 Patrick Taylor, "The Issue Is Fairness, Not Ideology, at CU," *Boulder Daily Camera,* August 28, 1987.

30 *Stanford University Campus Report,* "Faculty Political Preferences Surveyed," November 18, 1987.

31 *Stanford Daily,* "How Stanford Voted," November 8, 1984.

32 *Stanford Daily,* "Stanford Voter Breakdown," November 15, 1988.

33 "Politics of the Professoriate," *American Enterprise,* July/August 1991, pp. 86–87.

34 David Bryden, "It Ain't What They Teach, It's the Way That They Teach It," *Public Interest* 103 (Spring 1991), p. 52.

35 Theresa Johnston, "New Generation of Political Scientists Looks Toward the 1990s," *Stanford University Campus Report,* December 12, 1990, p. 7.

36 *Stanford University Campus Report,* "Faculty Political Preferences Surveyed."

37 *New York Times,* "A Reaffirmation of Principle," October 26, 1988, p. A5.

38 Millard, "CU Faculty's Liberal Tilt," p. 1.

39 John Taylor, "Are You Politically Correct?" *New York,* January 21, 1991, pp. 33–34.

40 Dinesh D'Souza, *Illiberal Education: The Politics of Race and Sex on Campus* (Free Press, 1991), p. 196.

41 Taylor, "Are You Politically Correct?" p. 34.

42 Ibid., p. 37.

43 *Wall Street Journal,* editorial, "The Stanford Mind," December 22, 1988.

44 Paul de Man, *Blindness and Insight: Essays in the Rhetoric of Contemporary Criticism* (Oxford University Press, 1971), p. 165.

45 Anne Matthews, "Deciphering Victorian Underwear and Other Seminars," *New York Times Magazine,* February 10, 1991, p. 57.

46 Stanley Fish, *Doing What Comes Naturally: Change, Rhetoric, and the Practice of Theory in Literary and Legal Studies* (Duke University Press, 1989), pp. 4, 164.

47 Suzanne Fields, "Stalked by the SSSP," *Washington Times,* November 15, 1990.

48 *Wall Street Journal,* editorial, "Politically Correct," November 26, 1990.

49 Ibid.

50 D'Souza, *Illiberal Education.*

51 Chester E. Finn, Jr., "The Campus: An Island of Repression in a Sea of Freedom," *Commentary,* September 1989, p. 23.

52 John L. Rosenfeld, AAUP California Conference Newsletter, Los Angeles, May 1988.

53 Jeff Gottlieb, "Hoover Fellows' Free Rein," *San Jose Mercury,* September 29, 1988, p. 1B.

54 "The Good Think-Tank Guide," *The Economist,* December 21, 1991–January 3, 1992, pp. 49–53.

55 John Leo, "The Academy's New Ayatollahs," *U.S. News & World Report,* December 10, 1990, p. 22.

56 *Human Events,* February 23, 1991, p. 18.

57 Matthews, "Deciphering Victorian Underwear," pp. 43, 58.

58 Jay Parini, "Academic Conservatives Who Decry 'Politicization' Show Staggering Naïveté About Their Own Biases," *Chronicle of Higher Education,* December 7, 1988, p. B1.

59 Taylor, "Are You Politically Correct?" p. 36.

60 Kenneth H. Bacon, "NEH Head Lynne Cheney Sheds Her Low Profile to Champion Educational Focus on 'Great Books,' " *Wall Street Journal,* November 14, 1990, p. A16.

61 *Stanford Daily,* June 5, 1985.

62 "Academic Freedom and Tenure: 1940 Statement of Principles and Interpretive Comments," *Academe,* May-June 1990, p. 37.

63 Denise K. Magner, "Gathering to Assess Battle Against 'Political Correctness,' Scholars Look for New Ways to Resist 'Illiberal Radicals,' " *Chronicle of Higher Education,* October 30, 1991, p. A17.

64 Folder describing the purpose of the National Association of Scholars.

65 Dorothy Rabinowitz, "*Vive* the Academic Resistance," *Wall Street Journal,* November 13, 1990.

66 Harvey C. Mansfield, Jr., "The State of Harvard," review of *The University* by Henry Rosovsky, *Public Interest,* Fall 1990, pp. 113–23.

67 Michele A. Paludi, ed., *Ivory Power: Sexual Harassment on Campus* (State University of New York Press, 1990), p. 5.

68 K. Wilson and L. Krauss, "Sexual Harassment in the University," *Journal of College Student Personnel* 24 (1983), pp. 219–24; cited in Paludi, *Ivory Power,* p. 3.

69 N. Bailey and M. Richards, "Tarnishing the Ivory Tower: Sexual Harassment in Graduate Training Programs in Psychology," paper presented to the American Psychological Association, Los Angeles 1985; cited in Paludi, *Ivory Power,* p. 3.

70 L. F. Fitzgerald, L. M. Weitzman, Y. Gold, and A. H. Ormerod, "Academic Harassment: Sex and Denial in Scholarly Garb," *Psychology of Women Quarterly* 12 (1988), pp. 329–340; cited in Paludi, *Ivory Power,* pp. 127–29.

71 Paludi, *Ivory Power,* pp. 129–30.

72 Ibid., p. 130.

73 *New York Times,* "Emory Is Reopening Inquiry into Charges of Sex Harassment," March 23, 1991, p. 8.

74 Sue Hutchison, "Stanford Accuses Doctor of Sexual Harassment," *San Jose Mercury News,* June 27, 1991, p. 1.

75 William McGowan, "School for Scandal," *Boston Magazine,* February 1991, pp. 60–61, 86–89.

76 Ibid., p. 89.

77 Ibid., p. 60.

78 Dorothy Rabinowitz, "Arms and the Man: A Sex Scandal Rocks Princeton," *New York,* July 17, 1989, pp. 30–36.

79 *Time,* November 14, 1983, p. 109; Kathleen O'Toole, "Karl Details

Successful Fight Against Sex Harassment," *Stanford University Campus Report,* October 30, 1991, p. 1.

80 Terry Karl, "Why Women Stick Around," *Boston Globe,* October 12, 1991, p. 23.

81 *Time,* November 14, 1983, p. 109.

82 Henry Rosovsky, *The University: An Owner's Manual* (W. W. Norton, 1990), p. 164.

83 Julian E. Barnes and Lan N. Nguyen, *Harvard Crimson,* October 24, 1991, p. 1.

84 O'Toole, "Karl Details Successful Fight."

85 Barnes and Nguyen, *Harvard Crimson.*

86 "Wide Sexual Harassment Found at Harvard," *New York Times,* October 28, 1983, p. A7.

87 Ibid.

88 Barnes and Nguyen, *Harvard Crimson.*

89 Rosovsky, *The University,* pp. 292–93.

90 Barnes and Nguyen, *Harvard Crimson.*

91 "Due Process in Sexual Harassment Complaints," statement approved by the American Association of University Professors, Committee A on Academic Freedom and Tenure, *Academe,* September–October 1991, p. 47.

92 Anthony DePalma, "Amid Inquiry, Ivy League to Stop Sharing Aid Data," *New York Times,* May 23, 1991, p. 1.

93 Jerry Seper, "Eight in Ivy League Settle Price-Fixing Case," *Washington Times,* May 23, 1991, p. A4.

94 Paul E. Gray, "Measure Need, Not Money," *New York Times,* July 22, 1991, p. A11.

95 Seper, "Eight in Ivy League."

96 Amy Rosenfeld, "Feds Investigating Stanford," *Stanford Daily,* September 25, 1989, p. 1.

97 *Fact Book on Higher Education, 1989–90,* American Council on Education, Table 95, p. 147.

98 Jeff Gottlieb, "Overcharge Estimate Climbs," *San Jose Mercury News,* November 15, 1991, p. B1.

99 Joel Shurkin, "Sailboat Costs Charged in Error to Government," *Stanford University Campus Report,* December 5, 1990, p. 1; John Wagner, "In Troubled Waters," *Stanford Daily,* December 5, 1990, pp. 1, 20.

100 Shurkin, "Sailboat Costs Charged"; Wagner, "In Troubled Waters."

101 Shurkin, "Sailboat Costs Charged."

102 Tracie Reynolds, "Stanford Research Out of the Ordinary," *Peninsula Times Tribune,* March 13, 1991, p. 1.

103 Ibid.

104 Jeff Gottlieb, "Congressional Probers Grill Stanford Leaders," *San Jose Mercury News,* March 14, 1991, p. 1A.

105 Ibid.

106 John Wagner, "House Subcommittee Lambastes Stanford," *Stanford Daily,* March 14, 1991, p. 19.

107 John Wagner, "University Cuts Bill for Indirect Costs," *Stanford Daily,* January 24, 1991, p. 1.

108 Donald Kennedy, remarks delivered at the April 3, 1991, meeting of the faculty senate, *Stanford University Campus Report,* April 10, 1991, p. 15.

109 Philip J. Hilts, "U.S. Warns 250 Campuses of Audit on Overhead Costs Linked to Grants," *New York Times,* May 10, 1991, p. A10.

110 Jeff Gottlieb, "Congress Reports More Universities Overcharged U.S.," *San Jose Mercury News,* May 9, 1991, p. 2A.

111 Hilts, "U.S. Warns 250 Campuses," p. A10.

112 Ibid.; "More Universities in Trouble: 12 Prestigious Schools Accused of Overcharging Government," *San Francisco Chronicle,* May 10, 1991, p. A3.

113 "Michigan University Billing Questioned," *San Francisco Chronicle,* September 11, 1991, p. A3; Colleen Cordes, "Draft Report Cites More Questionable Billing for Research Overhead," *Chronicle of Higher Education,* September 18, 1991, p. A33.

114 Colleen Cordes, "Allegations of University Abuses of Overhead System Continue as House Panel Releases a New List of Embarrassing Items," *San Francisco Chronicle,* May 10, 1991, p. 20; Martha Graham and Tracie Reynolds, "Stanford to Repay Government," *Peninsula Times Tribune,* May 9, 1991, p. A1.

115 Jack Anderson and Dale Van Atta, "U. of Pennsylvania Tagged by U.S. Probe," *Washington Post,* September 16, 1991, p. B15.

116 "Harvard Withdraws $500,000 of Overhead," *Stanford University Campus Report,* April 10, 1991, p. 4.

117 Jeff Gottlieb, "Congress Reports More Universities Overcharged U.S.," *San Jose Mercury News,* May 9, 1991, p. A27; *Chronicle of Higher Education,* April 24, 1991, p. A27, May 1, 1991, p. A20, and May 15, 1991, p. A20; *Stanford Daily,* April 23, 1991, p. 10.

118 Hugo Restall, "Dartmouth Accused of Abusing Grants," *Dartmouth Review,* May 15, 1991, p. 7.

119 Diane Curtis, "Stanford Centennial Year Marred by Allegations," *San Francisco Chronicle,* December 24, 1990, p. A7.

120 Andrew Pollack, "Under Audit, Stanford Will Repay U.S.," *New York Times,* January 24, 1991, p. A12.

121 "University Re-examines Indirect Cost Practices, May Cut Some Categories," *Stanford University Campus Report,* January 16, 1991, p. 1.

122 John Wagner, "The Man Behind the Controversy," *Stanford Daily,* November 28, 1990, p. 6.

123 J. Martin Brown, "Absurd Statements Suggest Other Agenda," *Stanford University Campus Report,* February 27, 1991, p. 6.

124 Joel Shurkin, "Massy to Resign, Study Cost Containment Ideas for Higher Education," *Stanford University Campus Report,* November 28, 1990, p. 1.

125 "Stanford Bills Justified, Trustees Say," *San Francisco Chronicle,* March 9, 1991, p. A5.

126 Tracie Reynolds, "Stanford Worries Increase," *Peninsula Times Tribune,* March 15, 1991, p. A5.

127 Christopher H. Schmitt and Jeff Gottlieb, "How Stanford Turned Grant Expenses into Big Money and Big Controversy," *San Jose Mercury News,* March 10, 1991.

128 "The Cracks in Stanford's Ivory Tower," *Business Week,* March 1, 1991, p. 65.

129 William E. Spicer, "Administrators Lacking Integrity in Cost Fight," *Stanford University Campus Report,* January 30, 1991, p. 10.

130 Opening statement of the Hon. John D. Dingell, chairman, Subcommittee on Oversight and Investigations, March 13, 1991; Wagner, "House Subcommittee Lambastes Stanford," p. 53.

131 Thomas Toch, "The Pitfalls of Big Science," *U.S. News & World Report,* March 4, 1991, p. 53.

132 Anthony DePalma, "Stanford President at Brunt of Storm," *New York Times,* May 10, 1991, p. A10.

133 David Dietz, "Auditor Who's Shaking Up Stanford," *San Francisco Chronicle,* February 13, 1991, p. 1.

134 Valerie Richardson, "A School for Scandal," *Washington Times,* March 20, 1991, p. E1.

135 Stephanie Stockbridge, "What Stanford Gives Outweighs Money Taken," *Stanford University Campus Report,* March 20, 1991, p. 8.

136 Mike Laris, "Faculty Poll," *Stanford Daily,* May 11, 1991, p. 1.

137 John F. Manley, "Image Under Kennedy Is Venal, Asserts Manley," *Stanford University Campus Report,* April 24, 1991, p. 10.

138 Scott Jaschik, "IRS Investigation," *Chronicle of Higher Education,* May 22, 1991, p. A24.

139 David Bianco, "Kennedy Focuses on Public Service," *Stanford Daily,* September 23, 1991, p. 1.

140 Jeff Gottlieb, "Mausoleum Mistake: Stanford Charged Tomb's Upkeep to Feds," *San Jose Mercury News,* September 5, 1991, p. B1.

141 Jaschik, "IRS Investigation."

142 *New Encyclopaedia Britannica, Macropaedia,* 15th ed., vol. 6, p. 909.

143 *Brooklyn Daily Eagle,* "Carnegie Charge of Paid Athletes Rouses Colleges," October 24, 1929, p. 1.

144 Douglas Lederman, "U.S. Subpoenas Data from 106 Universities in Big-Time Football," *Chronicle of Higher Education,* May 15, 1991, p. 1.

145 Report of the Knight Foundation Commission on Intercollegiate Athletics, March 1991, pp. 3–5.

146 Douglas Lederman, "Knight Commission Tells Presidents to Use Their Power to Reform the 'Fundamental Premises' of College Sports," *Chronicle of Higher Education,* March 27, 1991, p. 1.

147 Lederman, "U.S. Subpoenas Data."

148 Report of the Knight Foundation on Intercollegiate Athletics, p. 6.

149 A. Bartlett Giamatti, *A Free and Ordered Space: The Real World of the University* (W. W. Norton 1988), pp. 185–86.

150 Bonnie Angelo, "Big Campus, Big Issues," *Time,* April 23, 1990.

151 "Courses and Degrees 1989–90," *Stanford University Bulletin*, September 1989, pp. 9, 283, 288–91, 525.

152 Larry Gordon, "Stanford Plans to Raise Tuition, Cut Faculty and Classes," *Los Angeles Times*, January 30, 1992, p. A3; Steven McCarroll and Howard Libit, "Faculty Plan to Make Grads Teach," *Stanford Daily*, January 10, 1992, p. 1.

153 Tony Cooper, "Stanford Offers Walsh Its Head Coaching Job," *San Francisco Chronicle*, January 15, 1992, p. C1.

154 Ted Leland, "Bill Walsh's Return to Coaching Provides Great Boost to the University," letter to the editor, *Stanford Daily*, January 22, 1992, p. 4.

155 Louis Freedberg, "UCLA Coach Tops Public Payroll," *San Francisco Chronicle*, January 15, 1992, p. 1.

156 Mark Gonzales, "Snyder Leaves Cal to Coach ASU," *San Jose Mercury News*, January 5, 1992, p. D1.

157 Douglas Lederman, "Big Sports Programs Are Out of Control, Most Say in Survey," *Chronicle of Higher Education*, March 13, 1991, p. A35.

158 Joel Shurkin, "Allen Cox: A Life of Scientific Triumph Ends in Tragedy," *Stanford University Campus Report*, October 21, 1987, p. 9.

159 Bob Beyers, "Dean Cox Dies in Bicycle Accident," *Campus Report*, January 28, 1978, p. 1.

160 Mary Madison, "Suicide Suspected in Cox's Death," *Peninsula Times Tribune*, January 29, 1987, p. A-3.

161 *Stanford University Campus Report*, March 19, 1987.

162 Lisa Lapin, "Was Death a Suicide Born of a Sex Probe?" *San Jose Mercury News*, January 30, 1987, p. 1.

163 Madison, "Suicide Suspected in Cox's Death."

164 *New Encyclopaedia Britannica, Micropaedia*, 15th ed. vol. 7, p. 830, and vol. 16, p. 606.

165 Lapin, "Was Death a Suicide Born of a Sex Probe?"

166 *Stanford University Campus Report*, "Colleagues Honor Cox at Service; Probe Continues," February 4, 1987.

167 Ibid.

168 Lori Silver, "Memorial Service Honors Cox," *Stanford Daily*, February 4, 1987; *Stanford University Campus Report*, February 4, 1987.

169 "Memorial Resolution, Allan V. Cox 1926–1987," *Stanford University Campus Report*, April 8, 1987.

170 "Carolyn Lougee Named First Recipient of Allan V. Cox Medal," *Stanford University Campus Report*, June 17, 1987.

171 Ibid.

172 Letter from Tom Wasow to all Stanford faculty in humanities and sciences, engineering, and earth sciences, April 18, 1988.

173 *Stanford University Campus Report*, letter to the editor, November 4, 1987.

174 John Ruskin, *Modern Painters*, IX, 1872.

175 Crane Brinton, *A History of Western Morals* (Paragon House, 1990), p. 100.

SIX: Culprits and Solutions

1 *Composition of Governing Boards, 1985: A Survey of College and University Boards,* prepared by the Association of Governing Boards of Universities and Colleges in cooperation with the Higher Education Panel of the American Council on Education, 1986, p. 3.

2 Ibid., p. 15.

3 Leslie Spencer, "The Perils of Socialized Higher Education," *Forbes,* May 27, 1991, p. 303.

4 *Composition of Governing Boards,* pp. 20–24.

5 Richard P. Chait, Trustee Responsibility for Academic Affairs (Association of Governing Boards of Universities and Colleges, 1984), pp. 112–14.

6 Ibid., pp. vi, vii.

7 Allan Bloom, *The Closing of the American Mind* (Simon and Schuster, 1987), p. 382.

Index

academic freedom:
  assaults on, 151–52
  Committee on Academic Freedom, 151–52
  "1940 Statement of Principles on Academic Freedom and Tenure," 155–56
academic intellectuals:
  attributes of, 33–34, 35–36
  diminished quality of, 35–38
  elitism of, 124–29, 176–77
  ethical behavior and, 15
  gender of, 35
  integrity lost by, 123, 129–32
  journal reading neglected by, 80–81, 82–83
  numbers of, 18, 29, 32–33, 34–36, 119
  peer review employed for, 14–15, 30, 81–82, 120
  political views held by, 132, 137–46, 154–55
  prestige of, 16, 23, 37, 125, 131
  professional intellectuals vs., 11–26, 30
  public awareness of, 29–30
  quasi-socialist environment of, 14–15, 39

  scholarly temperament required by, 33–34
  sexual harassment by, 132, 157–67, 209
  as trustees, 198, 201, 204–5
  working conditions of, 39–40
  see also professors
academic journals:
  books vs., 106
  circulation figures for, 114–15
  impenetrable language used in, 79–80, 83, 87–90
  low readership of, 30, 80–81, 82–83
  number of, 82
  peer review process for, 81–82, 120
  publication schedule for, 115
  submission fees charged by, 114
  see also scholarship
Acadia Institute, 134
Acton, Lord, 72
administrators:
  institutional corruption and, 132, 167–87, 209–10
  limited authority of, 194–95
  salaries of, 42–44
  sexual harassment cases handled by, 161–66
  as trustees, 198

242

About the Author

MARTIN ANDERSON has had a distinguished career as both an academic and a professional intellectual. With undergraduate and master degrees from Dartmouth and a Ph.D. from M.I.T., he has been a professor at Columbia University's Graduate School of Business and is now a Senior Fellow at the Hoover Institution, Stanford University. While on leave from the academic world, Dr. Anderson directed the policy research efforts for three presidential campaigns and served as senior domestic and economic policy adviser to presidents Nixon and Reagan. Anderson has received numerous awards, among them Dartmouth's Presidential Medal for Outstanding Leadership and Achievement. He is the author of six books, most notably *Revolution* and *The Federal Bulldozer*. He lives in Portola Valley, California.